Burwood and Beyond

RUBY'S SKETCHES

The charming girlhood sketches of Ruby Riggin Dodd featured throughout this book were taken from her 1913 scrapbook. These drawings were first seen in the book, *Burwood,* published around the 1996 Tennessee 200 Bicentennial Celebration. We are delighted to offer them again in *Burwood and Beyond.*

BURWOOD AND BEYOND

Rick Warwick

Williamson County Historian

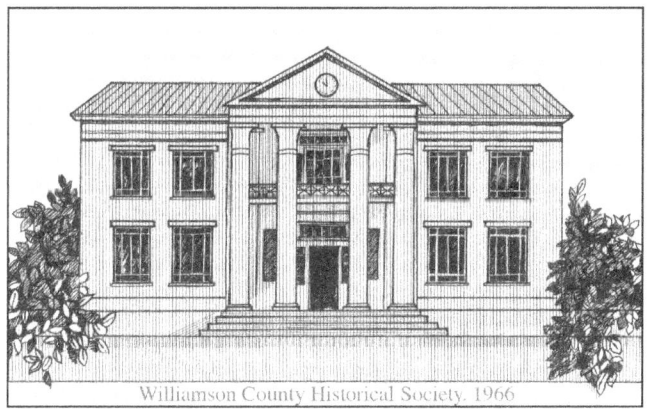

Williamson County Historical Society · Franklin, Tennessee

©2024

Burwood and Beyond

Copyright ©2024, Williamson County Historical Society. All rights reserved.
ISBN: 979-8-9863055-2-3
Library of Congress Control Number: 2024910194
3rd Printing

Marcia P. Fraser, Editor

Cover Design and Photo Editing by Peg Raciti

Interior Layout and Design by Marcia Fraser

Cover Images: Huff's Store by Anne Goetze

Williamson County Historical Society
P.O. Box 71
Franklin, Tennessee 37065
www.williamsoncountyhistory.com

DEDICATION

Judy Grigsby Hayes, daughter of Leonard Booker and Annie Lou Barker Grigsby, is a lifelong resident of the Burwood community. Without any exaggeration, it can be stated empathically that Judy is the most beloved member of the Burwood community. Her many contributions are both public and private. She was a successful Williamson County teacher, popular county commissioner, and helpmate to a radio executive, as well as the wife of the late Jim Hayes. Judy served with me as co-chair on the Tennessee and Williamson County Bicentennial Committee from 1995 to 2000. She has been a leader in the Williamson County Chamber of Commerce for decades, and an avid supporter of all the 4-H programs offered in the county. Judy is recognized across Williamson County for her devotion to the improvement of public schools, county parks, and county services. Judy is a role model for community service.

Judy is responsible for the publishing of this book. She is my model for the biblical cheerful giver. She exemplifies another biblical reference, "You will know them by their labors." Her good works have not gone unnoticed. Thank you, Judy Hayes.

A great admirer and friend,

Rick Warwick, Williamson County Historian

Contents

Title Verso xi
Introduction 1
Acknowledgements 3

Williamson County's Fourth Civil District

Samuel Akin, Early Settler of Burwood 6
Burwood, Forest Hill, Sycamore, Sugar Ridge, and Evergreen 8
Burwood Community Has a Fine Type of Citizenship 15
The Story of Burwood 19
Burwood Remembered, Johnson Hollow, and Sugar Ridge 22
Memories of My Life 26
Businesses in the Village of Burwood 37
Rural Scenes 47

Churches of the Fourth District

Leiper's Fork Primitive Baptist 55
Burwood United Methodist Church 57
Tent Meeting in Burwood 59
Evergreen Primitive Baptist Church 60
Pearly Hill C.M.E. and Pearly Hill Church of Christ 61
Murfree's Fork Primitive Baptist Church 62
Mt. Lavergne Methodist Church C.M.E. 63
Pearly Hill Baptist Church 64
Burwood Church of Christ 65
Lawrence Grove Baptist Church 66
Emanuel Pentecostal Church of Christ 68

Jones Chapel Church of the Nazarene   69

Old Hope Church of Christ   71

Schools of the Fourth District

Forest Hill   73

West End School and Williams Academy   79

Sycamore School   84

Burwood School   89

Mt. Lavergne and Pearly Hill Schools   107

Evergreen School   111

Families of Evergreen

The Pope, Campbell, and Beasley Families   119

Memories of Home on the Farm   124

Ollie Burns Remembers Hog Killing Days in Burwood   129

Military Veterans of the Fourth District

Locals Who Served Their Country During War   132

The Civil War   133

World War I   134

World War II   136

Korean and Vietnam Wars   143

Notable Citizens of the Fourth District

J. B. Akin   146

Robert Vance Akin, Sr.   149

Lottie Carter Ashworth   154

Perlina Locke Ashworth   157

George Roy Barker   160
Boyd Ridley Critz   164
William Coleman Jones   168
Percy Neal Lavender   171
John T. Lawrence, "Red"   176
Colonel Hardy Murfree   180
A.G. Overbey   183
T.F. Overbey   187
Myrtle Riggin Ragsdale   192
William Hamilton Sedberry   196

Notable Homes of the Fourth District

Fairview   201
The Collins - Layne Home   204
The Lamb - Lawrence Home   206
The W.P. Thweatt Home   209
The Willows   210
The Samuel P. Cannon Home   215
The Ridley-Beasley-Church Home   217
The Akin-Boyd-Dodd Home   219
The Vachel Barnhill Home   222
The Ashworth Home   224
The Pope-Lavender Huff Home   226
The Sparkman-Johnson Home   228
The Johnson-Morrow-Dodd-Huff Home   230
The Burnett Home   232
The Jacobs, Satterfield, Prince, Stanley, Brooks Home   234
The Barker-Plemons Home   236
The Pope-Barker-Duncan Home   238
Eastview   240

The Kate Norman Lawrence Kyle Home   245
The Pope-Martin-Pewitt Home   247
The Pope-Southall Home   250
The McRae, Shaw, Lavender, Barker Home   252
The Critz-Lazenby Home   254
The Shaw-Huff-Johnson Home   256
Hilltop Manor   258
The Cain Polk Home   261
The Byrd-Venable-Huff Home   263
The Sam and Ida Hay Johnson Home   265
The Helm-Akin Home   267
The Sparkman - Dodd Home   269
The Akin-Hutcherson-Norman Home   270
The Akin-Ragsdale Home   272
The Akin-Tomlinson Home   273
The Beasley-Hunt-Sparkman Home   276
The Si and Polly McCampbell Home   279
The Stephens-Garland Home   281

Tidbits

Cayce Springs, Summer Resort of the Fourth District   284
Ride-a-Thon   288
The Hawk Brothers vs. Lionel Johnson   297
Burwood's Baseball Teams of 1947   304

Fourth District Folks A Photograph Album

Names and Dates Featured in Familiar Faces   307
Familiar Faces   312

Index   379

INTRODUCTION

Rick Warwick at the grave of W.O.N. Perkins in Old City Cemetery

I have always found that history is best presented as a narrative accompanied by many period photographs. I hope you, as the reader, agree.

After a successful partnership with Judy Hayes with the publication of *Bethesda and Surrounding Communities*, Judy suggested that I revise the 1986 history of Burwood. This long out-of-print book was the product of a dedicated group of local folks interested in preserving Burwood's history. The book was published before the advent of personal computers, scanners, and digital printers. I accepted the challenge knowing that I could count on many of my old Hillsboro students from Burwood to be eager to gather old family photographs to supplement those used in the original Burwood book. Be forewarned, this book is a pleasurable history, not a scholarly tome.

The title *Burwood and Beyond*, will encompass the communities of Burwood, Forest Hill, Sycamore, Sugar Ridge, and Evergreen. The first section of this book will attempt to define the Fourth District with the realization that since 1836 these communities made up a political section of Williamson County. The two representatives from this section, known as magistrates, were elected at large to sit in the Quarterly County Court. Many may remember the late Coley Lavender of Burwood and Mack Hatcher of Thompson Station sharing that honor for many years.

The Fourth District, until recently, has been an important agricultural center of the county. From the early settlement of Williamson County, the fertile farms along the West Harpeth River and Murfree's Fork were major producers of grains, livestock, and tobacco. In contrast, the hilly western and southern sections of the Fourth District proved home to subsistence farmers, who tilled their hillside farms to support their large families, very much like their cousins in western North Carolina. Families living on the slopes of the Duck River Ridge, Johnson Hollow, and Perkins Road are good examples, who would be included in this analysis. From these hollows came the soldiers for our wars, workers for our factories, craftsmen, and store clerks for the cities. Those who remained in the community became the backbone of the workforce of Williamson County.

The small village of Burwood is the primary focus of this book. Several country stores over the years have opened and closed at the intersection of Carter's Creek Pike and Pope's Chapel Road, leaving Huff's Store as the lone commercial enterprise. Within sight of this intersection may be seen the old Burwood School, the Burwood Community Center, the Burwood United Methodist Church, and the Burwood Church of Christ. With the coming of 840, the surrounding area seems to be waiting for the encroachment that is sure to come. This change was unimaginable twenty years ago. Thompson Station from the east and Spring Hill from the south threaten the once sleepy burg. Rumors of a forthcoming giant truck stop and a new state highway connecting Spring Hill's factories with 840 endanger the tranquility the village has enjoyed for two centuries.

Rick Warwick,

Williamson County Historian

ACKNOWLEDGEMENTS

I want to thank those friends and former students for providing the wonderful photographs that have enriched this story. This was made possible by the likes of Claudine Haley Poynor, Louise Byrd, Dianne Carter, Dewey and Melissa Garland, Rose Marie Huff, Elmer Walls, Kennette Huff Sweeney, Shelia Johnson Meyers, Cindy Johnson Turnage, Connie Johnson Jones, Jon Harris, Tandy and Sherry Still Logan, Pat Logan, Ed Cannon, Angela McCullough Jefferson, Janet Booker-Davis, Suzanne McCampbell, Judy Hayes, Jackie Osborne McCandless, Faye Osborne Martin, Janice Inman Duff, Jerry and Larry Barker, Nancy Barker Craig, Sam Allen Dodd, James Redford, Ben Johnson, Rebecca Dodd Jackson, Thelma Battle, and Alice and Ollie Sparkman.

Special thanks to Marcia Fraser, Special Collections Librarian at Williamson County Public Library, for editing and designing the book; to Peg Raciti for creating the book cover and restoring photographs; and to Anne Goetze for providing the wonderful nostalgic photo art of Huff's Store on the front and back covers of this book.

I must acknowledge the committee that produced the first Burwood book: Anita Harris Grissom, Pat Gray Logan, Mary Rainey Martin, and Judy Grigsby Hayes. Their labor secured photographs and history, which provided the bones of this book.

Throughout the book, you will notice the charming drawings of Ruby Riggin Dodd, taken from her 1913 scrapbook. I thank her son, Sam Allen Dodd, for permitting their use in this book. Also, her two articles in this book are priceless with their local flavor and insight provided by one who lived a long life in Burwood.

Rick Warwick

RICK WARWICK

WILLIAMSON COUNTY'S FOURTH CIVIL DISTRICT

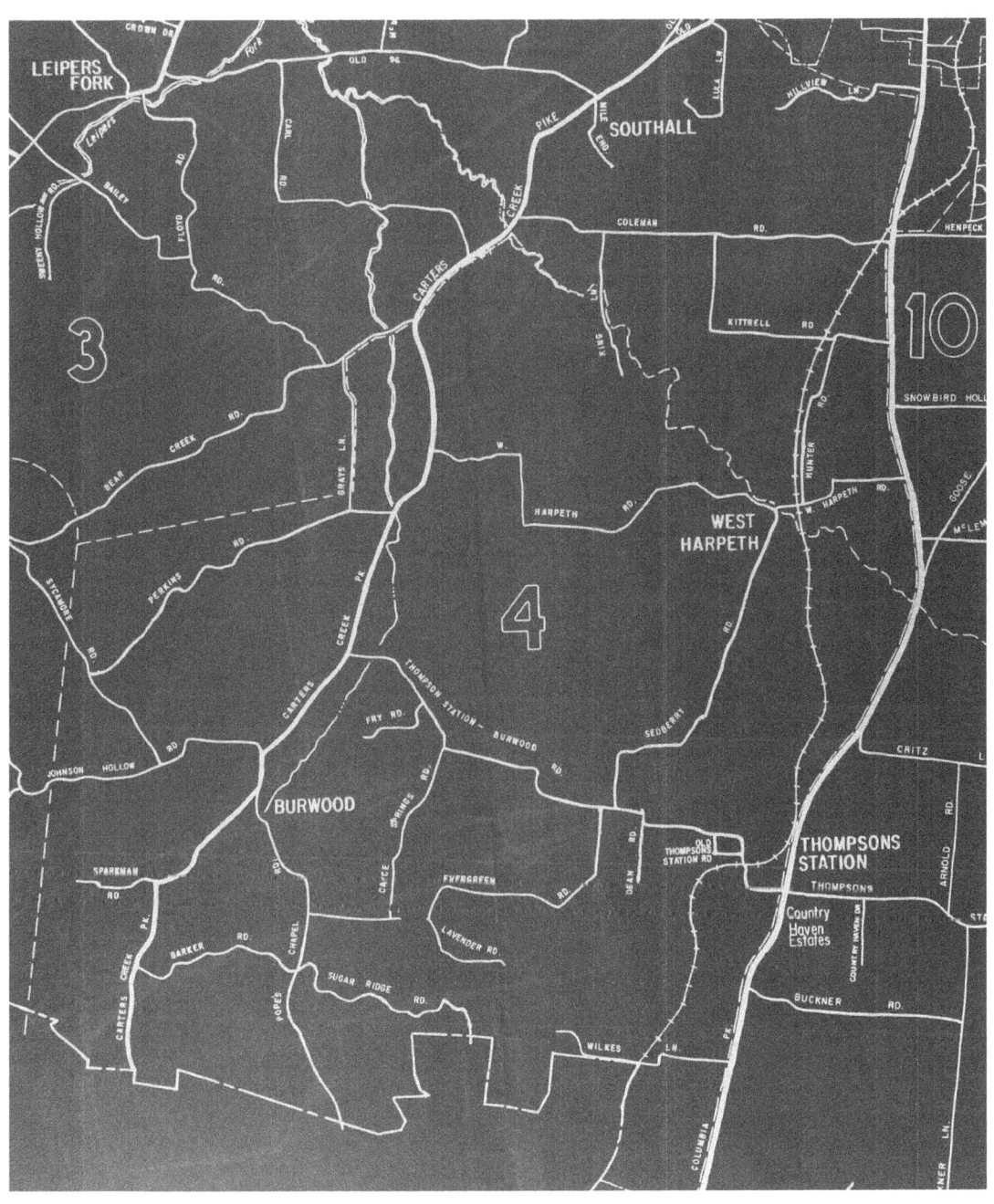

SAMUEL AKIN, EARLY SETTLER OF BURWOOD

LILA MAI AKIN RAGSDALE

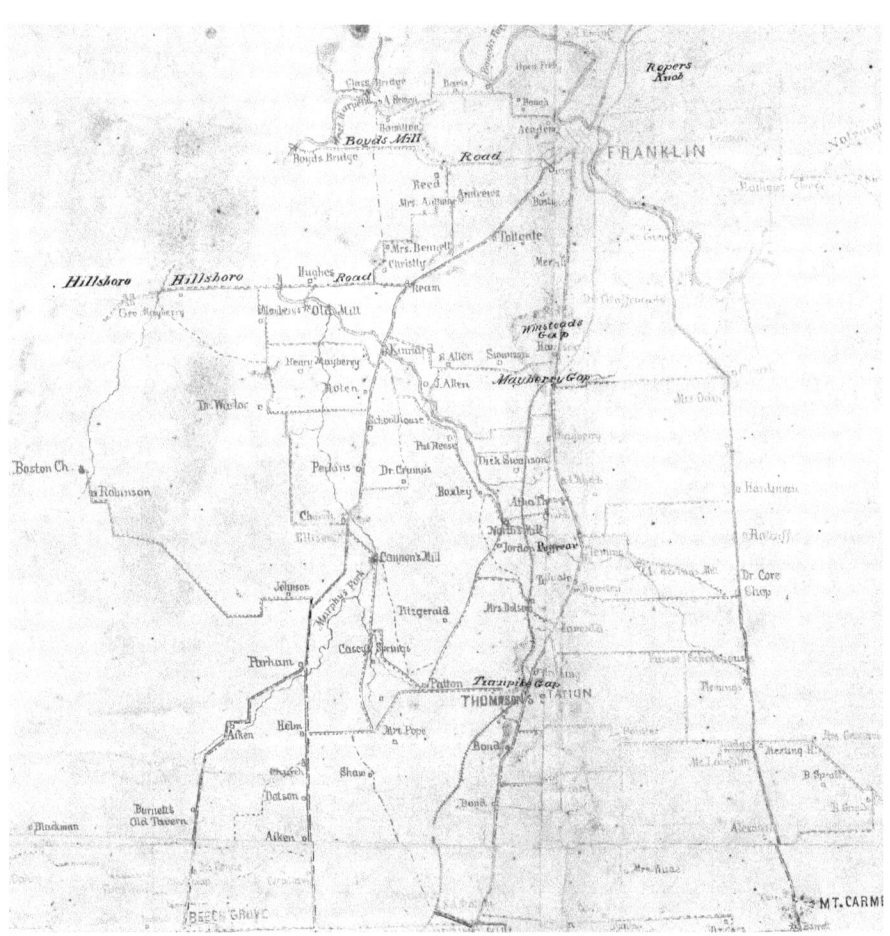

Williamson County map during the Civil War, by Merrill

Samuel Akin, one of the earliest settlers in the Burwood area was born in 1771 in South Carolina. In 1793, he married Dorcas Starr who was born in 1771.

It was unknown when they came to Davidson County, Tennessee, but, in 1801, Samuel Akin, living then in Davidson County, bought 60 acres of land from Thrasher McCollum for $100. This tract was located in the 4th Civil District on the headwaters of Murfree's Fork of the West Harpeth River. In 1811, he purchased 127 acres for $330 from Benjamin Carter, who had received a very large grant of land in Williamson County. In 1831, he bought from John Pope 25 acres for $80, giving him a total of 212 acres. The above information was obtained from old deeds in the Williamson County courthouse, Franklin, Tennessee. The Samuel Akin place was located a mile south of the present village of Burwood.

His will, a specific document written a short time before his death on February 11, 1844, is also recorded at the courthouse.

Samuel and Dorcas Starr Akin had 12 children, five sons and seven daughters. Dorcas Akin died in 1850, at which time only two sons survived. John Akin and Arthur Stewart Akin. By the terms of Samuel Akin's will, the land was to be divided equally between these two sons. John Akin was the grandfather of W.J. Akin and his brother Tim Akin, also of Millard and Vance Akin, brothers who ran Akin's Store for many years in Burwood, and John Akin was the great, great grandfather of T.T. Akin, Jr., a member of the Burwood Methodist Church.

Samuel Akin was one of the founders of the Methodist church in the Burwood area. He was one of the first trustees of Pope's Chapel Methodist Church, which began in 1818, and is the forerunner of the Burwood Methodist Church.

Ruby Riggin Dodd

BURWOOD, FOREST HILL, SYCAMORE, SUGAR RIDGE, AND EVERGREEN

RICK WARWICK

When Williamson County was established in October 1799, it was under the state rule that organized counties into militia districts. This changed in 1836 when the state legislature mandated that counties be organized into civil districts within which justices of the peace and constables shall be elected. In 1836, Williamson County had 25 civil districts.

Civil District Number Four was bounded as follows: Beginning where the road leading from Major Burnett's, to Franklin (Carter's Creek Pike) crosses the West Harpeth. Thence, west with said road, to Murfree's Fork. Thence, with the line of the third district to the east boundary line of the second district. Thence, south with said line to the Maury County line. Thence, east with the line of the same to the Columbia Road. Thence, north with the said road to West Harpeth. Thence, down said creek to the beginning. And designated, in like manner, the house of Joseph Yates at the Sulphur Springs (Cayce Springs) as a suitable place for holding elections, etc.

For most of our history, the Fourth Civil District was largely rural and a rich agricultural area of Williamson County. Some of the most productive farms were located along the West Harpeth River and Murfree's Fork. Before the Civil War, many of the farms were worked by slave labor resulting in a large population of freedmen living in the district after the war. The Fourth District had five Black and five White schools within its borders. By searching the county tax rolls, we can identify the citizens of the district, their acreage, the number of slaves, and total wealth.

THE TEN WEALTHIEST CITIZENS IN ACREAGE VALUE IN 1860

1. T.J. Watson – $80,850, located on West Harpeth Road
2. Patrick Reese – $73,575, located on West Harpeth Road
3. Thomas F. Perkins – $72,700, located on Carter's Creek Pike
4. Bird Fitzgerald – $40,100, located on Sedberry Road
5. Thomas Boxley – $39,600, located on West Harpeth Road
6. Thomas B. Bond – $38,300, located on Columbia Pike
7. James Allison – $37, 000, located on Carter's Creek Pike
8. W.P. Cannon – $35,750, located on Carter's Creek Pike
9. Thomas H. Bond – $28,800, located on Columbia Pike
10. W.H. Moss – $24,400, located on Thompson Station Road West

Will Akin's steam engine threshing wheat on Jim Cannon's farm

The following list of the 1860 Williamson County Tax Record will provide an inventory of the landowners in the 4th Civil District. This list will also include landowners in Burwood, Thompson Station, West Harpeth, and Forrest Hill. First, the property owner is listed, the number of slaves, the number of acres, plus the total value of the land, buildings, and slaves.

1860 Tax Roll of the Fourth District

NAME	SLAVES	ACRES	TOTAL VALUE
Allison, James	16	904	37,000
Akin, John		128	1,900
Akin, J.B.			
Akin, William M.			996
Bond, Thomas H.	10	528	28,8000
Bond, Thomas B.	17	609	38,3000
Burnett, W.W.	6	376	12,825
Burnett, J.J.	3	31	4,100
Burnett, Ann	3	70	3,900
Banks, Thomas		15	1,350
Barker, W.B.	2		4,600
Baugh, Phillip W.	7	184	16,600
Brown, C.M.			
Barker, G.W.	8	175	11,200
Boxley, Thomas S.	23	313	39,600
Boxley, D.W.			
Barker, G.H.	1		1,000
Beasley, J.J.	3	198	7,500
Banks, L.H.			574
Cowsert, B.F.	1		1,200
Critz, Zachariah	2		2,175
Cotton, William			
Critz, John			
Chainey, D.S.	1		2,860
Critz, Jacob	7	305	16,900
Cayce, William		106	2,150
Chapman & Morris			600
Core, J.G.			800
Colquit, John R.			1,000
Chairs, J.W.		172	7,500

Campbell, James			
Campbell, Janie	1		750
Crump, Martha	1		4,800
Crump, E.E.	3	100	7,000
Chainey, Mary		80	2,400
Chainey, E.B.	3		3,100
Chainey, S.J.	1		1,150
Crawford, J.W.	9	215	14,450
Crowson, A.J.			
Claud, John W.			
DeGraffenreid, L.D.	4		4,925
Dodson, B.F.	5		5,400
Dodson, Bird	8	250	11,200
Dodson, Mary	3	73	5,900
Dodson, T.W.	3	288	10,500
Dodson, A.J.	3		4,620
Dodson, B.E.	4		3,700
Drake, G.M.		66	3,700
Drake, C.	3	148	7,450
Gant, Ann		10	700
Hightower, R.R.	17	183	23,300
Helm, Henderson	7	195	10,460
Helm, Fielding	7	242	12,700
Jones, Ellis, Jr.			
Jones, Ellis, Sr.	7	322	12,100
Jacobs, Joseph R.		325	6,000
Jones, L.G.			300
Johnson, Lewis			
Johnson, John C.		56	1,120
Johnson, Elcain	4	465	11,261
Johnson, Jeff			
Johnson, Caroline		16	150
King, James, Sr.			500

Name			
Lile, C.T.	3	165	11,425
Loftin, A.M.			
Lamb, Drewrey		100	1,500
Lillie,			
McLemore, John D.	3		3,030
Mayberry, A.C.		196	5,700
Martin, J.L.	5	153	9,075
Moss, W.H.	9	342	24,400
Morrow, John		12	300
Morrow, J.J.			
Morrow, Robert			
McCollum, William			
Merrill, Wiley		23	250
Merrill, James			
Morton, Joseph			
Marlin, Joseph			
Nolen, Mary	6	183	11,775
Pope, John O.	3		2,300
Pope, E.	2		1,800
Pope, H.P.	3		2,800
Pope, E.W.	1	183	7,000
Pope, W.C.	8	253	15,100
Pope, T.A.			
Pope, Thomas A.	12	371	22,425
Pope, William A.	1		2,700
Parham, Peter	3	330	11,300
Parham, R.A.			
Parham, E.L.			
Pope, L.J.	7	230	12,500
Perkins, Thomas F.	34	1,504	72,700
Patton, William B.	6	338	17,610
Patton, J.B., heirs	4	197	10,000
Patton, Susannah	2	100	7,100

Name			
Puryear, Jordan, heirs		355	9,000
Parham, E.J.			
Reese, Thomas J.			
Ragsdale, H.H.		50	1,000
Ragsdale, John		20	500
Ragsdale, Hiram		45	900
Ragsdale, L.C.			
Ragsdale, J.M., estate			155
Reams, Joshua, Mrs.		29	1,450
Reese, Patrick	39	964	73,975
Ridley, J.B.	12	377	21,400
Sparkman, Eliza	2		1,500
Sparkman, E.R.		83	2,000
Sparkman, E.P.		85	2,100
Sparkman, Jesse H.		180	4,290
Sparkman, M.W.	1	121	3,650
Steele, Richard	12	656	30,955
Shaw, Burnice W.		260	4,000
Shaw, John A.		164	2,400
Shaw, W.A.			
Shaw, W.H.			
Steele, William M.			
Singleton, R.W.			
Thomas, Wesley			
Tucker, John A.			
Tucker, Thomas			
Terrill, heirs	8		7,050
Trimble, G.W.		1,423	2,550
Thompson, Janette	1		948
Thompson, Peter	1		1,000
Truett, J.M.			
Tatum, Richard M.			
Wren, William J.			

Watson, Stephen		12	484
Wilkes, John			
Wade, H.P.	9	233	17,800
Wade, Lucy			1,597
Wade, John F.			3,170
Wade, L.B.	14		14,100
Watson, Thomas J.	31	1,420	80,850
Witt, P.E.			
Warren, William			
Total	508		1,115,167

The Fourth Civil District was one of the leading sections of the county in the production of cotton, corn, wheat, hemp, tobacco, and livestock. With the coming of the Tennessee & Alabama Railroad in the mid-1850s with depots at West Harpeth, and Thompson's Station, local farmers had an advantage for wider markets and better product prices.

As early as 1803, a county road book mentioned a road running from Franklin to Samuel Akin's house in the gap of the Duck River Ridge. By 1850, the Franklin-Carter's Creek Turnpike was granted a state charter with two tollgates, one located near the rock quarry, a mile from the Franklin Square, and the second tollgate located across the road of the Leiper's Fork Primitive Baptist Church. The company maintained the roadbed and collected tolls until 1917, when it became a county road.

Ruby Riggin Dodd

BURWOOD COMMUNITY HAS A FINE TYPE OF CITIZENSHIP

WILLIAM S. WEBB

The Review-Appeal, May 26, 1938

Burwood is located in the Fourth Civil District of Williamson County ten miles south of Franklin and is a community of home-lovers, church-goers, and progressive people.

This community has two general merchandise stores, one grammar school, and three churches: Church of Christ, Methodist, and Baptist.

Burwood was first called Williamsburg after the Williams family in that section who were large landowners. Later when a post office was established there it was called Shaw, after Gus Shaw who was the first postmaster. When a second postmaster, R.V. Akin, Sr., a prominent merchant for many years, was appointed it was suggested by James Drake Pope, son of Squire Billy Pope, member of one of the oldest and most prominent families in Williamson County, that it be called Burwood, taking the name from the novel, *Robert Elsmere*, written by Mrs. Humphrey Ward. The village has been known by that name since that time.

Burwood Methodist Church, built in 1913

Near Burwood on the Carter's Creek Road once stood the old historic Pope's Chapel church which was badly damaged by a cyclone in 1910 and the building was torn down by the congregation and the windows and doors were sold to the Negroes of the community for a church building which is a short distance away.

After this old landmark was torn down the congregation built a Methodist Church at Burwood in which they are still worshiping. Pope's

Chapel was built on one-half acre of land given by Parson John Pope for a meeting house and school. A building was erected on the site in September of 1818.

Parson John Pope had it stated in the deed to this property where the church stood "that the pulpit in this house was to be free to ministers of any denomination of Godly and moral character." The meeting of other religious bodies in this building besides the Methodists ceased after Parson Pope's death. Parson John Pope was born in North Carolina and came to Tennessee early in the nineteenth century and settled in Williamson County in 1806 and purchased 2,000 acres of land near the Maury County line beyond Burwood. He was married twice; his first wife was Ann Whittaker of Virginia, and to this union were born eight daughters; his second wife was Ann Lukas and to this union were born six sons.

Dr. J.O. Shannon

Pope was not a regular ordained minister but was a lay preacher. He was a Protestant Methodist and was opposed to bishops and missions.

Lawrence Grove Baptist Church was built in 1917

Adjoining the site where Pope's Chapel stood was the campground where they held open-air services and camped for several weeks each year with people attending these services from all over the state. Parson John Pope died in 1828.

John O. Pope, the father of Mrs. J.O. Shannon, of Franklin, was Sunday School superintendent at Pope's Chapel for many years. Misses Edith, Mary, and Carrie Pope, granddaughters of Parson Pope, still reside in the Burwood community. Now where once stood the old historic Pope's Chapel church is an open plowed field.

Nearby in a large beech grove now stands the Lawrence Grove Baptist Church which was established in 1917.

The two magistrates in this district are V.I. Barnhill, a farmer of Burwood, and Dr. A. Gibbs, a farmer at Thompson Station.

The Rev. W.O. Largen of Thompson Station is the pastor of Burwood Methodist

Church and T.T. Akin is the Sunday School superintendent; the School teachers are J.B. Akin, men's and women's Bible Class; Mrs. Edgar Shaw, Young People's Class; Mrs. J.H. Cannon, Intermediate Class; Mrs. James Huff, Primary and Beginner's Class. Rev. Largen preaches the second and fourth Sundays of each month at this church. There is a Methodist Woman's Missionary Society with twenty members with Mrs. Will Akin, president; Mrs. J.H. Cannon, vice-president.

The Burwood Church of Christ was once called the West End Church and was moved a mile from its present location into Burwood in 1913. This church has fifty members who attend church and Sunday School services regularly. The elders are N.C. Beasley, L.D. Sullivan, C.A. Dodd, and Percy Lavender. Sunday School teachers are Mrs. Glenn Sparkman, Intermediate teacher; Mrs. Percy Lavender, Junior Class; Mrs. Allen Prince, Little Jewell Class; and N.C. Beasley, Adult Men's and Women's Bible Class. Elders Felix Sowell of Columbia, and Elam Kukendall of Nashville, preach each month at this church.

Burwood Church of Christ was built in 1913

Burwood High School (grades 1-12)

There was a four-year high school located here until 1927-28 when it was discontinued due to the lack of number of pupils to maintain the school. The present grammar school which has just closed its term for this school year had an enrollment of eighty students and the teachers were J.B. Akin, principal; Mrs. James Huff, primary teacher, and Miss Ruth Alexander, intermediate teacher.

There is an active ladies' home demonstration club here with Mrs. Allen Prince, president; Mrs. Mary Shaw, vice president; and Miss Ruth Barker, treasurer.

The Girls' 4-H Club has fifteen members with Miss Georgia Barker as president.

R.V. Akin, Sr., is president of the men's division of the Community Club.

During the Civil War, Jake Martin, Sr., organized a company of men at Burwood and Thompson Station which became a part of General Nathan Bedford Forrest's Cavalry and he and his men helped destroy a railroad for the Yankees. On account of Martin helping destroy this railroad, the Yankees burned his home in this community. He still has two sons living in this county.

The two chief sources of cash income for this community are farming and dairying which bring in scores of thousands of dollars yearly to the farmers. Burwood is a progressive community with a splendid type of citizenship of which any county might well be proud.

Akin Brothers' Store opened in 1911. Since 1937, Huff's Store has called this home.

THE STORY OF BURWOOD

LOUISE SHANNON DEDMAN

Louise Shannon Dedman

In 1806, Reverend John Pope with his second wife, Ann Lucas, and nine children, came to Tennessee from Edgecomb County, North Carolina. He owned land from Duck River Ridge on one side to the Indian boundary line on two sides. One deed was signed by General James Robertson in 1808. Pope was a circuit minister of the Methodist faith except he did not believe in Bishops and Missions. He preached in homes, in groves, or any place he could gather a few residents who had come into this unsettled area together. His land holdings extended as far as the law allowed settlers to go without infringing on land that had not yet been treatied by the Indians. His closest neighbor, two miles away, was Colonel Hardy Murfree, the Cannon farm now. The land was cheap, but fertile, as it had been granted for Revolutionary War service. He was paying taxes in Williamson County in 1805, and shortly after began hewing logs to build his home in the wilderness adjoining Indian Territory. He and his family cleared land for growing their supplies, including a distillery. Being a preacher, he preached in homes until his family grew and others were moving into the area. At that time there was a need for a house of worship and a school. He deeded ½ acre of land in 1818 to be used by any denomination or sec, as long as they did not infringe on another's beliefs as a place of worship. He specified foot by foot and board by board exactly how the building was to be constructed…the exact dimensions and the kind of material it was to be built with. Large camp meetings were held there which lasted for days and people came from miles away to Pope's Chapel, as it had been named, to worship according to their own beliefs. A large spring nearby made it a perfect place for a church and school, and it was constructed so well, that it was believed it would stand forever. In 1910, a tornado hit the area and damaged the building, which at that time was being used as a Methodist congregation. The area was growing, starting with the bringing of Rev. Pope's brother's family and slaves back here from Wake County, North Carolina after his brother died in 1811, and a small village had sprung up about a short distance from Rev. Pope's home called by several names including Williamsburg, for Dr. Williams. Dr. J.O. Shannon later began his practice with Dr. Williams. Pope had deeded lands to his children in that community as he had owned over 2,000 acres by that time.

There were five Pope homes on Pope Chapel Road, Evergreen, and Cayce Springs Road. With the death of Miss Carrie Pope in 1958, the last direct descendant with the Pope name left the area. There are yet Blacks, descended from the first who came to Tennessee with Rev. Pope or who came when Rev. Pope's brother died, living here… many on the same lands their ancestors farmed. They are a credit to their name and to their community.

During the war between the states, Rev. John Pope's grandson, John Osborne Pope, in trying to escape being captured by the Yankees, hid in the nearby woods, but one day got a chance to go home. He hid in the attic. When the Yankees were seen coming, a servant quickly took hampers of apples waiting to be stored for the winter and scattered them thickly on the stairsteps. As the soldier attempted to go upstairs in search of the escaped soldier, she spread all her 250 pounds plus her hands on her hips at the foot of the stairs and dared the Yankee soldier to walk on her winter supply of apples and ruin them. She must have been emphatic because the soldier went away, leaving the soldier and the apples in place.

In the Rev. John Pope's home, *Eastview*, cut in the wall of wainscoting, was a secret panel where important papers, old deeds, and a diary were hidden for safekeeping. The secret panel can still be seen and what was then an entrance hall is now part of the living room. The house has been weather-boarded over the yellow poplar logs, and the sheltered walkway to the separate kitchen, which was some distance from the house, has been torn down, removed, and added to the back of the house. The same batten door hangs at the foot of the small steep steps going to the upstairs bedrooms. The slave quarters and the distillery have been gone a long time, but the small rich plot of ground that Rev. Pope used for his garden beside this house is often used by the present owner as his garden.

Just beyond the garden is the family burial ground, with some forty marked graves and several unmarked ones. In front of the barn lay the bodies of the servants and slaves of the Pope family. The first recorded burial in the graveyard was Rev. Pope in 1829, and the last was in 1910.

As mentioned, the community that developed in this area was first known as Williamsburg, and later Shaw. It is said that the present name of Burwood was suggested by a grandson of Rev. Pope, James Drake Pope, who took the name from Mrs. Humphrey Ward's novel, *Robert Elsmere*, and *Burwood* it still is today.

As the Pope's children reached maturity, their father gave them each a farm near him, except for those who moved to his other holdings in the Western District. His sons Thomas Anderson and John Whitaker Pope were progenitors of the families who continue to live in the county. The homeplace, located at the intersection of Evergreen and Pope's Chapel Road, continued to be the home of Mrs. Ann Pope until she died in 1836, at which time it was to have gone to a son who had died, unmarried before that date. It was sold and owned for many years by Colonel Henderson Helm. At his death, it passed to other hands. Eastview was then owned by Edgar Shaw, who added on the kitchen area. It is owned by Leonard B. Grigsby.

Ruby Riggin Dodd

BURWOOD REMEMBERED, JOHNSON HOLLOW, AND SUGAR RIDGE

RUBY RIGGIN DODD

Ruby Riggin Dodd

John "Parson" Pope bought a large land grant from James Robertson in 1806. Parson Pope gave the land for a church, known as Pope's Chapel. This church was blown away by a tornado in 1910. There were large tent meetings. People came by wagons, buggies, horseback, and walking for miles around. In 1912 land was bought in what is now Burwood and in 1913 a new church was built. It became the Methodist church and is still in use today.

The settlers were coming from different directions and settling in what is now Burwood, located on the Carter's Creek Pike that comes out of Franklin, over the Duck River Ridge to Columbia. The road from Franklin was a toll pike. One toll gate was near the rock crusher in Franklin, one near the brick church, a few feet from the covered bridge over Murfree's Fork. This gate was kept by a little old lady who always wore a black bonnet. Her name was Mrs. Garner, grandmother of Robert "Dit" Garner who ran Lunn & Garner Shoe Store in Franklin. Mrs. Garner charged 25 cents for buggies, and 10 cents for horseback riders, and few people ever got by her keen eye.

Another early settler was Dr. Williams and his family. He built a home and store. Their son Eddie ran the store. Their home and land were across from Huff's Store. They had a family cemetery at the top of the hill behind the house, which included the Parham family. This community was named Williamsburg after Dr. Williams, who helped many. Dr. J.O. Shannon practiced here for 12 years. In front of Dr. Williams' home was a small office that Dr. Shannon used to store his medicine. He married a local girl, whom he saw when she was five years old, and he waited to marry her until she was 21. That girl was Georgia Pope.

On the Pope land, West End School was built, and used until about 1916. A church, known as the Burwood Church of Christ, was built near the school and later moved to Burwood, where it became the new Church of Christ in about 1914.

There were other schools, too. A one-room school around the curve is now remodeled into a home. This was known as the John Morrow place, and now is the Robert Huff home where Nannie Huff continues to reside. There was another school, known as Sycamore, that also served as a church. All faiths could worship in this building. In the summer, they would build brush arbors and have revivals under them.

A sawmill was a necessary part of life. Will Akin ran a sawmill on the banks of the creek on Pope Chapel Road with the help of Bob Clark, who also ran a grist mill. At the start of the day, at noon, and at quitting time for miles around you could hear the whistle blow, and the cutting sound of the saw cutting logs. When extra help was needed in the summer for the sawmill, gristmill or to help Will Akin run the thresher, they worked with wagon and mules for $3.50 and a man alone $1.00 per day.

Later, Williamsburg's name was changed to Shawtown for an old Civil War veteran, William Shaw, who with Calvin Dodd began another store in the community. Shaw's son, John, lived in Thompson Station and brought the mail by horseback. It was stored in one side of the store. When folks came to the store, they could also get their mail. Prices were different then – sugar was 10 cents a pound, coffee was 15 cents, tobacco 5 cents, and 10 cents per plug.

Peddlers came and bought some of the farm produce such as eggs, chickens, ducks, and geese. The peddlers carried many of the items needed at home like sugar, soda, coffee, tobacco, candy, etc. They carried their produce to Nashville to sell. The trip was so long that it took them a day to go and one to return.

Members of the Baptist church would have Associations in the fall that would last for 2 or 3 days. Other families would often take in visitors to help. They would use domestic materials to make covers for straw for these visitors to sleep. These became known as "Baptist Pallets."

As the years went by, another store was run by two brothers, Vance and Millard Akin. When the old store gave way, a new one was built across the road. They had the only telephone and people came from miles around to use it. This store is still in use today, owned by Ken Huff. The old rolling ladders are still in use today, and the balcony which was the center for clothing and shoes.

Cayce Springs was a place where people came for picnics and on the Fourth of July, there would be a big celebration for the old soldiers. Many people spent the night in one of the log cabins nearby. A hotel had burned several years ago.

In later years, Dr. Joe Parks came to the area and built an office on the corner of the Millard Akin yard. It is said that upon a return from a trip to California, he had found a new name for Shawtown…that being Burwood.

Then came the Jew Peddlers, who walked with big packs on their backs. They mainly sold socks, cloth, pins, lace, buttons, thread, and other such like. In a few years, they came back in wagons with more stuff to sell.

In the winter a song leader would come and teach singing classes at night for $1 for two weeks. After these classes, people continued to gather in their homes to sing. Ladies had quilting parties. It took a lot of cover. The families were large, and the wood fires did not keep the homes warm as we like them today.

Men would help each other. They would go to friends' homes and cut wood until they all had enough. When a person was sick or died, friends and neighbors would come and help and sit with the family all night.

In front of the store was a blacksmith shop and garage. Another church was built on the other side of the road known as the Burwood Presbyterian Church. It was moved from Burwood around 1936.

More doctors had come to Burwood. Dr. Leslie and Dr. Miller. They made their visits by buggy and horseback. A dentist by the name of Dr. Lamb came and rented a room at the Shaws, and, put up his office about once a year. This was in the mid-1920s.

The W.C. Jones family ran a type of country packing house. They killed hogs, salted the meat down, cooked the lard, and sold the meat and lard to the public. When they sold out, they would kill again.

A high school was built around 1912. They had ball games, horse shows, and community fairs where the men and women could show their year's work. First, second and third prizes were given. There were also Ride-a-Thons starting about 1940 as well as log pulling and other activities to help the community and its people.

Burwood is a nice place to live – in the past and now!

Johnson Hollow, By Estelle F. Johnson

Johnson Hollow got its name from Elcain Johnson, Sr., and his son, Elcain Johnson, Jr., who lived there back in the early 1800s.

When Elcain swapped his Stetson hat for a sow and pigs, he made such a good trade that it started him buying land. Before he died, he had done so well that he gave all his children, as well as two former slaves who always stayed with him, land for a home in or near what is known as Johnson Hollow.

Sugar Ridge, By Larissa Pope

Sugar Ridge got its name from the many Sugar Maple trees all over the hills. Each year these trees were tapped, and the sap was boiled into maple sugar. There was not a good road across the ridge, but dozens of wagon trails led down on both sides of the ridge. One of the main areas for gathering sap was the area around the home of Lottie Carter Ashworth and signs of old wagon roads can still be seen. Even in recent years, "Miss Lottie" was still tapping her maples, and making her syrup. One giant maple tree in her yard still shows the scars. Over the years, folks referred to the hill with all the Sugar Maples as Sugar Ridge, and the name remains unchanged today.

Ruby Riggin Dodd

MEMORIES OF MY LIFE

RUBY RIGGIN DODD

Ruby Riggin Dodd (1901-1999)

There was a little country store at the foothills of Theta in Maury County, where Ruby Ava Riggin (Dodd) was born, on February 28, 1901, to William J. and Susan Mahala Ashworth Riggin. This community consisted of one church and one grocery store. The little store sat on the banks of a stream known as Snow Creek where the forks of the road divided – this was called Union. Mom and Dad lived in the back of the store. When I was about six or eight months old Papa would take me up in his arms to a deep hole of water, under an old beech tree, and let me paddle and play every day, that was the doctor's orders. I was cutting my teeth and that would cool down my temperature (no fans to keep cool).

Dr. Cox lived at Theta and rode horseback sometimes. My mother used to ride horseback up here to Grandpa Ashworth's where Uncle Fate lived just west of Thompson Station Road in Burwood.

We moved away from Snow Creek when I was about two years old and came to Williamson County. We lived in Ridley Hollow, as far back in the woods as you could go, where the owls hooted all the time. There were about six or eight gates to open. Dad tried to farm while there. We moved again when I was about four years old over on the hill where Jim Elick Porter (Grandad's old farm) used to live by Evergreen Road. I think Dad ran a peddling wagon then, which was a slow go, too. Then a little later on, we moved into a log cabin at the end of West Harpeth Lane. I started school at Thompson Station, I reckon about seven years old. I walked to school when it was pretty with other children in the neighborhood. Kate and Sally Norman were older than me so they kept an eye on me. When the weather was bad, I would ride up behind Dad on an old mare named Dutch who had pneumonia and died. I remember they would wrap her in old quilts and put hot rocks around her.

Will Riggin 1875-1959 Mahala 1874-1958

I had no brothers or sisters to play with, so I learned to content myself and play alone, or play with neighbor children around the hill where Dorris and Buddy Huff lived. I was afraid to go by myself, so I would walk up against the fence, drag a stick along the wire to make a noise, and look back every step or two. One doesn't know how much to appreciate brothers and sisters. It was a little lonely, but I had a pretty little black and white dog I loved very much. Dad was cutting wood one day and when the tree started to fall it made a squeaking noise, and my dog thought it was mice under there, so she ran beneath the tree, and it fell on her and killed her. I was shaken up, my playmate was gone.

When I was about eight, we moved to the place Tom Byrd has now. I started school at Sycamore and went there until I was twelve. This place had a nice orchard. Dad built an outdoor toilet that was a little better than going to the barn or a gully. Dad began farming pretty well and hired a boy to stay with us and help him. He raised sheep too. Mother raised turkeys and bought her a big range cookstove which took up one corner of the kitchen. Dad bought a steel tire buggy, which sounded like a wagon cracking rocks, but Mom would put me in a pretty little frilly dress (I don't know what they wore), however when we would dress up, crawl in the buggy, and start down the road, you could hear us coming. I was raised to go to church. We had prayers every night before going to bed.

Around the year 1909, a storm came through the Boston community and Hillsboro (Leiper's Fork), and the community was torn apart.

We bought lots of things from Jew peddlers and the market wagons or peddling wagons. We raised all kinds of garden vegetables so we didn't buy too much. We had milk, butter, chickens, hogs to kill. We did not have Christmas trees, but I got quite a lot in my old ribbed black stockings I wore with buttoned-up shoes. I remember my first sweater. It was an old gray, baggy cotton one. Kids wouldn't wear it to the barn now, but I wore it to school. This old house had two big rooms and a dog trot. Mom papered one room with dark red paper and shining designs in it, but that was our company room, or used it when we were sick and had the doctor come to check on us. The other room was very large with a big open fireplace, the cook stove was on the left side and my cot was on the right side. The kitchen table was in the middle of the room. Mom and Dad's bed was in the back corner on the right side, one window between my cot and their bed. She stretched wire in a square around their bed, took some material, and made a curtain around it. No one knew what was behind there.

We kept warm and had plenty to eat, roasted potatoes in the open fireplace, a wire hung in the middle of the fireplace, there we hung pots on it and cooked food. Mom was known by everyone for her good cooking, so on Sunday, she prepared our dinner, and we went to church. While we were gone someone came in and helped themselves to lunch.

There were tent meetings in the summertime, so we would walk and go if close enough, also go on wagons away from our community. In the wintertime, a guy would come in the neighborhood and teach people to sing. He would stay about ten days to two weeks and stay around with the people in the community. He would make a few dollars (he charged about a dollar each), but all learned how to sing, old and young would go. After the teacher would leave, people would go to the homes of different ones every week and sing. When I was around thirteen my grandfather died so we moved up to the hill where Bulldog used to live to be with Aunt Nancy and Grandmother "Mammy." Then I had a room upstairs. Things were somewhat different, the house was almost new, had two bedrooms upstairs, one bedroom downstairs, a kitchen, a dining room, and what was called then a front room.

Burwood school was built about that time (1916), and I started to school down there. I met a host of kids from every direction from Carter's Creek, Boston, all around Overbey's store, etc. I had never been to a school that was taught by a man, so I didn't hardly know what to do. His name was Mr. Logue, he was a fine fellow about middle age. New teachers came and new children boarded and went to school there. We had music teachers and voice teachers, and some crafts were taught. A little bit of drama (ha). We had plays that were very entertaining, musical programs, duets, solos, piano duets, most anything anyone was interested in. The schoolhouse would be full when anything was scheduled. Future farming programs. Box suppers first, and others came from different places. I got my piano when I was fifteen years old.

Entertainers came to Burwood School and had musical concerts. Names like Uncle Dave Macon, Johnny Wright, Wood Peartree, and speakers of all kinds, clubs. We had ride-a-thons, fairs, and horse shows. People of the community would have a fair every fall. The ladies would enter their canned goods, cooking, sewing, chickens, and craft work. Children in school would make things to be judged. The judges would present the best with a blue ribbon, and red and yellow for second and third place. Also, we had hog-calling contests, sack races, and contests for babies, etc. Name it, Burwood had it.

A storm hit the Sugar Ridge community around 1916-17 and blew Uncle Riley Lavender's house away.

When girls would play basketball, they had to wear big black bloomers and long stockings. In the summertime, boys would play baseball on Saturday afternoons. They had to work all through the week. They went to church on Sundays.

In the wintertime, we had parties every once in a while, like opossum hunts, come back and sing, playing rook, and someone would have a square dance. Very few were allowed to stay out later than midnight. When we were not in school, everyone had to work. People in those days had large families. I think Glen Sparkman and I were the only ones that didn't have brothers and sisters.

Girls were not allowed to go out with boys alone. I was about seventeen or eighteen before I could go with a crowd or have company at home.

Ruby Riggin Dodd and Callie Mai Hawkins

Dad bought me a pony and buggy, the buggy was a wicker-back runabout, (pony named Jeff). We would go to Franklin, Theta, Thompson Station, anywhere we needed to go. We had lots of company in those days when I grew up. Young and old, when Christmas would come, we would go somewhere every night until school would start up. One time, Cammie Akin and I went to Southall to Aunt Ada Ormes's, a snow came, and we had to stay a week, that was in November, one snow would come, then another. We would all walk and go places at night, that was fun. We would walk to church sometimes too. The snow would build up under the horses' hooves and they could not stand up, it would pack so hard. I remember going home with one of my friends on Sunday from church, which was customary, most of the time. About four or five of us kids got in the buggy to go riding. There was only the postman that had a car and we saw him coming. We all jumped on and hitched the old white horse to the fence, guess we were more afraid than old Nell. We all jumped over in Gus Sparkman's yard (now Doug and Patsy Johnson's home).

I had lots of friends and relatives, but yet I grew up and was lonely, with no one at home but older people. We went somewhere really often. I had lots of company, boys and girls. I spent nights with my friends, rode around on Sunday afternoons, and went to ballgames, here and there. We had big dinners, went to parties, played *Blindfold, Catch the Train, Spin the Plate, Musical Chairs, Pop the Whip, Broken Sentences*, etc. This was in late 1916. Also, *Tidy Up* and *Skip to my Lou*. We went on hayrides, all kinds of good wholesome games.

Other girls in the community sang, and we had a girl's quartet. Ethel Clark played by ear, so we played and sang our time away. Ethel's sister, Robbie, sang alto, Cammie Akin sang tenor, and I sang bass. Ha! Also, we had a male quartet consisting of Homer Meaders, Cam Akin, Wilson Ashworth, and Will Riggin.

I played for both churches for years, twice a day, evening services, morning services, and at night. At every funeral when they used to have them at the church. When I was twelve years old, I joined the Methodist church at Burwood, I went every Sunday and Sunday night too. So, the piano players had all left to teach, so I started when I was sixteen to play at the church, and continued until Billy was born, then he would sit on the seat real close to me and hold my coat tail, afraid I would get away, I reckon. I still played on for several more years. After Sue and Allen came along, I did not play every Sunday, others would help out, when they would be home.

Carl S. Dodd and I were married on December 20, 1924. We lived at home until Billy was born on November 20, 1925. We spent all his money on this old house, and we moved here in March of 1926. We had lots of fresh air in summer and winter. Billy had the croup the first night we were here. Carl went up to Claude Johnson's and got Lela. She came with her apron on and Vicks salve in her pocket to doctor him. I kept a big roiling fire all the time, he was croupy, half of the night that winter. I would put on Carl's long johns under, and old long outing gown to keep warm. Carl would possum hunt several times a week. He had an old hunting dog

Ruby Riggin and Carl Dodd

named Woodrow. Carl would catch anything he could skin and sell the hides. After things warmed up later in the year, Jim and Bob came and built the kitchen and dining room. Charged about a dollar an hour. Carl worked on his Dad's farm, raising corn to feed cattle and to grind for our meal and chicken feed. We raised everything to eat. I would can berries, apples, peaches, and cherries, and work until midnight in the summertime canning. We put barrels of apples in cold storage for winter. We bought oranges by the crate, raised everything, peanuts, popcorn, and melons, and sold what we didn't use. I made homemade soap, candies, cookies, cakes, and pies. We drank sassafras tea in the spring of the year to thin our blood, not too many blood clots in those days. We bathed in the old wash tub; or big pan. Lye soap was made to wash clothes or take a bath. Washed dishes and heated water in the old black iron kettle in the yard. Boiled the ham in the big lard stand. We didn't have the money to buy things.

We bought this old place and it took all the money we had, plus the house needed a lot of work. So, when Billy was crawling around, we went to Gray's store at Bingham and bought two rockers, six chairs, one grass rung, and odds and ends of other furniture. A little black iron stove about the size of the top of a washing machine that was so low that Carl made a little frame to sit it on. A kitchen cabinet, furniture from home, and Carl's mama. I had to get up early for Carl to go plow up at his Dad's place every day. We had a horse, old Stocking was his name. He had four white feet and legs. We had a nice rubber tire and top buggy. We did not buy anything on credit. We paid our grocery bill by the month regular. We finally got a little one-seated Ford car. After Sue was born, we bought a four-door Ford.

Carl and Ruby Dodd's house

We still did not buy things on credit, except the Sparkman place, and we finally got that paid off when Billy was about four years old. After that, we began to have doctor's bills to pay. Around 1932, I had a miscarriage and had to hire some help. Sue was born in 1933, Dale came up here from Santa Fe (Maury County) to stay with us for two or three weeks. When Sue was about eighteen months old, Carl took pneumonia and was not able to put in his crop. Dad moved in the old house, Sparkman house, and got everything going until Carl was able to work. They stayed on for some time, and Dad ran the grocery store in Franklin. Then in 1936, Carl had an operation in January at St. Thomas Hospital. Then in April 1936, Sam Allen was born. Dale came back and stayed four weeks with us. By that time, Sue was trying to help Dale cook and a baby to see after. Billy was in school. I had quite a bit to do. Mom was sick quite a bit. Mamie was bedfast, and things began to get pretty hard to see after both places, I had the bag to hold. Dad worked until dark. So, when Mom got better they moved to Franklin and ran a butcher shop.

Things changed up quite a bit. Children growing up. All were in school at Burwood. Time went on, still lots to do. Get up at four o'clock, cook breakfast, hurry, hurry. Milking to do, catch the school bus at six o'clock. Work all day and get ready for another meal. Wood to get in. Water to bring in, same old merry-go-round. When summer came, work in the field, gathering in food, berries, apples, peaches, watermelons, corn, peanuts, beans, and canning again. Chickens to feed, more cows to milk, hogs to slop. Hot weather or cold, plenty to do.

Sue Dodd Locke, Ruby Riggin Dodd, Sam Allen Dodd and Billy Dodd

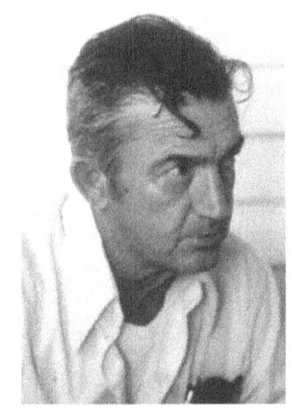

Billy Dodd

Sue Dodd

Sam Allen Dodd

Now! Children are all ready to go to Franklin High School (late 1940s and early 1950s). Get on the old yellow bus. Hurry up, time for the bus. Where are my shoes? Snow on the ground, slip, and slide, get more wood. Breakfast over! Where is this? Where is that?

I am still making tracks, cooking, and washing, making up beds! Watching after everyone! Still waiting on the family, cooking, children going and coming here and there.

Billy and Esther married, and have one son, Bobby. Sue and Jay are married and have two boys. Sam Allen is married and has two sons. History of my family as of today.

Still on a merry-go-round. Grandchildren now. Work all day trying to build houses for themselves, past dark until bedtime. I have settled down alone in the same old house, where I have lived many years, ever since March 1926. Carl passed away in 1985.

Tidbits of Ancestors

I never knew my father's mother and father. Grandma was Henrietta Shaw before she was married to Robert Bruce Riggin. She died when my dad was very small. Grandpa married again to Sarah Jones. When Dad was about six years old. He and Aunt Ada Ormes were the only children of Henrietta Shaw and Bob Riggin. After Grandpa and Grandma Sarah were married, they had two girls, Aunt Callie and Aunt Myrt. They lived in the old house on the corner where Uncle Jimmy Ball and Aunt Laura lived. Callie married Tom Huff (Mr. Rob Huff's brother). Myrt married Jim Ragsdale and had two sons. Callie had four children. Poppa and Aunt Ada went to Boston to live with Uncle Oscar Shaw and his wife, which was not very good for them. After Dad grew up, he came back to live with Grandma Sarah and the two girls. Aunt Ada married Charlie Ormes; and had three children: Charlie, Eliza, and Ned.

Perlina Ashworth with her children

I knew my mother's parents, for we lived with them sometime between moves. My Grandfather Josephus Ashworth was Scotch-Irish and came from Virginia. His mother's people were Caseys who originated from Illinois and had relatives in the West or at least in Oklahoma. I remember when I was small some of the kin came to see us, and his wife was part Indian, with long black hair parted in the middle, all slicked down, so long she could sit on it. My Grandad was in the Civil War. My Grandmother was a tiny little wisp of a woman, kind, loving, and cared for me and my children until she was taken to a nursing home in Franklin. Before her marriage, she was Perlina Branch Locke and her mother was a Jones. When her mother died, she was raised by her Aunt Mary Jones Hassell. During the war, she lived in Spring Hill. When they were fighting, Aunt Mary told them to get on each side of the chimney so the bullets would not hit them. The ground was frozen, and the soldiers were marching with their shoes worn out. The soles were just flopping as they marched by.

When grandmother and grandfather were married and after five children were born, they decided to go West as many others did. So, they proceeded to go by wagon train to Texas, which was a very dangerous journey. While crossing the Red River, one of the horses became frightened and almost turned the wagon over in the water. While in Texas, they lost three children, little Willie, Sena, and Emily. They came back to Tennessee, where Walter, Jim, and Wilson were born. They lived at the Ashworth house on the pike, where Mother and Dad married. Grandad bought the old place next to Evergreen School, lived there for many years, sold everything, and moved to Nashville when I was small.

We had to ride the train to visit them, which was a big treat for me. I got to go to Kress's 5 & 10 Cent store. The first wedding I ever saw was in Nashville. We went to church at the old Tabernacle, where they attended every Sunday. Aunt Nannie and Wilson went to Tarbox School.

My Dad was born in this community (Burwood). His name was William Jonathan Riggin. He married Susan Mahala Ashworth and had one child, Ruby Ava Riggin. His father was named Robert, "Bob," Riggin. He married Henrietta Shaw, she had two sisters, Cornelia married a Barker, and Dolly Pea married a Nellums from Spring Hill. One brother, William Shaw. Lots of connections if you can find them. W.J. Riggin had two half-sisters, Callie and Myrt, also, one sister Ada. Grandpa

Will J. Riggin (1875-1959) and Mahala Ashworth Riggin (1874-1958)

Bob married again to Sarah Jones. Myrt married Jim Ragsdale. They had two boys, Mack and Albert. Callie married Tom Huff and had several children. (Alexine, Eugene, Louise, and Malcolm) The Akin family was also connected to Dad. Grandpa Riggin's sister Callie married Uncle Jim Akin, Vance and Millard's father.

Dodd Family Tidbits

Carl Shannon Dodd was born to Calvin Washington (1859-1926) and Ida Sophronia Beasley Dodd (1862-1928) on January 3, 1900. He was raised in Burwood on a farm. His father ran a store where Charlie Huff lives now. The Dodds lived where a trailer is now located since the home burned some years ago. Calvin Dodd built another home on the curve where the Balls used to live. They sold that house and built a larger home up in the hollow, where the boys could have a farm to use growing up. The Dodd family came from around Boston. I don't know too much about the family. They scattered after growing up. Carl's brothers farmed on this side of the ridge until grandchildren began to scatter from Franklin to Columbia. War came (WWII) and some had to go away for some time. Most of them are close enough to visit when they wish.

Calvin Washington and Ida Beasley Dodd

Calvin Dodd – Jim Ball Home

Last Writings

Wednesday, November 22, 1995.

Thinking of days past and gone by. I could even write. I could sing. I could play the piano. They were the days of no responsibility. I grew up a normal person. Now, thinking about how times have changed, I have had a life that has taught me to care for others. I have three wonderful children who have cared for and watched after me. And no one has grandchildren any more helpful and thoughtful than mine have been. May God bless Little Jessica to follow on with the rest of them.

Bobby Dodd, oldest grandson

Sam Allen Dodd, Christine Burns, Sue Dodd, and Neil Barnhill

Bobby Dodd and Lou Huff

Charles Ormes (1868-1947) Ada Lee Riggin Ormes (1873-1941)

BUSINESSES IN THE VILLAGE OF BURWOOD

RICK WARWICK

1878 Beers Map of Williamsburg showing the commercial center of what would become Burwood.

The intersection of Carter's Creek Pike and Pope's Chapel Road has a long history as the commercial center of the Burwood community. The first post office was located here in 1878, in a store owned by W.A. Shaw, who was appointed the first postmaster. The 1878 Beers map indicates the Shaw store was located south of the present Huff store, a blacksmith shop was in the corner of the intersection, a sawmill-cotton gin across the road, and an office for Dr. W.W. Williams, for whom the village was named, located opposite the blacksmith shop. On August 3, 1893, *The Review-Appeal* reported the killing of Joe Fitzgerald near Capt. Margart's store at Shaw.

The old Akin Store across the ditch from the present Huff's store. It was operated by Vance and Millard Akin before building the present Huff store, in about 1911.

Akin Brothers' Store opened in 1911

Businesses in the Village of Burwood

The old John Shaw Store was possibly the site of the killing of Lionel Johnson by Fred and Charley Hawk on February 10, 1913, then known as Lavender's Store.

The general store owned by Mr. John Shaw went out of business in 1935. For a while, in 1936, Mr. L.D. Barnhill was in the grocery business there. In January 1937, Mr. and Mrs. W.H. Short, (Bill and Annie Lee) opened a general merchandise business in the old Shaw store. To the left was an old blacksmith run by Mr. Bill T. Huff. There was also a set of scales to the right, where people could bring their wagons or trucks of farm goods to be weighed. The old blacksmith shop was torn down in 1937 and the scales were taken up soon after that. The old gas pump at the store was a hand pump, commonly used before electricity came to the country. The tank held 10 gallons and then you had to pump it full again.

The Shorts built a new store and house across the road, on the old Burwood Cumberland Presbyterian Church lot in the late fall of 1939. The church had been moved there from its original home across from the Leiper's Fork Primitive Baptist Church in 1918. The Short Store continued until August 7, 1963, when they retired and moved to Franklin. The store still stands vacant today.

In 1941, Mr. L.D. Barnhill bought the old Shaw store. He made an apartment on one side and ran a poolroom on the other. In 1945, L.D. sold the store to Mr. R.G. Huff and the entire store was made into two apartments, as they remain today. L.D. bought the Billy T. Huff place, on the hill near the Burwood Church of Christ and built a new home there in 1946.

The evolution of the old Shaw store – Barnhill's poolroom, two apartments – now a single dwelling may have been the location of Lavender's store, the scene of the murder of Lionel Johnson by Fred and Charlie Hawk in 1913.

The old store building located next to Robert Byrd's house was possibly the first store operated by Millard F. Akin, built in 1883, and took in his brother, Vance Akin, as a partner in 1888. In 1911, they built the present Huff store.

Myles Brown and Billy T. Huff standing in front of the old blacksmith shop in 1938.

Old blacksmith shop operated by Myles Brown and later Billy Huff. It closed in the 1940s.

The "Little Store" was built for James Huff in 1933 on Carter's Creek Pike across from the Johnson Hollow Road intersection. Billy and Esther Dodd tried their luck here. One of the last was David and Betty Plemons. The store later burned.

The Bill Short Store in Burwood was built in 1939 and continued until he retired in 1963.

Annie Lee and Bill Short sitting on the porch of their new store built in 1939 and run until they retired in 1963.

Milton Clark stands in front of the former sawmill where his father, Bob Clark, helped Will Akin. Bob Clark also ran the grist mill which was located behind the Osborne home further down the creek. The cotton gin was located at the same location as the grist mill, years before. The 1878 Beers map indicates that the mill was next door to Dr. W.W. Williams, being the same site as the home of James and Jessie Grigsby Huff.

The Joe Pope store on Cayce Springs Road closed in 1941.

Joseph Lucius Pope, Sr. was born in Thompson's Station in 1903 and married Fannie Mae Fitzgerald in 1924. They farmed their land until the 1980s and had six kids: Mary, Joseph, Jr., Robert, Louis, J.C, and Ethel. The property was originally part of a 20-acre parcel purchased by Osborn Pope in 1882 for two mules valued at $200. Osborn was the son of Patience Pope, an enslaved person of African descent. Joe Pope, as a grandson of Osborn, received a part of the land, and he donated part of it for the establishment of Joe Pope Road in the late 1980s. The remaining property passed to his children, and much of it remains in the Pope family.

Robert Huff, Jr., Ken Huff, and Robert Huff, Sr.

Lou and Ken Huff, Leonard Grigsby, and James Ragsdale discuss the local news.

Ken and Lou Huff restock the shelves.

Lou Huff, Burwood School secretary and cashier at Huff's Store.

Ken Huff and Glen Huff

Charlie Huff making sandwiches.

RURAL SCENES

RICK WARWICK

Judy Grigsby with her 4-H project

Brown Cannon and a friend driving a horse and wagon

Riley Lavender with Mac Allen, a Tennessee Walker raised and trained by Lavender

Curtis Barnhill, Thomas and Ola Fry, and grandson in the strawberry patch on Thompson Station Road

Grace Jones and Flossie Barnhill in front of a crop of tobacco

Blacksmith Will Jones with horse and buggy on Columbia Pike. Who would do that now?

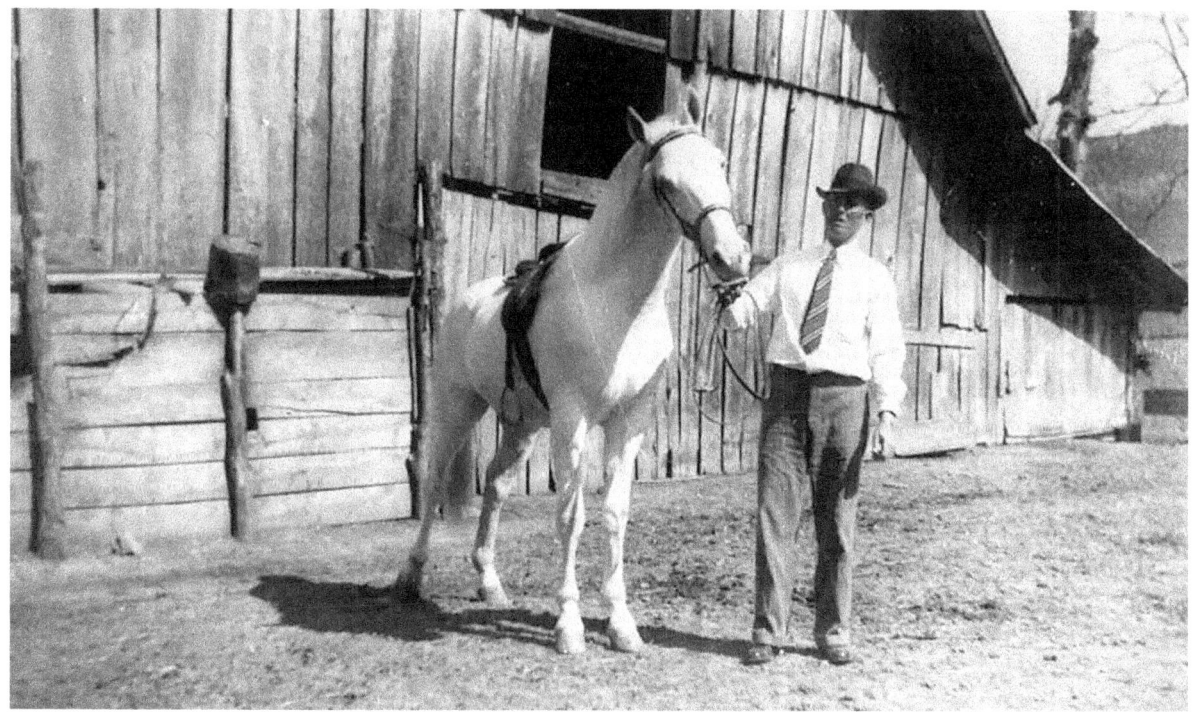

Horse trainer Ollie Sparkman, Sr. (1884-1959) with horse raised by Ridley Jones.

Ollie and Gertrude Dodd Sparkman and friend on Carter's Creek Pike, ca. 1910

Ollie Sparkman, Sr. farm on Sparkman Road, south of Burwood

Tenant families hand-picked cotton until local farmers stopped raising it due to low prices and the arrival of the boll weevil.

Curtis Amos of Forest Hill Community with a pair of mules going to the creek for water.

Fresh milk, buttermilk, cottage cheese, and butter keep the country folks happy. In the 1950s, Williamson County led the state in the number of Grade A dairies. Small farmers sold their surplus milk to the cheese plant in Franklin.

Randal, Ernest, and Wayne Davis

Lucile Johnson holds the cow as her nephew fills the bucket.

Sam Allen Dodd and Neil "Big Dog" Barnhill

Brown Cannon and a fine example of horseflesh

Clyde Andrews and his sister Jennie relied on mule power before the tractor. Williamson County rivaled Maury County in the production of mules.

Curtis Amos and Diamond Smith of the Forest Hill community with mules and wagon

Remember when the first cold spell came … we knew it was time to kill hogs. Tenderloin and biscuits were served for lunch. The making of sausage, lard, and cracklins came later. The salting down of shoulders, hams, and sides came after the meat had cooled overnight.

R.H. Barker, Sr. and crew scalding a hog

James Wade and Doc King

R.H. Barker, Sr. oversees the hog killing

CHURCHES OF THE FOURTH DISTRICT

Leiper's Fork Primitive Baptist Church, whose congregation was organized in 1824, began its physical church home in this building in 1916.

LEIPER'S FORK PRIMITIVE BAPTIST

LULA FAIN MAJOR

Leiper's Fork Primitive Baptist Church

Leiper's Fork Primitive Baptist Church

The sign on the front of this building shows that Leiper's Fork Primitive Baptist Church had its beginnings on July 22, 1824. However, they did not have a church building of their own until 1916 when, through a swap, this building became their church home.

A church meeting house was already on this lot when Thomas F. Perkins deeded an acre here in 1848 to the denomination called Disciples of Christians, and these Christians in 1916 deeded their interest in the building to the Primitive Baptists.

The brick building faces Carter's Creek Pike; Perkins Road is on its south side and Murfree's Fork of West Harpeth on the other. Unusually, the two front doors are on the long side rather than at the end. The church's record of Saturday before the third

Sunday in August 1916 states that this building was known as Pleasant Dale or the Brick Church.

Editor's note: This building should not be confused with the Pleasant Dale Presbyterian Church U.S.A. (1888-1917) across the road, which was moved to Burwood to become Burwood Cumberland Presbyterian Church. This church building is no doubt the oldest house of worship in the Fourth District.

Dewey Garland, whose grandfather, Elder Malachi Johnson, was the minister here for 36 years, remembers these leading elders in his lifetime:
Elder Malachi Johnson, Sr., from 1914 until he died in 1950.
Elder Oakley Johnson from 1950 until he died in 1963
Elder S.T. Scott, Sr.
Elder Otis Lee Newton
Elder S.T. Scott, Jr.
Elder Clifton Johnson
Elder Travis Williams, current

Carter's Creek Pike at Perkins Road in 1965

Text: *Sketches of Antebellum Churches of Williamson County*, by Lula Fain Major, Williamson County Historical Society, Journal No. 22, 1991

BURWOOD UNITED METHODIST CHURCH

LULA FAIN MAJOR

Burwood United Methodist Church

Burwood United Methodist Church, photo by Anne Goetze

In the summer of 1818, John Pope gave one-half acre of land to Samuel Akin, John Moore, and James Patton "for the good cause and express purpose of encouraging and promoting useful knowledge and the religion of Jesus Christ." Trustees were to have a house built for the worship of God "and School house when the same may be occupied in that way." This acreage was on the headwaters of Murfree's Fork near Anderson's Big Spring.

It was on the acreage John Pope gave that the Methodists and other denominations worship. The church came to be called Pope's Chapel as did the road.

In 1910, a tornado damaged the building. The congregation then worshiped in a schoolhouse. In 1913, the present sanctuary was constructed on 1 acre and 18 poles bought the year before for $167.80 from Mr. and Mrs. W.A. Shaw. At this time, it was renamed Burwood. It is within sight of Huff's store.

Inside Burwood United Methodist Church

Text: Sketches of Antebellum Churches of Williamson County, by Lula Fain Major, Williamson County Historical Society, Journal No. 22, 1991

TENT MEETING IN BURWOOD

Burwood Tent Meeting of all denominations, 1912

Old-time Tent Meeting at Burwood ca. 1915. A.B. Church made the following identifications. 1st row: Noble Boyd, unknown, Iulas Sparkman, Ollie Porter Sparkman, Abram B. Church, Timothy Akin, seated, Elmer Church, Abe Church, Frank McMinn, W.A. Shaw, J.B. Akin, Sr., David Jones, J.B. Akin, Jr., Butler Sparkman, Marsha Robinson, Ruth Akin, James Thweatt, Robert Akin, Mrs. Lucy Sparkman, Mrs. Tishie Sparkman, Mrs. Mary Akin, Miss Belle McMinn, Mrs. Maggie Jones, 2nd row: Bernard Shaw, Prentice Elmore, Carl Dodd, Bernard Elmore, Lou Barker, Ewell Clark, John Will Akin, Ed Thweatt, Edgar Shaw, Bill Short, Eph Ragsdale, Cliff Jones, Tiny Andrews, Mr. and Mrs. R.V. Akin, R.V. Akin, Jr., unknown, Lela Jones Johnson, unknown, Estelle Johnson Baker, unknown, John Ella Huff, Mr. and Mrs. Claude Sparkman, three unknown, Louise Shaw, Johnny Elmore, Cammie Akin, Dixie Shaw, Anola Thweatt, Lila Mae Akin, Ollie Mae Pope, Ethel Clark, Joella Akin, Jim Tanner, Jennie Lee Elmore, Robbie Clark, Mrs. R.D. Lawrence, two unknown, Mrs. Noble Boyd, back row, several unknown, Mary Lou McMinn.

EVERGREEN PRIMITIVE BAPTIST CHURCH

Evergreen Primitive Baptist Church, est. 1876, was built in 1946 on Evergreen Road.

Evergreen Primitive Baptist Church was organized in 1876. The first elder was Berry Wilson, followed by Elder Henry Jordan. Early deacons were Lish Darden, Sam Amos, and Henry Oden. Later deacons were James Fitzgerald, and Joe Pope. The present church building was built in 1946. The 1996 membership roll consisted of Percy Beasley, Rosie Lee Beasley, Cora C. Ladd, Fannie Leach, Cheryl Kittrell, Janie Leach, Chad Kittrell, Janie Kittrell, Jana Dodson, Joshua Dodson, Lucille Haynes, Denise Fitzgerald and her three children – Trey, Denae, and Jasmine, Elizabeth Booker, Louis Pope, Leroy Brown, James Biggers, Henry Fly, Dennis Fitzgerald, Andrea Patton, William Murdic, James Fly, and Elder Maurice Brice. The Evergreen Primitive Baptist Church is in fellowship with the Lynn Creek Primitive Baptist Association.

PEARLY HILL C.M.E. AND PEARLY HILL CHURCH OF CHRIST

Pearly Hill C.M.E. and Pearly Hill Church of Christ (Extinct)

Located on Johnson Hollow Road

On January 12, 1892, J.T. Polk sold a lot to trustees Solomon Pope, Henry Carothers, John Burnett, Robert Polk, and William Pope. In 1953, the building was sold to a new congregation known as the Pearly Hill Church of Christ. Sadly, both congregations are extinct.

MURFREE'S FORK PRIMITIVE BAPTIST CHURCH

Murfree's Fork Primitive Baptist Church appears abandoned today.

Located on Perkins Road off Carter's Creek Pike

Murfree's Fork Primitive Baptist Church. This may be the adjacent fellowship Hall.

On June 6, 1887, Thomas F. Perkins sold to Deacons Robert Bradley and Robert Perkins for one dollar a half-acre lot for a church and school. The cornerstone of the present church reads: "Murphree's Fork P. B. Church rededicated August 14, 1983, Elder T. Givens, Pastor." The school closed many years ago and the church appears abandoned since Thomas Givens died in 2019.

MT. LAVERGNE METHODIST CHURCH C.M.E.

Located on Sugar Ridge Road

Mt. Lavergne Methodist Church (Colored Methodist Episcopal Church), now extinct, was located on Sugar Ridge Road. In 1946, Bessie Cunningham sold for $30 a half-acre to church trustees Rufus Reese, John H. Carothers, Dig Steele, Council Helm. The lot was located on Sugar Ridge Road on the north, Fleming on the east, Mount Taber Lodge on the west, and Ollie Lawrence on the south. In 1967, the Mt. Tabor Lodge sold its interests in the building to church trustees Fred Carter, Zandine Phillips, and Calvin Johnson.

Mt. Lavergne C.M.E Mothers and Deacons

PEARLY HILL BAPTIST CHURCH

Located on Sycamore Road, the last Pearly Hill Baptist Church also housed the school that closed between 1952 and 1954.

The original two-story building for Pearly Hill Lodge and School, now extinct.

BURWOOD CHURCH OF CHRIST

Burwood Church of Christ was built here in 1913. Many local citizens are buried in the adjoining cemetery.

Located on Carter's Creek Pike

The first Church of Christ was located at the west end of Evergreen Road and was called West End Church of Christ. It was next to the West End School. In 1913, the land was bought for $200 from W.A. Shaw and his wife by trustees: Riley Lavender, James Shaw, George McKee, John Morrow, and N.C. Beasley for the Burwood Church of Christ to be built at its present site. The West End Church was torn down and the useable materials were hauled by mule wagons by Abraham Church, Carl Dodd, Billy Holt, and others to the present site. Logs were given from the Calvin Dodd property, cut, and hauled by Bud Fuller to the Will Akin sawmill for further cutting. As usual, there were two doors, one for women and one for men. In later years, Sunday School rooms were added and later a baptistry was added.

The following families have been worshiping here from the beginning: Barker, Lavender, Shaw, Morrow, Beasley, Sparkman, Church, Dodd, Holt, Grigsby, Barnhill, and Duncan.

LAWRENCE GROVE BAPTIST CHURCH

Located at the corner of Pope's Chapel Road and Barker Road

In September of 1917, it was voted that the new church be given the name Lawrence Grove Baptist Church. About two acres of land that had previously been the old Methodist Pope's Campgrounds were given to the trustees of the church by Ollie Lawrence for the erection of a house of worship. In 1919, Claude Sparkman and S.A. Robinson donated logs from their land, which they cut in a local sawmill and the building was begun. The first service was held in the new church in July 1919. Today, the church enjoys an active, growing congregation.

Easter egg hunt at Lawrence Grove Baptist Church

Easter Sunday at Lawrence Grove Baptist Church

EMANUEL PENTECOSTAL CHURCH OF CHRIST

Brother Dan Wise is the minister at Emanuel Pentecostal Church of Christ on Perkins Road.

Sister Inez Tywater Jones among the local families of Jennettes, Johnsons, and Ragsdales

JONES CHAPEL CHURCH OF THE NAZARENE

LUCILLE RAINEY

Located on Johnson Hollow Road

Jones Chapel Nazarene Church on Johnson Hollow Road

The Nazarenes in Burwood started meeting in the Sycamore School as early as 1900.

The school closed in 1949. In 1950, Mr. and Mrs. Wiley Jones donated the land where the present church building was built with the hands of the members. In 1959, the first two Sunday School rooms and the addition on the front were completed. It was also re-dedicated, and the name was changed from Sycamore to Jones Chapel. In 1981, four new Sunday School rooms, the fellowship room, new carpet, and pews were added.

The Spiritualaires (shown right) call Jones Chapel home: William Andrews, Nancy Andrews Atkinson, Ronnie Johnson, Gary Fewell, and Arnie Ryan.

Jones Chapel Church of the Nazarene in the early 1950s

Ruby Riggin Dodd

OLD HOPE CHURCH OF CHRIST

Old Hope Church of Christ

Located on Sycamore Road

In 1974, a group of about forty neighbors along Sycamore Road decided to organize a congregation of Christians in their neighborhood. Herbert Marlin gave the land for the building, a very neat one nestled among the trees in this area just off Bear Creek Road.

Dillard Howell was the first preacher to serve the church; Wayne Chadwell and Tony Stafford have also preached here. Leaders in the congregation have been Clint Holt, Grover Hargrove, and Terry Peach.

For the curious: yes, there is a New Hope not far away, two, in fact—New Hope Church of Christ and New Hope Baptist Church.

SCHOOLS OF THE FOURTH DISTRICT

FOREST HILL, WEST END, SYCAMORE, BURWOOD, PEARLY HILL, MT. LAVERGNE, AND EVERGREEN

The 4th Civil District is unique in Williamson County in that it had five public schools for Black students and five public schools for White students as follows: Pearly Hill School on Sycamore Road, Mt. Lavergne School on Sugar Ridge Road, Evergreen School on Evergreen Road, Murfree's Fork on Perkins Road, and Thompson's Station School for Black students; Forest Hill School on Carter's Creek Pike, Sycamore School on Sycamore Road, Burwood School on Carter's Creek Pike, West End School on Pope's Chapel Road, and Thompson's Station School at Thompson's Station for White students. This doesn't consider Williams Academy at Burwood, the one-room log school at the home of Mrs. Nannie Huff, and Forest Hill Female Academy on Carter's Creek Pike of the mid-19th century which may not have been public schools.

The Nannie Huff home, located on Carter's Creek Pike and Johnson Hollow, was the site of an early one-room log schoolhouse.

FOREST HILL

RICK WARWICK

Forest Hill Female Academy

The Forest Hill Female Academy school was organized in 1853 and operated by female teachers from New England. The school became a public school after the Civil War. The trustees included T.F. Perkins, Sr., W.P. Cannon, C.H. Kinnard, Samuel S. Morton, H.G.W. Mayberry, Alexander Gray, and Dr. H. Oden.

Forest Hill School

Forest Hill School was built between 1900 and 1910 and closed in 1949.

Forest Hill School was located near Glen Overbey's Store on Carter's Creek Pike and is thought to have been built between 1900 and 1910. The school still stands today and has recently been restored by the present owner. The school closed in 1949 with Mrs. Gladys Whitley as the teacher. Mrs. Whitley remembered Supt. W.P. Scales came one morning and told her to gather the books and the students as they were moving to Burwood. The building was later used to store grain and hay from the Overbey farm.

Forest Hill School, 1911

1st row: Buck Brooks, Joe Lillie, Paul Johnson, Joe Carl Andrews, Lennie Polk, Sam Cannon, and O.B. Carl;

2nd row: Emma Overbey, Eunice Overbey, Mabel Polk, Allie Mai Smith, Clara Carl, Ruth Johnson, Mary Overbey, and Louisa Sullivan;

3rd row: Teacher Miss Sybil Lillie, Emma Johnson, James Brooks, Ada Johnson, Bessie Brooks, Herman Lillie, Sam Maury, and Leonard Lillie.

Forest Hill School

Forest Hill School, 1899, Miss Jane Bowman, teacher

1st row: Unknown except Brown Kinnard on right;

2nd row: Lemuel Cooke, Ethel Gray, unknown, unknown, Louise Bailey, Bessie Cooke, Mabel Gray, unknown, Rose Hardison, Cynthia Kinnard;

3rd row: Herman Lillie, unknown, Sibyl Lillie, Jim Cameron, Miss Jane Bowman, unknown, unknown, unknown.

Forest Hill School, 1936, Miss Annie Lou Barker, teacher

Forest Hill School boys, 1930s

1st row: Lester Marlin with dog, Allen Marlin, unknown, Ernie Jennette, Jim Layne, unknown, Si McCampbell, T.C. McCullough;

2nd row: Melvin Marlin, unknown, unknown, Clayton McCampbell, Johnny McCampbell, Glen Marlin, and Buddy Huff

Forest Hill

Forest Hill School, 1948

1st row: Boyd Beard, Doyle Beard, Donald Martin, Ellis Davis, Dennis Martin, Bernice Martin, William Anglin, Ed Geasley, Lorene Martin;

2nd row: Alton Martin, Grace Anglin, Mildred Beard, Bennie Hamby, Vivian Gray, Martha Jean Martin, Milton Geasley, Clay Byrd, Betty Ann Johnson, _____ Sullivan;

3rd row: Buddy Martin, Dorothy Martin, Latha Osborne, Willie Mai Martin, Christine Johnson, Lela Martin, Prudie Beard, Mattie Lou Davis, Mrs. Gladys Whitley, unknown;

4th row: Mrs. Alva Jefferson, Benton Martin, Connie _____, Odelene Geasley, Betty Jo Blair, Annie Lee Walls, Douglas Martin, Claudine Martin, Mary Nell Walls.

Forest Hill School, Mrs. Whitley's Class, 1948

1st row: Bennie Hamby, William Anglin, Clay Byrd, Doyle Beard;

2nd row: Grace Anglin, Dennis Martin, unknown, Ruth Beard, Vivian Gray, Martha Jean Martin, Betty Ann Johnson, Ellis Davis, Milton Geasley, Bernice Martin;

3rd. Mrs. Gladys Whitley, Latha Osborne, Annie Lee Walls, Delton Anglin, Marie Anglin, Mildred Beard, Alton Martin.

WEST END SCHOOL AND WILLIAMS ACADEMY

RICK WARWICK

Williams Academy

Little is known about Williams Academy, located on Carter's Creek Pike, near the Williams Post Office, except that it was named for Dr. William Washington Williams, who practiced medicine in the community. The charter of incorporation of 1879 named the trustees as follows: Simon Watson, George W. Barker, Joe Ashworth, W.C. Pope, Henderson Helm, J.C. Johnson, W.W. Byers, and James Watson. The purpose was to establish a library, promote painting, music, or fine arts, to encourage literature, and scientistic understanding. The exact location is not given.

West End School

The West End School closed about 1915.

West End School, 2024

West End School was built in 1885. It is located on the former Parson Pope property on Pope Chapel Road. It was a two-teacher school, but at times one teacher taught all grades. It was heated by woodstove and water from a well near the school. There were also several springs nearby for water. West End closed about 1915 after the frame Burwood School was built. The old stage and blackboards can be seen today. In 2023, the building underwent a complete restoration under the direction of owner, Judy Grigsby Hayes.

West End School, circa 1910

1st row: unknown, Farris Huff, unknown, Glen Lavender, J.B. Akin, James Huff, Joe Butler, Edgar Shaw, James Thweatt, Roy Barker, Joe Greer Nichols, George Shaw, unknown;

2nd row: Greer Shaw, Ruth Short, unknown, Odell Church, Dixie Shaw, Teacher Cynthia White, Lera Thweatt, Ethel Clark, Cammie Akin, Ethel Morrow, Verda Huff, unknown;

3rd row: Era Huff, Martha Robinson, Ruth Akin, Maggie Mae Akin, Ethel Short, unknown, Abe Church, Robert Robinson;

4th row: Ollie Porter Sparkman, Cliff Latta, Park Huff, Henry Sparkman, unknown, Clarence Latta, unknown, Carl Dodd, unknown.

West End School, with Mr. John B. Gray

1st. row: Dixie Beasley, John Will Akin, Park Huff, Bernard Shaw, Prentice Elmore, Vallie Elmore, Lizzie Lawrence, Willie Lawrence;

2nd. Birdie Harmon, Missie Sparkman, John Ella Huff, Charlie Hutcherson, Ewell Clark, Frank Waddey, Roxie Hutcherson, Lou Anna Beasley;

3rd: unknown, Louise Shaw, John Ella Elmore, Mr. John B. Gray, Abigail Chappell, Rollie Pope, Cliff Hutcherson;

4th row: Robbie Clark, Cammie Akin, Vernette Chappell, Marie Elmore, Dixie Shaw, Johnnie Lee Elmore, Ethel Clark, Ollie Mai Walton, Lilia Mai Akin;

5th row: Jim Walton, Pate Chappell, Tommy Nichols, unknown.

West End School, 1911, Mrs. Eugene Barker

1st row: James Thweatt, Glenn Lavender, Robert Robinson, Walter Faw Short, George Shaw, James Huff, Roy Barker, Arthur Huff, Edgar Shaw, Ollie Porter Sparkman, Park Huff, John L. Barker;

2nd row: Ruth Akin, Ethel Short, Azille Boyd, Willie Beth Elmore, Ruth Robinson, Eva Huff, Anola Thweatt, Robbie Clark, Joella Akin, Jessie Sparkman, Willie Beasley, Ruth Short;

3rd row: Nona Sparkman, Ruby Sparkman, Lera Akin, Louise Shaw, Dora Lawrence, Verda Huff, Jessie Elmore, Zun Dodd, Henry Sparkman, Clarence Latta, Carl Dodd, Pate Chapell;

4th row: Jennie Lee Elmore, Vernetta Chappell, Cammie Akin, Lou Wille Boyd, Bill Short, Bertha Tomlinson, Ethel Clark, Marie Elmore;

Top row: Johnnie Elmore, Blanche Lawrence, Dixie Shaw, Miss Leona Hardison, and Mrs. Fannie Barker, teachers.

SYCAMORE SCHOOL

RICK WARWICK

Sycamore School, located in Johnson Hollow, closed in 1949, as seen here in 1960. Sycamore School was established in 1885 with a deed by Lewis L. and Susan Johnson to directors Elisha Johnson, John Polk, Robert Morrow, W.S. Inman, and H.J. Johnson. It was used as a union church. It was heated by a wood stove and got its water from a spring. It closed in 1949. In 1922, records show that 28 double desks and some benches were on the school inventory. In 1922, there were 11 boys and 13 girls with the teacher being James Sparkman.

Sycamore School, 1905

1st row: Porter Jennette, Eva (Polk) Geasley, Alma Sparkman, Deamie Fry, Lula Johnson, Emmer Lee (Johnson) Huff, Ollie Kelley, Marvin Rollins;

2nd row: Etta Ragsdale, Della (Johnson) Jennette, Teacher Mrs. Gertie (Dodd) Sparkman, Willie Bell (Geasley) McCoy, Vunia Johnson (Jennette), Earnest Holt, Vance Ragsdale, Cal Hassell;

3rd row: Miss Sparkman, Elsie Johnson Jones, Beal Kelley, Ross Geasley, Park Jennette, Carl Dodd, Nelson Polk, Zan Dodd;

4th row: Louella Johnson Jennette, Birdie (Fry) Huff, Bud Holt, Prince Geasley, and Wesley Inman.

Sycamore School 1913

1st row: Paul Hassell, Florena Rader, Bessie Johnson, Hayward Johnson, Lem Ragsdale, Leslie Price, Oakley Price, Clellon Ragsdale, Jasper Rader, Oakley Johnson;

2nd row: Willie Hicks, Cora Gray, Olene Hargrove, Bertha Johnson, Rosie Whitehead, Hallie Rader, Ida Huff, Eva Byrd, Annie Lee Fry, Gordon Huff, Erby D. Hargrove, O.B. Hargrove, Bob McCandless;

3rd row: Ethel Ragsdale, Grace Huff, Ruby Riggin, Ila Johnson, Lillian Whitehead, Earl Huff, Ed McCandless, John Lynn, Gene Johnson, Herbert Rader, Barnett Johnson, Adie McCandless, Cub Johnson;

4th row: Teacher Bessie Smith, Gertie Johnson, Eva Johnson, Emmalee Johnson, Effie Price, Bertha Hargrove, Lena Gray.

Sycamore School, Miss Pauline Barker, teacher

1st row: James Ragsdale, Eugene Martin, Dorothy Jones, Gertrude Andrews, Joe Carl Andrews, Clifton Martin;

2nd row: J.B. Jones, Lonnie Martin, Lela Jones, Vivian Stofel, Pauline Stofel, Dallas Johnson, Wesley Inman, Teacher Pauline Barker (Duncan)

Sycamore School, 1947

1st row: Melvin Williams, Joe Crafton, Dan Jennette, Lloyd White, Donnie Joe Craft;

2nd row: Gilliam Williams, Wayne Johnson, Wilma Jones, Bessie Craft, Faye Ferguson, Norma Williams, Shirley Curtis, Jessie Curtis, Mildred Jones;

3rd row: Harold Johnson, Ralph Crafton, Sam Allen Dodd, Ester Dodd, Teacher Miss Clydie Geasley, Heddy Geasley, Jessie Ruth Baker.

BURWOOD SCHOOL

RICK WARWICK

Burwood High School was built in 1916 as a three-room school for grades 1-12. M.F. Akin and R.V. Akin sold 3 acres for $375.oo to W.C. Jones, M.F. Akin, and J.P. Morrow, school directors of the 4th District. Water was provided by a well and heated by wood stoves. In 1922, it was reported that Burwood School had 100 double desks and some benches. The value of all materials was valued at $650.00 In 1922, there were 51 boys and 45 girls with S.C. Veach, Nonnie Orr, Ora Smithson, and Ula Martin being teachers. In 1928, the high school classes were moved to Franklin. This building was replaced in 1956 with a brick structure. It closed in 1976 due to low attendance.

Old Burwood School (1916-1956)

Burwood School, 1917-1918

1st row: Greer Shaw, O.B. Carl, Buford Robinson, Jack Lillie, Howard Latta, Robert Akin, Edwin Thurman, Joe Carl Andrews, R.V. Akin, Jr., Patterson Nichols, Farris Huff, Timothy Akin, George Shaw, James Huff;

2nd row: Elmer Church, Howard Stanley, Joe Lillie, Emma Overbey, Ruth Akin, Christine Good, Eunice Overbey, Ruby Wright, Opal Blackburn, Frances Burnett, Ethel Byrd, Mary Overbey, Sunshine Nicholas, Lucille Byrd, J.B. Akin;

3rd row: Mary Campbell Burnett, Eva Byrd, Maggie Mai Akin, Lillian Boyd, William Huff, Jim Robinson, Annie Lee Fry, Principal G.W. Reed, William Burnett on post;

4th row: Clarence Latta, Azile Boyd, Teachers Miss Grace Drumright, Miss Mabel Gray, Miss Lila Mae Akin, Ruby Riggin.

Burwood School, 1920

The Burwood Presbyterian Church can be seen on the left. Miss Eula Mai Anderson, teacher

1st row: Mary Lou McKinnon, unknown, Jessie Ashworth, Robbie Lee Barker, Louise Hutcherson, Charlotte Johnson, Kathleen Johnson, Josephine Lawrence, Pauline Huckabee;

2nd row: Bernice Johnson, unknown, George Taylor, Inez Huff, Elizabeth Church, unknown, Barkley Johnson, unknown;

3rd row: Robert Byrd, Thomas Tomlinson, unknown, J.D. Elmore, Dayton Southall, Percy Sparkman, Kenneth Blackburn, Thomas Fry

Burwood School, Mr. Brownie Boyce, teacher

Identifications of students are not complete.

Clara Trimble, Edgar Shaw, unknown, Cliff Latta, Clarence Latta, Robbie Clark, Ruby Riggin, Ethel Morrow, Azile Boyd, Roy Barker, Howard Stanley, George Shaw, Glen Sparkman, Dixie Shaw, Elmie Flowers, Aura Burcham, Anola Thweatt, Jessie Sparkman, Joella Akin, Ethel Clark, Lucille Akin, Emma Johnson, Mattie Lee Hicks, Martha Robinson, Elizabeth Akin, Velma Trimble, Ruth Akin, Emma Overbey, Mr. Brownie Boyce (teacher), Ada Johnson, Eunice Overbey, Tim Akin, Frances Burnett, Nell Cannon, Leila Akin, Lillian Boyd, Mattie Mai Akin, George Shaw, J.B. Akin, Farris Huff.

Burwood School, Teacher Jessie Grigsby Huff, 1939-1940

1st row: Mary Pewitt and Marie Pewitt;

2nd row: Alene Still, Virginia Ann Dodd, Keith Southall, J.B. Beard, L.C. Jones, Joe Thomas Adkisson, Malcolm Nichols;

3rd row: Mrs. Jessie Grigsby Huff, teacher, Marie Barnhill, Dorothy Jean Huff, Ruth Zan Dodd, Evelyn Dodd, Margaret Sullivan, Corinne Haley.

Burwood School

1st row: Josephine Scott, Lois Byrd, Georgie Barker, Evie Scott, Cliff Sparkman, J.C. Dodd, Woodie Lawrence;

2nd row: Junior Dodd, Hugh Prince, Bill Lavender, Robert Caldwell, Paul Lawrence, John W. Barker, Clyde Caldwell;

3rd row: Ella Scott, Jeanne Barnhill, Louise Stofel, Geneve Sullivan, Lucille Stofel, Stella Prince, Jettie Ashworth, Teacher Vera Sullivan.

Burwood School, Miss Ruth Alexander (Mrs. Bob Sewell), 1939-1940

1st row: R.B. Capshaw, Clarence Haley, Henry P. Sparkman;

2nd row: Hasting Capshaw, Howlett Polk, Wilma Sullivan, Evelyn Dodd, Mary Louise Campbell;

3rd row: Bobby Huff, Rebecca Dodd, Tom Prince, George Beard, Luther Dodd, Celia Sullivan, Edward D. Dodd, Margaret Beard;

4th row: Kenneth Huff, N.C. Jones, George Dodd, Dewey Latta, Ottis Dodd.

Burwood School, J.B. Akin, Principal, 1939-1940

1st row: Jean Pewitt, Mary Cannon, Molly Sullivan, Esther Barnhill, Tic Akin, Bill Dodd, Sterling Sullivan;

2nd row: Anderson Buckner, Darnell Huff, Theresa Scott, Odell Beard, Sadie Haley, Bobby Sullivan, Frankie Short, Margie Short, Elizabeth Sparkman, Blanche Latta;

3rd row: Principal J.B. Akin, Leslie Beard, Roy Barker, Thomas Byrd, James Pewitt, Claude Southall, Brown Cannon, Claude Still, Bates Southall, Cal Dodd, Guy Sullivan.

Blue Ribbon Day

In May of 1940, the Williamson County Health Unit sponsored a Blue Ribbon Day event at Burwood School to recognize those students who had completed their health card successfully. Students had to receive all their vaccinations, maintain good dental hygiene, practice clean physical hygiene, and develop good study habits. Blue, Red, and White ribbons were awarded in the order of completing the student's pledge cards at the beginning of the school year. A day of baseball and volleyball games and a filling picnic lunch made it a day to remember. The following photographs were found in the Williamson County Health Department archives. Special notice should be given to the first Burwood School bus which appears to be a flat-bed farm truck with a wooden frame covered in metal, and benches inside for seating. It is believed L.D. Barnhill owned the truck and drove the makeshift vehicle to Franklin High School. By 1943, the county school board furnished a regular bus with Edward Dee Dodd as the driver.

Burwood School Blue Ribbon Day Event with students, teachers, and parents enjoying a softball game.

Burwood School Blue Ribbon Day Event with students, teachers, and parents enjoying a softball game. Notice the boys' outhouse to the left. May 1940.

Health Department officials in front of Burwood's makeshift bus.

Burwood School 1935, Miss Mary Lou Cannon, teacher

1st row: Bill Zan Dodd, Martha Sue Inman, Thomas Byrd, Roy Barker, Linton Holt, Jr., Celie Sullivan;

2nd row: Molly Sullivan, Esther Barnhill, Mary Inman, Odell Beard, Frankie Short, Bates Southall, Cal Dodd, Billy Dodd;

3rd row: Guy Sullivan, Owen Sullivan, Bobby Sullivan, Vivian Stofel, Anderson Buckner, Hugh Dodd, Leslie Beard, James Southall;

4th row: Glen Huff, Kenneth Latta, Eugene Stofel, Neil Barker, Miss Mary Lou Cannon, teacher, Pauline Stofel, Pud Stofel, James Prince.

Elmer Walls, Mrs. Jessie Huff, Velmer Walls, and Betty Huff

Elmer Walls, Velmer Walls, Mary Inez Walls, and Rosie Walls, 1958

Burwood School 8th Grade Girls, Class of 1962. Brenda Sullivan, Nancy Plemmons, Barbara Ambrose, Nancy Johnson, Doris Taylor, Rose Marie Huff, and Judy Fox, with Rev. Thomas Vance and Mr. Richard Griggs.

Burwood Girls Basketball, 1966-1967, Coach Howard Johnson

1st row: Kathy Stovall, Lynn Drake, Peggy Sullivan;

2nd row: Virginia Holt, Nelda Baker, Pam Andrews, Connie Johnson;

3rd row: Linda England, Sandra Andrews, Debbie Crutcher, Sue Osborne;

4th row: T.C. Brown, Anita Harris, and JoAnne Martin.

Burwood Elementary School   1968-69   Thompsons Station, Tennessee

Burwood Girls Basketball 1968-1969

Standing: Patty Crafton, Kennette Huff, Jane Ragsdale, Pam Andrews, Linda Carothers, Coach Howard Johnson, Kaye Gillespie, Linda Crutcher, Charlene Jones, Sandra Sullivan, and Fay Harrison.

Cheerleaders: Kathy Stovall, Vickie Johnson, Dianne Ingram, Debra Johnson, Reba Holt, Karen Stovall

Burwood Boys Basketball and Cheerleaders with Coach Howard Johnson

Cheerleaders: Karen Stovall, Kim Gillespie, Suzanne McCampbell, Patty Crafton, Kathey Stovall, Kaye Gillespie, Charlene Jones, and Linda Crutcher.

Boys Basketball Team: Ricky Johnson, Gary Fewell, Emery Jones, James Beard, Ricky Shelton, Lee Jennette, Coach Jay Howard Johnson, _____ Oliphant, Bob Hargrove, Charles Holt, Mark Hargrove, Tommy Sullivan, and Ricky Davis.

Burwood Boys Basketball 1965-1966

1st row: Martha England, Faye Johnson, Nellie Hargrove, Betty Sue Fly;

2nd row: David Crutcher, Randy Gillespie, Carroll Sullivan, Kenneth Andrews, Pete Harris;

3rd row: Ronald Johnson, Jerry Sullivan, Allen McKee, Glen Beard, Lon Bucky Sullivan, and Coach Howard Johnson.

Burwood School 5th grade, 1972-1973. Mrs. Amanda North, teacher, and Principal Richard Griggs.

1st row: Danny Wise, Terry Hartley, unknown, Michael Brown;

2nd row: Terry Cox, unknown, John Curry, Demetria _____, Daphne Lazenby, unknown, Monica Johnson, Lisa Wise;

3rd row: Calvin Sullivan, Jerry Candler, Howard McLemore, Ricky Crafton, Jeffrey Marlin, James McKissick, Brenda Harrison, Teresa Edwards;

4th row: Elvis Beard, Pat Steele, Dorothy Oden, unknown, Charlene Harrison, John Steele, Delores Miller, Brenda Walker, Kenny McLemore, and Nathan McKissack.

Burwood School 1973-1974, 8th grade, Mr. Howard Johnson, teacher.

Kneeling: Bobby Barker and Randy Shedd;

Sitting: Carolyn Oden, Patricia McLemore, Kathy Johnson, Debbie Martin, Polly Harper, Kaye Hartley, Teresa Martin, Vicky Geasley, Tina Jennette, Wanda Steele;

Standing: Mr. J. Howard Johnson, Mike Johnson, Dennis Southall, Jeffery Williams, Henry Holt, Dorothy Curry, Mike Burns, Evelynn Lee, Gerald Falk, Velma Brown, James Sullivan, Gail Carlton, Martha Lee, Eddie Lee Harrison, Nancy Whitfield, Tony Stutts, Mike Farmer, Tandy Logan and Kerry Sweeney.

MT. LAVERGNE AND PEARLY HILL SCHOOLS

RICK WARWICK

Mt. Lavergne School

Mt. Lavergne School on Sugar Ridge was built between 1910 and 1920. In 1922, there were 22 girls and 20 boys on the roll with 17 double desks and benches. Mrs. Lottie Carter Ashworth was the teacher for its entire history. The school closed in 1953 with the teacher and students transferred to Thompson Station.

Mt LaVergne School, 1948

Mt. Lavergne School on Sugar Ridge, Miss Lottie Ashworth, teacher

1st row: Eules Carter, James Jamison, Thomas Burns, Robert Steele, William Carothers, John Willie Leggs, L.E. Burns, Howard Carothers;

2nd row: Elizabeth Burns, Cam Alexine Carothers, Annie Pearl Carothers, Willie Lawrence, Sarah Jamison, Annie Lee Carothers, Mattie Sallie Dotson, Docia Carothers, Sarah Dotson, John Thomas Jenkins;

3rd row: Mrs. Ashworth, William Carothers, Leslie Pope, Vallie Steele, Early Burns, Sadie Carothers, Alberta Burns, Dorothy Carothers, May Susie Steele, Katie Watson.

Pearly Hill School

Pearly Hill School for Black Students was located on Johnson Hollow Road in a one-room frame building. Students from surrounding farms walked some distance to attend.

In 1922, there were 17 boys and 13 girls with 13 double desks and some benches. It closed in 1952.

Pearly Hill School 1929-1930, Miss Mary Wilson, teacher

1st row: Elthomas Terrell, Otis Guinn, Robert A. Helms, Robert "Deedie" Crump, William D. Beasley;

2nd row: Robert A. Campbell, Russell Cunningham, Anna M. Johnson Mayes, Samella Terrell Redd, Johnnie G. Campbell, Alice L. Rainey Hobbs, Mary E. Helms Fitzgerald;

3rd row: Annie F. Helms, Larissa Campbell Pope, Katie Campbell, Teacher Mary L. Wilson, Hattie L. Helms, Hattie Fleming;

4th row: Paul Terrell, John O. Polk, John W. Fleming, William J. Crump, and John W. Terrell.

Pearly Hill School, 1948. Miss Mary Alice Dotson, teacher.

The names of students have been listed earlier but not in the correct order. Until the proper order can be found, the students will be listed here as found in the 1986 Burwood book.

1st row: William Scruggs, Walter Pope, Lucious Pope, John Willie Perkins, R.S. Johnson, Charles Pope, Buck _____;

2nd row: Louise McKissack, Geraldine Patton, John Pope, Pointer Cunningham, Mag Helm, Josephine McKissack, unknown, John Wesley Helm;

3rd row: Harold Nevils, Earl Scruggs, Fannie Patton, Dorothy Scruggs, Tommie Jean Helms, Annie Pope, Teacher Miss Mary Alice Dotson, Hester Scruggs, Emily Johnson, unknown, and _____ Cannon.

EVERGREEN SCHOOL

NANCY MUELLER

Evergreen School was built in 1965 and closed in 1976 due to low attendance.

Integration pains helped close area's last elementary school

Thompson Station – Over on Evergreen Road, just a few miles west of where a new multimillion-dollar school will soon be, the flag still waves from the flagpole of a county school auctioned off only four years ago, after sitting empty for most of its existence.

That the Thompson Station area is urgently in need of another elementary school today is an irony that may be lost on newcomers, but not those who remember the odd history of Evergreen School, built in 1965 and mothballed by the county only 10 years later, never to reopen.

"That school," says county commissioner Clyde Lynch, "was abandoned before it was even paid for."

Today, Evergreen—which is newer than either Franklin High or Pinewood Elementary—houses the fan club and recording studio of singer Billy Ray Cyrus, who bought the school building and its 16.8 acres from Williamson County for $120,000 in 1994.

Although schools in the Bethesda – Thompson Station – Spring Hill area were rapidly filling up in 1994. Lynch says there was never any talk of reopening Evergreen.

"It wasn't growing at all down there," he says. "You didn't have all that development there that you have and there wasn't any need. Even if you had the land now, you'd have a lot of objections to it, because of the location.'

Thompson's Station native, Joe Johnson, Jr., who recently won a seat on the county school board, remembers Evergreen very well.

Two of his five children attended classes there before it was shut down and Johnson was among several town residents who crowded the school board meeting one night in 1976 when the vote was taken to close Evergreen.

"There were classrooms there that never were used," said Johnson, who also joined an unsuccessful lawsuit to keep the school open. "It was a terrible waste."

There is very little written documentation of the school's history and some references to the building called it, Thompson's Station School" instead of Evergreen.

Johnson recalls that Evergreen was built just before racial segregation of county schools was ended.

"When Evergreen was built, there was a school for Black students in Thompson Station. It was an old, old building and it (Evergreen) was built to replace it." He said.

Ken Fleming, who oversaw the closing of Evergreen in his first year as school superintendent in 1976, believes Evergreen was actually built in part to avoid desegregation.

"Let's face it. The Thompson's Station school was built in the wrong place in an effort to fight integration." Fleming said at the time, "and it didn't work."

Today, Fleming says, It was built as a school for minorities and it was sort of like, "This is nicer than any white school around now why don't ya'll be happy That's my unfounded opinion, and I haven't had to admit I can't prove it, however, I'll admit that I still hold that opinion."

The 1965-66 school year is the first for which the county school system has an enrollment record for Evergreen. The school is recorded as having classes for [grades] 1-8, with seven teachers and 201 students.

A history of Thompson's Station, *Hold Us Not Boastful* by Sue Barton Oden, indicates that by 1967, segregation had ended, and Evergreen was operating as the desegregated and sole elementary school for the town.

Its one and only principal, according to Fleming, was Freeman Cooper, who at the time was the school system's only Black principal and who would later wage a protracted highly published legal war with the county and Fleming over the job assignments he received after Evergreen closed.

Enrollment at Evergreen began to drop after it became a desegregated school.

By 1971, the headcount had fallen to 131 students. The racial composition of the student body was almost 70% Black and 30% White.

"The parents that could afford to carry their kids to Franklin to school would bring them to Franklin, said Lynch, who recalled that Evergreen had no enforced attendance zones.

By September of 1976, enrollment at Evergreen, which had become a K-4 school, had dropped to only 82 students, and a companion school for grades 5-8 in Burwood was down to only 64, according to a letter sent to Fleming from the state Department of Education urging that both schools be closed, and their students reassigned elsewhere "to logically assure equal education opportunity."

The school was shut down by Sept 30, shortly after the lawsuit filed by Johnson and others was dismissed.

"We kept it open one day longer than they wanted," Johnson remembers. "It was a community school, you know."

Fleming remembers the condition of the building as excellent. "It had terrazzo floors. It was so nice and it's hard to justify ceasing to use something so nice, but the students just weren't there," he said.

However, it would be another decade before the Saturn car plant arrived in nearby Spring Hill with hundreds of newcomers and their school-age children. Johnson said, "You could see the growth coming (1976) ... people were moving in wanting to get out of Nashville. I felt like they were going to be sorry, eventually, if they closed it."

Around 1988, the county allowed the National Guard to use the Evergreen building as an armory, but for most of the time between 1976 and 1994, when Cyrus bought it, the schoolhouse sat empty."

"There's the question, does closing the school kill the community? Or can a school that's unpopular kill a community?" says Fleming, who believes that friction between the community and Cooper cost Evergreen its life as a school.

"He was not popular, and I'm convinced to this day it wasn't because of his race," he said. "And you can't force people to send their children to where they don't want to go.'

Last spring, someone quietly submitted "Evergreen" to the county board as a suggested name for the new elementary on Highway 31.

The suggestion wasn't considered for long. Instead, the new school will be called "Heritage Elementary."

"I wouldn't have minded if they called it Evergreen," says Johnson. "Maybe it would remind the board members from here on of the mistake that was made, so it won't be done again."

Willie Kinnard Dotson, 1st

Julia Otey Hudson, 2nd

Janie Mai Cannon, 3rd

Thelma Radcliffe, 4th

Amanda H. Patton North, 5th

Mrs. Jimmie Gentry, 6th

Christopher C. Cross, 7th

Freeman Cooper, 8th

Eva Myers Cain, Sp. Ed.

In the fall of 1976, Burwood and Evergreen Schools were closed due to low enrollment.

The students and teachers were sent to either Hillsboro or Bethesda. The following students were welcomed at Hillsboro School. These photos appeared in the 1976 and 1977 Hillsboro annuals.

Bo Andrews　　Delores Brown　　David Burns　　Deborah Burns

Dorothy Curry　　John Curry　　Nannie Curry　　Dee Dee Davis

L.T. Davis　　Wanda Davis　　Betty Fleming　　Jackie Fleming

Robert Fleming　　Steven Gibson　　Brenda Harrison　　Charlene Harrison

Charles Harrison　　Eddie Harrison　　Faye Harrison　　John Harrison

Alfred Johnson　　Belafonte Kinnard　　Evelyn Lee　　Martha Lee

Robert Lee　　Angela McCullough　　Arlena McCullough　　Vanessa McCullough

Evergreen School

Howard McLemore

Danny McKissack

James McKissack

Jamie McKissack

Larry McKissack

Nathan McKissack

Patricia McKissack

Patricia McKissack

Finis Sparkman

Rena Sparkman

Wanda Steele

Dwight Walker

FAMILIES OF EVERGREEN

Mary Graham and Elijah Tate (1821-1896), Cayce Springs blacksmith

THE POPE, CAMPBELL, AND BEASLEY FAMILIES

The Burwood community once had many African American families living among their White neighbors. Some worked as tenant farmers, and day workers while a few were able to own their own homes and small acreage. Many were descendants of former slaves who, after the Civil War, remained on the farms of their former owners. The three families represented here were respected members of Burwood. They worshiped in their churches which included, Murfree's Fork Primitive Baptist Church on Perkins Road, Pearly Hill Baptist, Church of Christ, C.M.A. churches on Sycamore Road, Mt. Laverne Methodist Church on Sugar Ridge Road, and Evergreen Primitive Baptist Church on Evergreen Road. Their children attended schools in the same communities as their churches. Only Evergreen Primitive Baptist Church is still active. The decline in the number of Black families in the area is due mostly to economics—homes in Burwood are too expensive.

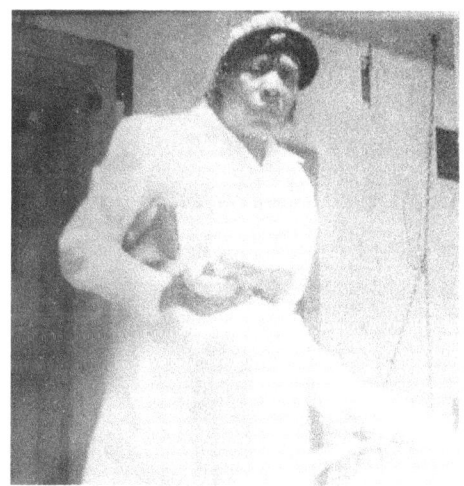
Fannie Mai Pope, wife of Joe Pope

Joseph Lucius Pope

Joe Pope, Jr.
(1930-2019)

The Booker Family – front row: Linda Booker, Janet Booker-Davis, Charlotte Booker Hall, Monroe Booker, Mary Pope Booker, Claudia Booker Lisenby, Gwen Booker Jones, Sherry Booker Reynolds; back row: Brenda, Joe, Cyrus, Robert, Barry, and Karen Booker

Brothers Joe and Leslie Pope with Joe's great-grandchildren Damail and Ormari Pope pose here on Joe's front porch.

Nannie Pope Quinn

Lavinia Pope with her grandchildren, John Lee Patton, Fronie Patton, Annie Patton, and Thelma Patton

Will Campbell of Evergreen Road at 101 years old

Alberta Campbell of Evergreen Road

Lucinda Campbell Rucker, daughter of Will and Alberta Campbell, taught school in Williamson County for many years.

Will Campbell with his mother, Ellen Campbell.

Alberta Campbell with Annie Mai and Callie

Samuel A. Campbell (1889-1959)

Percy and Rosie Lee Covington Beasley lived on Evergreen Road. Percy drove the school bus for Hillsboro School and worked his small farm.

Riley Beasley (1884-1940), deacon of Connection Hill Primitive Baptist Church

Alfreda Beasley, daughter of Percy and Rosie Lee Beasley, graduated from college and teaches in the public schools.

Dwight Beasley, son of Percy and Rosie Lee Beasley

MEMORIES OF HOME ON THE FARM

ANGELA MCCULLOUGH JEFFERSON

Sadie Louise "Ease" Pope McCullough, Angie Jefferson, Stevie Gibson, Tenisha Clausi, Arlena Clausi, and Sharon Oden

My Grandmama, Ollie Mai Patton, passed away on July 8th, 1969. Her death led my mother, Sadie Louise, or "Ease," to move back home to care for her father, Leslie Pope. With her, she brought 4 kids and another on the way. Sharon, Stephan (Stevie), Arlena, Angela (Angie), and Vanessa had the blessing of being taught many life skills and work ethics by our grandfather and mother at the humble home located at Route 1, Box 255 (Cayce Springs Road), Thompson Station, Tennessee.

Mama was an *amazing* cook! She commonly used basic salt and black pepper in her dishes and her skill in balancing them in different ways allowed for noncompetitive deliciousness on every plate. I recall a visit from a couple of traveling salespeople who showed up around dinner time and my mother was frying chicken. She offered them dinner, and to my surprise, they accepted the offer. I recall them raving about her cooking, which our family had the pleasure of enjoying every day. My personal favorite was her caramel cake; no one made the icing as she did, and I appreciate her so much for giving us a taste of simple pleasures that came so easily to her.

She called it a cake if it had 2 eggs or a pudd'n if there were one. If we were out of buttermilk the alternative was to put a splash of lemon juice or vinegar in whole milk. If there weren't enough candles for the birthday cake, it would be okay to use what you had.

When it came to playing with others daily while at home our option was with one another. I kind of chuckle about this to myself, because sometimes there was a desire to enjoy the company of our cousins, but that was not as often as it may have been desired because the cousins closest to our ages all lived in Franklin, and occasionally visited.

Sharon is the oldest of my siblings and we share the same graduation day in 1974; she graduated from Franklin High School, and I graduated from kindergarten at Thompson Station Elementary School (Evergreen). In the Fall, she left to attend Tennessee State University.

Leslie Pope on the farm

Stevie is the second eldest and he worked daily alongside Grandaddy from about the age of 4 until our grandfather's passing. I remember seeing him drive the farm equipment and truck at a very young age. Amazingly, anyone could learn how to drive a 'standard shift' vehicle, but as a kid, he learned. The road to the house was a gravel lane, and at the end of the work or school day, Stevie would pop rocks with a tobacco stick or play basketball near our garden.

Arlena, Vanessa, and I were stairsteps in birth order. The attention that we needed or the reference to the 'girls' was all about us. Arlena often kept up with Stevie as much as she could, playing basketball, running races, and other sports stuff.

When Mama cooked chitterlings, we locked ourselves in Grandaddy's room all day! We wanted no part of it. There was a purple velvet couch that belonged to our grandmother, and we'd rub it in one direction or another to have bumps or no bumps.

During a school break, I remember that we put baby powder on the linoleum and skated in our socks. I loved milk and drank it like water, hence my pudginess and Mama had to manage my consumption!

I loved the family time we shared growing up out there. Grandaddy brought home buckets of beans and other produce and sat for hours, it seemed, shelling peas, or breaking beans for Mama to can. Aside from these activities, we ran on gravel rocks and tried to stay out of Stevie's way when he popped rocks with tobacco sticks at the end of the school or workday.

It was super special when we were able to spend time with our nephew Brent, who was born when I was 8 years old; he was our baby, and we could not love him enough!

Some of my earliest memories include the only farm dog that I liked, Tracy. My sisters and I enjoyed playing with her. One day she was gone; she'd gotten sick, and the next step was to have her put down. Of course, as very young kids we were unaware of this action and the farm methods of executing it. At some point we learned about Tracy's disposition and where she was buried. To this date, we affectionately recall that dog as the only one.

Granddaddy allowed us girls to earn a little bit of cash at the end of the tobacco season picking up residual tobacco leaves, then making bundles that we would slide onto the sticks that he or Stevie would hang in the barn. I remember the strong smell and fullness that took over the space during this annual season and the glow from the sun burning through the cracks of the barn's planks. I don't remember how much we got paid for our work, but the memory of the experience is priceless, and I hadn't considered that there would be an end to these moments. In retrospect, I wish that I had appreciated everything about farm life sooner than now.

Each year, Granddaddy grew corn, beans, tomatoes, potatoes, and strawberries. After Mama got home from work, we were directed to the garden to harvest the offerings. Before the chickens went in for the night, we gathered the eggs and shelled corn for them to eat.

Today, a few apple trees remain on the farm. I remember in our front yard having immediate access to peach, almond, and walnut trees. These trees were messy, but enjoyable fruit and meats. I learned how to enjoy and cook with each of these bountiful blessings from my mother. Knowing when the nuts or fruit are going to be center stage or treated similarly to a flavoring spice makes a difference in my approach to recipes presently.

The road or sometimes referred to as the lane. I recall walking down to Uncle Joe's to buy soda (sometimes we referred to it as pop). He kept a variety of Nehi orange and grape options, Kick and RC cola. All were icy cold, and we returned the bottles to him for the 10-cent deposit on the bottles. During the school year, Uncle Joe kept a roaring fire going in the wood stove while we waited for the bus in the mornings. Mr. S.O. Gillespie was my first bus driver and later it was Mr. Perk Beasley; both were patient and considerate of the moment and waited if we weren't at the end of the lane immediately. Uncle Joe kept watch at the window for the bus or reminded us to watch. Sometimes, Granddaddy would warm up the truck and drive us to the end of the lane to wait for the bus to arrive.

Farm life as I know it was foundational to much of what I know today, and I would not be the person that I am without it. My appreciation for the upbringing that I received developed over the years. I shamefully shared some of my experiences with a colleague once who grew up during the same period in Watts, California. The response was something like, do you know how many kids wanted to have the life experience that you got? This moment was a paradigm shift for me and my enhanced appreciation of all the joy and blessings that Granddaddy, Mama, and Uncle Joe gave to me, and my siblings, and I am and will be forever grateful.

Leslie Pope (1908-1993) married Ollie Mai Patton (1914-1969) in 1930. They had three children Mary Frances, Sadie Louise, and Lee Pope.

Leslie's parents were Lucious and Mary Gray Pope. Their children were: William Henry Pope, Mable Patton, Elizabeth Amos, Howard Pope, Vallie Pope, Sorchum Pope, Joe Pope, Leslie Pope, John Pope, and Alowena Pope.

Ollie Mai Patton Pope was the daughter of John Patton (1874-1964) and Emma Bradford Patton(1874-1960).

Besides working on his farm, Leslie worked at the Dortch Stoveworks, and Magic Chef in Franklin until his retirement in 1964.

W.G. Alexander, Magic Chef manager, Will Campbell, Leslie Pope and Ollie Mae Pope, Mary Frances Pope, Sharon, and Sadie Louise "Ease" Pope McMcullough, Joe Dodson

CHEF SHIPPERS: The men who load the railroad cars and tractor-trailers with Magic Chef ranges for trips to faraway points are shown in this picture. Kneeling, left to right, are Henry McKissick, Joe Pope Jr., Leslie Pope Arthur Nowlin, Andrew Merritt; standing, Willie F. Smithson, Kenneth Peach, Herb Forster, traffic manager; Charles Patton, Hollis Mangrum, Richard Curry, Robert Hardison, Walter Patton, and Henry Lane.

Magic Chef Shippers with Joe Pope, Jr. and Leslie Pope

OLLIE BURNS REMEMBERS HOG KILLING DAYS IN BURWOOD

THELMA BATTLE

Ollie Burns of Cayce Springs

There were two meat packers out there near Burwood. Two white men owned their own companies. One of the men was Mr. W.C. Jones and the other was Mr. Jim Cannon. They killed about three hundred or four hundred hogs apiece every year. My Papa, Walter Burns, worked for both men at killing time. They'd kill hogs every spell because we didn't have seasons then like we do now. It seems like the weather stayed cold longer than it do now. They'd have a hill full of meat. It seems like acres of meat. They'd lay that meat out on planks.

At first, they (the meat packers) just gave the chitlins away. My Papa would go in the wagon sometimes and come back with a wagon full of chitlins, but he didn't get that pile of chitlins from all that hog killing. Somebody else would go get a wagon full of chitlins and it would still be some left.

Papa would bring them chitlins home and they hadn't been cleaned. He'd take that wagon full of chitlins to the creek. Us children (siblings) would be there at the creek all day by ourselves. Our parents had to go to work. We couldn't build no fire. They (parents) didn't allow us to fool with fire. We'd take a knife and split the chitlins open and empty them into the creek. Shucks, it (the flow of the water) would wash it (the contents) on out of there. They'd be just as pretty and white.

Mamma had plenty of tubs around there for us to have. We'd put them chitlins in a tub. We'd put enough of 'em in there that we was able to carry to the house. And we'd bring the empty tub back to the creek. The creek was about 50 yards from the house or something like that. We'd end up having three full wash tubs of chitlins.

Mama cooked them chitlins outdoors in two big black kettles. They had to keep a fire going around them kettles til they was good and done. She had a large paddle that looked like one of them boat oars that she used when she made lard. She'd used that paddle to turn over in the kettles whilst they was cooking. Shucks Mamma canned them chitlins in jars…and we would eat chitlins year 'round!

Them meat packers discovered how popular chitlins really was … and they started keeping 'em for they selves and selling them. Them meat packers hired a Black man named Mr. Beasley to clean all them chitlins. He was Daniel and Charlie's daddy, but I don't remember his first name. They'd have Mr. Beasley sitting beside the creek cleaning chitlins all day.

The regular time for us Casey Springs families went like this most of the time: Old man Doug Martin would kill hogs today, and he'd leave the scalders down … and we'd (Burns family) kill hogs the next day. And somebody else in the community would use the scalders after that. We'd have a big time cutting up the meat and putting it on the roof. The lean meat called the trim went to the sausage meat. And we'd shape the hams up where they'd look like hams do today.

Hog killing

Courtesy of *Hog Head Cheese, Chitlins, and Puck* by Thelma Battle, published by the Williamson County Historical Society, 2019

MILITARY VETERANS OF THE FOURTH DISTRICT

Billy Sedberry, WWI medic

LOCALS WHO SERVED THEIR COUNTRY DURING WAR

Col. Harding Murfree came to Williamson County in 1807 from Murfreesboro, N.C. He settled on his 5,760-acre land grant, which covered most of the land from Kinnard Springs, Peckerwood Hollow to Burwood. He also owned another 640-acre land grant just north of the village of Burwood. At his death, he owned over 40,000 acres, making him one of the richest men in Williamson County. Right in the middle of his large acreage was a 640-acre land grant of Hugh Leeper, centered around the Beaver Spring, known later as Forest Hill plantation of Thomas F. Perkins, and later, the farm of Frank Overbey.

Another large North Carolina land grant for Revolutionary veterans was the 3840-acre grant of Daniel Carter (1761-1826) that included the headwaters of Carter's Creek, located southwest of Burwood on the south side of the Duck River Bridge. The turnpike that passes through Burwood from Franklin to Columbia carried the name of Carter's Creek Pike.

From the military rolls of the War of 1812, it appears these men from the area served for a period – Samuel Dodd, Matthias B. Murfree, Joseph Stovall, Joel Riggin, Benjamin Carter, and Daniel Carter.

*THEY GAVE THE GREATEST
GIFT OF ALL
– THEIR LIFE!*

THE CIVIL WAR

It would be difficult, if not impossible, to list all the men who served in the Confederate Army from the Fourth District, but here is a list of the known who served.

James B. Akin	Zachariah M. Drake	Samuel F. Perkins
William P. Akin	Alexander N. Gray	Thomas F. Perkins, Jr.
James P. Allison	James A. Hassell	John Wesley Polk
Josephus Ashworth	Elisha M. Hassell	William Augustus Polk
George H. Barker	Samuel H. Huff	Ephraim F. Ragsdale
William W. Burnett	Jefferson Johnson	Michael A. Ragsdale
Thomas Henry Byrd	Lewis L. Johnson	John Osborn Shaw
Newton Cannon	Willis R. Johnson	Thomas E. Shaw
Samuel P. Cannon	William Latta	William A. Shaw
John M. Cayce	Jacob Thomas Marlin	William H. Shaw
David S. Chaney	George W. Marlin	Phillip Southall
Ezekiel J. Chaney	Joseph B. Marlin	Calvin Sparkman
William T. Chaney	James K.P. McKee	Carroll Sparkman
George Kinnard Crump	James H. Merritt	Jacob G. Sparkman
Bird Dotson	Wiley Merritt	George M. Stovall
Presley Dotson	James R. Morrow	

James Bruce Akin

Lewis L. Johnson

Thomas F. Perkins, Jr.

WORLD WAR I

Several men from the area were drafted or volunteered for the U.S. Armed Services. The following are among the Williamson County Roll for Veterans of World War I.

William Kelly Smith

Clifton Jones

Sam Church

Those Who Served from the Fourth District

John W. Akin	Turner Jennette	Hardy Pope
R.H. Barker, Sr.	Percy Jennette	Raleigh Pope
Sam Church	Claude Johnson	C.W. Prince
Ewell Clark	Clifton Jones	W.H. Sedberry
J.A. "Zan" Dodd	Brown Kinnard	William B. Shaw
Fred Hawk	A.G. Overbey	William Kelly Smith
Percy Jennette		

World War I

Raleigh Pope and Clarence Price

Percy Jennette and his father, Jesse Jennette

Paul A. Jones

John Polk and R.H. Barker, Sr.

John Alexander "Zan" Dodd

Turner Jennette and Claude Johnson

WORLD WAR II

Many local men and women joined or were drafted into the U.S. Armed Forces during World War II. The following are photographs provided by their relatives. Their service should be remembered.

Odie Hargrove

George F. Walker and Lonnie T. Martin

Earl E. Jones

Fulton Johnson

Christine Haynes and Maude Southall, WAC

Glover C. Andrews

World War II

John Mack Geasley

Marvin F. McKennon

Jefferson McKennon

Walter Polk

Nannie Jennette Huff, WAC

Arthur "Si" McCampbell

James Edward Johnson

John T. "Red" Lawrence

Percy "Perk" Beasley

Charles W. Lawrence

Nathan Lawrence

O.V. (Jody) Rainey

James Skinner, Tommy Jennette, and Abram Johnson

Walter Howard Andrews

R.H. Barker and Neil Barker

Robert Andrews

Eugene Polk

Milton Clark

World War II

James Johnson and William Johnson

Abram Johnson

Local Servicemen Lost in WWII

Curtis Brown

Benny Hargrove

Louie G. Williams

Prisoners of War

George Milton "Mutt" Clark was a prisoner of war for 9 months and 17 days during World War II. He was captured in France, with 3 fellow servicemen, during an offensive. There were many times when their food consisted of only one loaf of bread to be divided between ten men. Later, when he was placed on the hard labor detail, he was given more food.

Many times, Mutt felt he would not live to see home again. So you can imagine how happy he was to be liberated when the Americans came in April 1945. He was especially happy and surprised to see a familiar face when he spotted Bates Southall also waiting to board the ship to come home.

Submitted by Judy Hayes as told to her by Mutt Clark

George Milton
"Mutt" Clark P.O.W.

Calvin Dodd, a Prisoner in Two Camps

Calvin Dodd

After spending nine months in two different prisons where he suffered from hunger for the greater part of the time, PFC Cal Dodd is again a private citizen.

He reached home last Thursday from Fort Douglas, Utah, where he received his honorable discharge and is at Burwood with his parents, Mr. and Mrs. Zan Dodd.

Dodd said he lost thirty pounds while a prisoner but gained it back after being liberated. His time was spent while in prison working on the railroad and clearing debris in towns bombed by the Allies. This last job he was always glad to do, only wishing there were more to clear. Last Christmas Day he was so hungry it made him sick to think of all the good things to eat the folks "back home" were enjoying.

Last May, Dodd was returned to the United States and given a sixty-day furlough which he spent with his parents, and was then sent to Miami, Florida, to rest camp. The remainder of the time he was stationed at Fort Bragg, N.C., and several camps in California, Montana, and Utah, until receiving his discharge.

Two weeks after graduating from Franklin High School he was called to service, and trained at Camp Hood, Texas, and Fort Lewis, Washington. On his return to the United States on the *USS George Squires*; other Burwood boys aboard the ship were Bates Southall and Milton Clark.

Bates Southall and Calvin Dodd, Local Prisoners of War Meet

I was aware that Milton Clark and Dr. J.O. Walker's son had been taken prisoners before my capture in the Vosges Mountains of southern France on September 30, 1944. Every new camp that I reached, I looked for him and made inquiries as to whether anyone knew of had seen him.

In early November 1944, I reached a camp in Limburg and had been there only a week or so and was confined to an overcrowded prison compound, which was filled with double bunk beds with only space enough between them to walk sideways. Rations were very light, and we were limited to one slice of bread and one tablespoon of marmalade for breakfast, a small bowl of carrot soup or, alternately, a small bowl of soup made of green material similar to grass, and a cup of barley coffee at night.

Cal Dodd and Bates Southall

Needless to say, with limited food and exercise space, and with lots of time on our hands, there was little to do except swap recipes for food and cat nap and dream of preparing the recipes and then awaken hungrier than ever.

Early one morning a guard came into our barracks and asked for 10 volunteers to sweep the barracks. No one volunteered. I decided, in order to escape boredom, that I would rather sweep than lie around on my bunk. So, I stepped forth and James H. Hamilton, one of the six captured with me, followed suit. We soon had the 10 men requested to clean the barracks.

We were on our way to the storage room, where the cleaning supplies were kept. We observed the guards unlocking the gates of the work compound and a group of men, in columns of two, waiting to exit from the work area into the street we were using. The guard ordered us to move from the narrow street to the road shoulder; so that we would not impede the movement of the work gang.

As was my customary practice, I was idly scanning each face to determine whether I recognized anyone from my regiment; since I did not know their fate after my capture, as we had been surrounded by the Panzer Division, and also to see if "Mutt" was in the group. As I looked, I thought that I saw a familiar face and decided it could not possibly be Cal Dodd, as I did not know he was in the service, and the person who was approaching was badly in need of a haircut and shave, and like myself, had lost considerable weight. In disbelief, I continued staring at him. He was looking directly at me, with the same look of disbelief that I felt; until he was within 10 paces of me. When I blurted out, "Aren't you Cal Dodd?" he replied, "Yes, and you're Bates Southall." Cal then advised me he was on a work detail and would be back through our area around 4:30 and to bring a friend and fall into their column and go to his compound. Having no way of telling the time, or whether they would arrive at the designated time, Hamilton and I took turns watching for the work details. When they arrived, we fell into their column and went to the work camp with Cal, where we remained until we were shipped to Poland on box cars to a farm. We remained at the farm until we began our march from the Baltic Sea to the Elbe River, where we were liberated on April 12, 1945, the day that President Roosevelt died.

When we met, Cal Dodd and I pretended that we didn't know each other, for fear that we would be separated. Cal had gotten a can of turkey for Christmas that he was serving for his birthday. No matter how hungry we got, we saved that can of turkey to celebrate his birthday.

I attribute my safe return home firstly to God and the prayers of my family and friends and to the unselfishness of Cal Dodd and James H. Hamilton, who shared their hoarded food with me after mine was stolen by a Frenchman, prior to our march, which began February 19, 1945, and ended April 10, 1945.

Bates Southall submitted this article for publication in the preceeding Burwood book, published in 1986.

KOREAN AND VIETNAM WARS

Kenneth Huff, Korea

A.B. Church, Jr., Korea

Robert B. Capshaw, Korea

Dennis Martin, Korea

Benton Martin, Korea

Emery Eugene Johnson, Vietnam

Howard Hatcher Cotton, Vietnam

Edward Leon Capshaw, Vietnam

Danny Martin Is Killed After Year And Half in Vietnam Area

The Review-Appeal, December 11, 1969

Danny Gail Martin, U.S. Army Vietnam. Born 10-31-1948. Died November 20, 1969.

Army Specialist 5 Danny Martin, 21, a resident of Burwood, was killed Monday, Nov. 20, in Vietnam. According to the Defense Department announcement after press time last week, the soldier was killed when the bulldozer he was operating struck a buried explosive.

The son of Mr. and Mrs. Jesse Martin, he attended Burwood Elementary School and graduated from Franklin High School in the class of 1967. He had been in the Army for 2 ½ years and in Vietnam for 1 ½ years where he served in the 81st Light Equipment Maintenance Company of the 81st Maintenance Battalion. He was married to Miss Sharon Anglin, a Franklin High School senior.

In addition to his wife and parents, he is survived by several brothers: Benton Martin of Maury County, Donald, Delmer, Delbert, all of Burwood, Dennis Martin, who is with the U.S. army in Germany, David Martin of Kansas City, Mo., and Gillman Martin of Franklin; four sisters, Carolyn, Janice, and Debbie Martin, all of Burwood, and Mrs. J.W. King of Franklin; and his grandmother, Mrs. Ever Martin of Burwood.

Funeral services were held Wednesday afternoon at Franklin Memorial Chapel with Elder Milton Lillard and James Davis. Burial was in the Sparkman Cemetery in Boston. Military services were held.

NOTABLE CITIZENS OF THE FOURTH DISTRICT

James Bruce Akin holding Jim, Nancy Riggin Akin holding Mittie, Vance, John, Millard, Ed, Ida, and Lena Akin.

J. B. AKIN

JANE OWEN

The Review-Appeal, February 12, 1942

J.B. Akin

The prosperous settlement of Burwood in the heart of a rich farming section was not always thus named. Back in the early days, it was known as Williamsburg. When W.A. Shaw became postmaster, he had the name changed to Shaw. In the early 1890s, R.V. Akin was made postmaster and, through his instrumentality, the burg became known as Burwood and by this, it is still called. No post office has been there for many years; the mail is delivered by Clayton Arnold, a rural route carrier out of Thompson Station.

Since the place first became a settlement, the name Akin has been identified with progress. Several generations ago, the first of the name came from Carolina before that section was divided into two states, and settled in the Fourth District of Williamson County where several Akin families continue to make the village famous.

For forty-five years, two brothers, Millard and Vance Akin, were partners in a general merchandise business where, for miles around, farmers and their wives bought most of their groceries, dry goods, hardware, seeds, etc., paying for them in the main with butter, eggs, meat, lard, and other products from the farm. Even ginseng, sassafras, sage, pepper, and hides were received in payment for merchandise.

They were sons of J.B. Akin, for three years a soldier in the Civil War who saw service under General Hood in the Battle of Franklin and at Murfreesboro. While in this section, he managed to get leave to spend a night at home. When he reached the house, he was afraid to make himself known for fear he would not be recognized and be shot for an enemy, so he slept under the butterbean arbor in the garden and appeared at the door before breakfast time. He had concealed his saddle in a hollow log and his young

J. B. Akin

son, Millard, found it, saw the brass trimmings shining, thought it was an ogre, and no one had to tell him to make all speed for home.

Millard and Vance worked side by side for almost half a century and were pals from childhood, though there were seven years' difference in their ages, Millard being the oldest and Vance the fifth of a family of twelve children. In November 1934, death severed this close companionship, when the oldest brother rounded out a full, useful, happy life and quit the walks of men. His son, J.B. Akin, teacher of science and athletic director for 4 ½ years in Ashland City High School, came home to be with his mother, Mrs. Lula Boyd Akin, and to help his uncle close out the business which took more than a year to complete.

J.B. felt very much at home to be back in his old community where he called every man his friend and every door was open to him. Here he was born and began his education under Miss Fannie Buchanan and Joe Sparkman. After he reached third year high school under such men as James Fitzgerald, S.C. Veech, Garret Reed, and others, he entered Battle Ground Academy the last year "Daddy" Peoples was headmaster and finished under Prof. George I. Briggs. He went to the University of Tennessee, Knoxville for four years, receiving his B.S. degree in 1930 and majoring in science and physical education. He was a member of the Chi Sigma Delta and the Pi Kappa Phi honorary scholastic fraternity and made his home while there in the fraternity house.

Katherine Beckett Akin

As his parents had three other children to educate, he worked before and after school hours and on Saturdays to help defray his expenses. He jerked soda in a drug store near the campus and even took a job in an undertaking establishment. His hardest task here was when his employer sent him and Ed Howard of Thompson Station, also a student in U.T., on a call to dress a body. It took them several hours and he says it was the hardest work he ever did.

In the fall of 1930 he went to Ashland City to teach and while there married Katherine Beckett of Columbia, at the time secretary of the late O.L. Dortch, founder of Dortch Stove Works in Franklin. They went directly to housekeeping using the many lovely wedding gifts to add beauty to the home along with the new furniture bought with their savings. That Christmas they came to Burwood to spend the holidays and while here all their earthly possessions went up in smoke.

Undaunted, they bought more household goods on the installment plan and went to work in earnest to get out of debt.

After returning to Burwood and about the time he and his uncle closed out the business, the principal of Burwood School, G.W. Reed, died and J.B. took over, a position he held for five years. He and his wife and daughters make their home in the ten-room house his father built to take his bride to many years ago. In 1938, when electricity was first extended to Burwood, this was one of the first homes to install it. They enjoy all the comforts of a townhouse and the cleanliness and health of the country. Here his hobby is his milk house, modernly equipped with electricity. A radio keeps the milkers entertained and the ten Jersey cows contented during the milking hour. Milk is picked up by a truck and carried to market. He raises grain and pasturage but has not undertaken tobacco.

Mrs. Akin takes great pride in her flock of White Leghorn chickens, flower, and vegetable gardens, the care of her home, husband, and their two children, Janice, 8, a member of the third grade in Franklin Elementary School, and a pupil of Mrs. Josephine Garner, and Polly Vance, 4, not yet old enough to go to school but plenty old to rule the home, which she does in no uncertain terms.

Last fall, J.B. joined the faculty at Franklin High School where he teaches general science, biology, and physics. He also assists Prof. Yates with coaching football. He finds in the school a very fine corps of teachers, splendid to work with, and he is thoroughly enjoying every responsibility he has, especially the football work, for next to his wife's cooking, he likes athletics.

Descending from such grandparents as J.B. and Nancy Carolyn Akin and Abner and Sophronia Boyd, it has always been an inspiration to live up to their examples by J.B., his brother, Robert, captain in the United States Army, stationed at the air base at Jackson, Mississippi, his sisters, Joella, principal of the training school in East Radford, Virginia, College, and Ruth who married George Hackett, shop teacher in Knoxville High School. It is with Ruth their mother makes her home, but often visits the others.

Both Mr. and Mrs. Akin are members of Burwood Methodist Church. He is teacher of the Bible class composed of men and women. His wife works with the young people, is past president of the Missionary Society, and is now superintendent of the Bible Study, as well as a member of the Burwood Demonstration Club. They have practically the same tastes in recreation and reading. Their aim in life is to abide by the Golden Rule, to "live by the side of the road and be a friend to man." This they do in every sense of the word for their home is not many yards from the Carter's Creek Road and all who pass know a welcome awaits them and a helping hand is ever extended to those who need it.

ROBERT VANCE AKIN, SR.

JANE OWEN

The Review-Appeal, August 8, 1946

Robert Vance Akin, Sr.

If it "takes a lot o' livin' in a house to make it home," then the one which Mr. and Mrs. Vance Akin will soon vacate at Burwood to come to Franklin, where they will be nearer their children, is indeed a home in capital letters. Mr. Akin believes in having the cage ready before catching the bird so purchased the present home with 86 acres and when, on October 20, 1909, he married Miss Margaret Hull, daughter of Frances Marion and Mary Mangrum Hull, of Columbia, he had a place to take her. It was here their children were born and reared, where many teachers of the nearby school have found a pleasant place to live during the school terms, preachers have been ever welcome to stay during protracted meetings, and in days when traveling men made their visits to country stores by means of horse and buggy, they too found a welcome at the door.

Every corner the eight rooms in the Akin home speaks of comfort, especially the bedroom where so much of this happy couple's time is spent. Here they have the radio and telephone. In a cozy corner by the fireplace in a built-in seat under the window where books, magazines, and papers are kept ready for use and prominent among them is the Bible. A rocking chair close by shows that this is a favorite spot.

In all the years Mr. and Mrs. Akin have lived in this house, the roots have grown deeper and deeper until it is indeed a gnawing at the heartstrings when they think of leaving the place which holds so many fond memories, but they are not growing any younger and Mr. Akin finds cows, hogs, garden, and other responsibilities are too much for him. As much as they dread leaving, they realize their children know best and are willing to do their bidding, and will soon be in their newly purchased home on Fair Street where their younger son, James Hull Akin, can be with them.

Mr. Akin is the fifth of eleven children born to J.B. and Carolyn Riggin Akin, who lived in the Fourth District of Williamson County, near Thompson Station. Nine of the children lived to be grown and the five left are in or near Franklin.

Lena Aline Clark (1869 -1955), Mittie Akin Pope, (1873-1960) Jim Akin (1871-1960), Vance Akin (1867-1952), Cam Akin (1879-1945)

When asked if he had lived his entire seventy-nine years in the fourth district, he moved his chair to a better position, settled himself more comfortably, hitched his suspenders to an easier angle, and replied, "When I was three years old, my parents moved to West Tennessee where we lived seven years in Lake and Crockett counties between Reelfoot Lake and the Mississippi River, where mosquitoes, tadpoles, and bullfrogs were plentiful and quinine was as common on the table as salt. I well remember one day when, as a boy of seven, I went to the orchard late in the fall searching for apples. I saw one hanging on a limb and was determined to have it. After throwing several rocks to no avail I climbed the tree intending to shake the limb until the prize fell, but my foot slipped, and I did the falling. The seat of my pants caught on a snag and there I hung in mid-air. Finding

I could not get up or down under my own power, I used the only method available. I began calling in such distressed tones that my family, thinking wild cats were after me, came in a hurry and I was soon on the ground again. I did not realize until then that jeans were made of such strong cloth.

"I was always in some sort of trouble but managed to come off without serious damage. One day when driving the cows up for the evening milking and contrary to my father's orders, I was riding on the gate. It fell, catching me under it in a puddle of mud and slime. The cows and hogs rushed through the opening and, when I came out, I resembled one of those tadpoles so common in Crockett County. I was never considered a strong child, but I withstood more than any of the others.

"The climate did not agree with my mother so, in 1879, we returned to Williamson County. I attended school at Thompson Station with Miss Mickey Thompson as a teacher, finished my educational efforts at Cayce Springs, and farmed with my father for a while before going into general mercantile business at Burwood with my brother, Millard, who was older than I. For nearly fifty years we worked side by side and, after his death, his son, J.B. Akin, and I continued the business for a while. I realized I was getting old, and I missed my brother so much and J.B. wished to return to teaching, so we sold out.

"We began business in a small store, selling everything from a paper of pins and baby shoes to all kinds of farming implements used in those days. Our trade outgrew the building, and we erected a larger one. As time advanced, so did we and, when automobiles became more plentiful, we added gas and oil. Many a thousand dollars changed hands and I remember one year – and it was not during a boom – our sales amounted to $20,000, which was good business for a country store. Millard and I both lived close enough to go home for lunch and we were always on time.

"Once a week we sent our wagon to Nashville filled with country produce for we bought everything the people in the community brought—butter, eggs, chickens, turkeys, geese, ducks, hides, furs, cotton, feathers, wool, even chestnuts and ginseng. We never passed up anything and always found a ready market for all commodities on the Nashville market. It took two days to make the trip and the wagon would return filled with merchandise. My brother and I would go down in a buggy a day or two ahead of the wagon to do the buying.

"If I had all the money owing us yet I'd buy more than one house in Franklin. But there are plenty of honest people left in the world. After all these years people are offering to pay their debts. One man came to me with $11.50 he had owed for years and the only reason he had never paid was simply because he never had anything to pay with—a very good reason. Another man came to my house on a Sunday afternoon to pay me for a pair of shoes he had long ago worn out. I tell you, it isn't always dishonesty that keeps a man from meeting his obligations. I have faith in my fellow men even if some did refuse to pay up, but if they can live and die with it, I certainly can without it.

"All the years my brother, Millard, and I were partners we agreed on everything, seeing eye to eye, and there never was any rough stuff pulled by people around the store. One night, officers came looking for a man but fortunately, he had just left our place; and had gone to another store where the shooting took place.

"I have never held a public office but for forty years have been a notary public, have written many deeds and wills for my neighbors, and while in the store, was almost a pharmacist, issuing all kinds of drugs, weighing out calomel and quinine, etc. For thirty years, I have been a director of the Williamson County Bank and am the oldest in age and number of years of service. I am a voting Democrat, a member of the Burwood Methodist Church, serving as Sunday School superintendent, and my wife is a worker in the Woman's Society of Christian Service. Leaving our church ties is going to be another wrench at our heartstrings when we move away."

R.V. Akin, Jr.

Cornelia Akin

Both Mr. and Mrs. Akin were pensive as they looked about the room seeing things so dear to them and knowing much of the accumulation of years must be discarded. The guest sat quietly by, respecting their silence. Mrs. Akin, no doubt, was remembering the first steps taken in that very room by her children, for it was there each one of them was born. She comes from the same family tree as Cordell Hull, only from a different branch, but they both inherited the sterling qualities of good citizenship, right living, and dependability. She was born at Williamsport and lived next door to Dr. J.O. Walker's parents. Her grandfather, Rev. Roland Hull, a Baptist preacher, came south before the Civil War, married a Maury County girl, and never desired to return to his native state of New York except for occasional visits. He was one of Tennessee's first prohibitionists and, until his death, fought for its supremacy as he rode horseback on his circuits in many parts of the state. When she was in her teens, her parents moved near Columbia, and it was there she completed her education and met and married Mr. Akin.

Mr. and Mrs. Akin realized the importance of an education and were determined to see that their children received one. R.V., Jr., the oldest, graduated from Battle Ground Academy and attended the University of Tennessee before he entered the automobile business in Franklin. He married Cornelia Williams, one of those who found a home with his parents while a member of the faculty at Burwood School. They have the only grandchild in the family, Vance, III, seven years old and a bright pupil at Franklin Elementary School, where his mother was a popular teacher for several years.

Note: This article has been shortened but it can be read in full in *The Review-Appeal* on microfilm or online.

Vance Akin-Robert Byrd home

LOTTIE CARTER ASHWORTH

DEBORAH COLLINS

The Williamson Leader, January 11, 1976

Mrs. Lottie Ashworth taught for 46 years.

In just a few months America will be celebrating its 200th birthday. One person in Williamson County who has witnessed almost 100 years of American growth, and particularly progress around the Franklin area, is Mrs. Lottie Ashworth.

Mrs. Ashworth, whose home is located at the southern end of the county on Sugar Ridge, refuses to give her exact age.

"I keep that a secret," she says. "Why, young people wouldn't pay me no mind if I told 'em my age. They'd say, 'You too old to be tellin' me my business. I already know about it.'"

"Sometimes I say I'm 16 plus," she cheerfully concludes.

When questioned about the changes and progress made in Franklin during her lifetime, Mrs. Ashworth provides a variety of observations.

She recalls that the first time she went to Franklin was in a horse and buggy. "It took about two hours. It takes me longer than that when I go in my old car now. The traffic is so bad."

The spry old woman has two vehicles at her disposal—and she drives both. One, a 1949 Hudson car, is now a collector's item.

"When I bought that car, everybody said, 'What do you want to buy that for? You won't never be able to sell it.' "Now I can hardly keep it. Everybody wants it," she says.

Her other vehicle is a 1960 Dodge pickup truck. "If the car won't start, I go in the truck," she says. I go to Franklin every week as often as I can so I can keep up with what's happening there."

Mrs. Ashworth says that she remembers when the route she traveled to Franklin was a road among cultivated land and farms. "Now there are houses and stores along the road," she observes.

Remembering downtown Franklin, she recalls that the courthouse has been remodeled and that a lot of shops are gone where she used to shop.

"Some of the shops have changed buildings and locations and such. The banks have changed around and all from where they used to be," she says.

She went on to say that she liked to shop better before the modern ways of self-service were adopted by stores." I can't hardly find what I need, and it takes me longer to shop now," she says. "I like it better when the store folks wait on you at the counter.

The two-story farmhouse in which Mrs. Ashworth lives is the same one in which she was born.

Lottie Ashworth's home on Sugar Ridge

"My daddy was the first settler on Sugar Ridge," she notes. "The ridge gets its name from the maple trees here. Time was when you could look out this time of year and see people gathering the syrup everywhere. Now hardly anyone does it. I claimed to 'em that I was gonna get out and tap some trees this year, but I haven't had a chance to yet."

Being one of 10 children, Mrs. Ashworth recalls that she always knew she wanted to help people when she grew up. "That's why I decided to be a teacher," she says. "Although I retired in 1956, I spent 46 years in the classroom."

Mrs. Ashworth received her early education in Williamson County but had to finish her high school at the Agriculture and Industrial College (now Tennessee State University) in Nashville. "They didn't have a high school for my people in those days," she recalls. She obtained her teaching certificate from there and spent most of her teaching years in the Williamson County system.

Once establishing herself as a teacher, she met and married Frank B. Ashworth, who is now deceased. "I made sure he knew I wasn't going to give up my job when we married, I waited until I was over 21 to marry because I feel that people don't really know enough to get married until they are passed that age," she says.

The Ashworths had no children but reared two foster children. "We always had children who just stayed with us some," she says.

A woman of many musical talents, Mrs. Ashworth plays the organ, guitar, and autoharp. She recalls that 30 or 40 children used to come to her house, and she would give each one a little instrument to play. "We put on shows and things,' she says. "Some of those children are gone now. Many are ministers and I still get Christmas cards from some of them," says Mrs. Ashworth.

She still has the instruments in a box in her living room.

In recalling her teaching years, Mrs. Ashworth notes that methods have changed from the time when she was an active teacher.

"I remember when all the children walked to school. I taught in a one-room school for 32 years. I used to cook in the classroom because I knew that some of the children didn't eat right at home and I wanted to help," she says.

Going on, Mrs. Ashworth remarks that even now she finds herself doing things for other people more than for herself.

"I don't care what day or time I stop to think, it seems like everything I do is to benefit someone else," she says. "But I enjoy it and that's what I always determined I would do," she explains.

One change in the school system that bothers Mrs. Ashworth is the matter of public prayer. She always believes the trouble our country is having today is because people have forgotten the "source" that founded it.

"Our forefathers always put God first," she says. "There's not enough emphasis on Him now. People worry more about self instead of Him."

A woman of many interests, Mrs. Ashworth lives a quiet life on her farm. After retiring from teaching, she raised ducks and turkeys to sell. Later, she switched to raising calves and still follows this pursuit along with the help of a nephew.

PERLINA LOCKE ASHWORTH

JANE OWEN

The Review-Appeal, July 10, 1941

Perlina Locke Ashworth

Nonagenarians in the county are indeed few and still fewer have hopes of gaining that distinction. Since life is not numbered by years but by deeds, many live a short full one while others accomplish a great deal less in a much longer span of existence.

This has not held true in the case of Mrs. Perlina Locke Ashworth of Burwood, who will, on September 14, celebrate her 90th birthday. She is the mother of eleven children, eight of whom are living. From the time she was a little girl up until five years ago, she led an active life and even yet directs a number of household activities from her bed.

Mrs. Ashworth was born in the neighborhood of T.F. Overbey's home on the Carter's Creek Road. Her parents, Wilson and Sally Ann Jones Locke, died when she was a very young girl and she made her home with her uncles and aunts until she was seventeen when she married Joseph Ashworth, a young Maury County farmer seven years her senior. She met him at Old Goshen Methodist Church when she first went to make her home with her uncle, Lige Hassell.

Visited one evening recently at the home of her daughter, Mrs. W.J. Riggin, she smiled a welcome from her bed where she has spent the greater part of the last five years. She was not expecting visitors but could not have been more "dressed up" if she had. Her spotless nightcap was as white as the locks it partially covered. The only color about the bedding was the yellow and green embroidery on the pillowslips, the work of a granddaughter, Virginia Ashworth. She is of the old school and prefers white counterpanes to the colorful ones now so much in use. By her side was her pocketbook (for she still likes to have her own change), a box in which she keeps her trinkets, and her greatly beloved Bible which she reads daily without the aid of glasses. Near her bed burned a bright kerosene lamp, the blaze showing that the one who trimmed the wick certainly knows how it should be done.

As "Old Mother," as she is lovingly called by her 24 grandchildren and 12 great-grandchildren, recalled the days of her childhood, it was not an especially happy one for she and her sister and brother were separated after the death of their parents and they were passed around periodically from one relative to another, not that they were mistreated in any way but they developed no deep-rooted home ties. She learned in those years what stabilizing effect a home must have and decided that, if she ever became the mother of a family, she would make of it a happy, worthwhile one, and she kept her promise.

Josephus Ashworth (1845-1914) and Perlina Locke Ashworth (1851-1950)

Her account of the skirmish at Spring Hill during the Civil War was very vivid. She was living then in the home of an uncle, Oliver Jones, and watched the soldiers throw up breastworks. She was frightened but was too much interested to leave the scene. She stood on the bank of a creek as Company D, Brown's Division of the 32nd Tennessee passed by and begged for news of her cousins, Joe and Bill Marlin, as the soldiers fled by, but received none. Later she learned that one of the boys had been wounded and the other was left to care for him. She watched the soldiers eat raw pumpkins and parched corn as they tramped along.

Mrs. Ashworth's husband died in 1914 and, since then, she has made her home with her daughter, Mrs. Riggin. Her oldest son, A.L. lives near her; Wilson, the youngest, is a city mail carrier in Franklin; Walter lives in Nashville; James and Charlie in Greensboro, Alabama; Bolton, in Cheatham County; and Nannie, who married John Hawkins, lives at Carter's Creek. They visit her often and she enjoys their visits.

When her children were growing up, she said she measured them by Solomon's Rule and found that it worked. She knitted all the hosiery worn by her family, spun the cloth for their clothing, and made the garments as well. The suits she made for her boys fitted as well as ready-made ones. She never kept account of the number of quilts she pieced but does know that each child and many of the grandchildren have some in their homes.

Mrs. Ashworth's droves of turkeys, ducks, and geese were the envy of the neighborhood, and her flocks of chickens were always large. Her girls helped her with the household affairs and the boys were busy assisting their father who was an industrious farmer.

Mr. and Mrs. Ashworth were members of the Methodist Church from youth, and they never thought of missing services. If the horses were overworked during busy seasons, they took their children with them and walked; otherwise, they went in the spring wagon. Their home was always open to preachers and every Sunday found them with a house full of company for Mrs. Ashworth was famous for her good table. She canned and dried fruit in the summer and her supply always kept her table through the winter.

Mrs. Ashworth was the neighborhood doctor, and the weather never was too hot or cold to keep her from an expectant mother when sent for. Often no doctor was in attendance, and she never lost a mother or infant.

Once during their married life Mr. and Mrs. Ashworth saw their home go up in smoke, destroying all their dearly beloved possessions. They did not become discouraged, worked all the more diligently, and by good management, soon had another start.

Mrs. Ashworth remarked, "My husband and I had limited opportunities and for that reason we wanted our sons and daughters to have a better chance than we, not have to do everything the hard way. It took a great deal of work to do it, but it was not a burden for it was a labor of love and only what we wanted to do. When the heart is in the undertaking it is not drudgery, and much satisfaction is derived from seeing the task well done. I am proud of my children and I feel that I have not lived in vain."

Mrs. Ashworth looks forward to the visits of her pastor, Rev. E.D. Trout, who goes often to her home to talk with her on the subject nearest her heart—the Home that awaits her, "the house not made with hands, eternal in the Heavens."

GEORGE ROY BARKER

JANE OWEN

The Review-Appeal, August 24, 1950

George Roy and Pearl Troope Barker

George Roy Barker, 49, better known, however, as Roy Barker, was on August 3 elected Circuit Court Clerk of Williamson County and will enter upon his duties on September 1. He will not begin unprepared due to the kindness of the present office holder, Dot Skelley Boulware, who by her long term of office, knows the business from A to Z and invited him to come to the office where she is helping him in every way possible to become as familiar with the work as the short time allows. The new incumbent will ever be grateful for this friendly gesture on the part of Mrs. Boulware.

The oldest of six children of G.W. and Blanche Lavender Barker, Roy was born at Burwood where both branches of the family resided since coming to Middle Tennessee from Holland, France, and Ireland when that section of the county was a canebrake. The names of Barker, Shaw, and Lavender have since that time been linked with the community up-building.

Roy was five years old when his brother, John, was born. Though he had become accustomed to being the one and only in the family he gladly welcomed the arrival of the newcomer. Then at intervals of 2 1/2 years or thereabout came four sisters – Cornelia, now the wife of Knox Norman; Christine who married Earl Morton; and Margaret, who is Mrs. Melvin Whittaker, all of whom live in Columbia, and the youngest, Georgia, wife of Floy Taylor, of Nashville.

The brothers and sisters were educated at Burwood when that section had a flourishing high school. They were joined along the two miles of road separating home and school by other children of the neighborhood. The morning trip was usually made in peace as all were anxious to arrive on time so that there would be no staying in at recess for being late, but the return trip gave them plenty of time for fist and rock fights. He says one snowy day while in the act of making a snowman, Cal Dodd popped him with a hard mass of snow. As Cal was so much larger than he, to fight back was of no avail, but he did get in a good hold when the larger boy stooped over for a new supply of snow, and the scratches Roy left with his fingernails on Cal's face were painful for days.

The two-story frame house where Roy's parents lived, which was also the home of his grandparents, is close to the scene of Pope's Camp Grounds, where in former years the Methodists worshipped before erecting the church building in Burwood, and has been in the family for many, many years. At present, the other son, John, has charge of cultivating the 150 acres.

When Roy reached 19 years of age, he decided he wanted to quit farming and go to work for Akin Brothers, general merchants at Burwood., who were kind, considerate, southern gentlemen of the old school and were most patient in teaching him the ins and outs of the business. He was anxious to learn, and life moved along smoothly. The firm bought the first truck ever purchased in that section and sent Roy to Franklin to drive it home. It was the understanding with the buyers that the tank was to be filled with gas when delivered. Roy drove it to Burwood and the next morning after much hand cranking, for it was of that type, the engine refused to run. All day and into the night he and others in the village tried in vain to get it going but to no avail. Finally, a young lad made a wonderful discovery and yelled, "By golly, it ain't got no gas." A more crestfallen group of men and boys than they would be hard to find.

It was not long before the firm sent Roy to Nashville with a load of produce and to bring back merchandise. Doss Johnson went along for the ride, and as they were descending a steep hill, Roy discovered the brakes were burned out. There was nothing to do but keep the truck on the road and the farther they went the more momentum they gained. Doss said afterward he held on to his hat and all that he could see was tombstones flaring up before him on both sides of the road. By the time they reached the bottom of the hill and started up another, the truck was really making time and a half. When it finally stopped of its own accord both men sat for a while staring into space and Doss broke the silence with, "Boy, I saw nothing but destruction ahead of us. You managed fine to bring us out alive."

In 1920, Roy came to Franklin to clerk for John Moran in Moran's Drug Store, forerunner of Gray Drug Company. He secured room and board with Mrs. E.W. Daniels along with Sam Church, Percy Jennette, and Billy Henry, who also hailed from Burwood. No one dared leave his room without the others for fear of what would happen to his belongings in his absence. It was in the days when the food was put on the table, each person helping himself and did not have it doled out on a plate as is now the custom. If you did not get enough at the first helping, there was always more in the dish.

Hearing of the opportunities Detroit offered and looking for greener fields, Roy took off for Michigan one fine morning, but it only took him a short while to discover "all is not gold that glitters," and back to Franklin he came. It was not long before he was soda-jerking for Johnnie Shea and it was during this stay of two years he married Pearl Troope, a native of Columbia, but living at the time at Burwood, and with whom he attended school. One fine spring Sunday morning, April 16, 1922, to be exact, they halted Rev. J.R. Stephens as he was on his way to church. In the presence of two witnesses, they soon had the ceremony over and went on their way rejoicing.

John W. Barker (1873-1952) and Blanch Lavender Barker (1876-1974)

The desire to return to the soil became so very, very strong that the Barkers turned their faces toward Burwood, and until 1945, Roy cultivated his father's farm. His sons, John William and Roy Edwin, had a chance to know the joys of farm life. Both graduated from Franklin High School. The older son married Grace O'Riley, of Nashville, where he is with an insurance company. The younger son will graduate in December from the University of Tennessee, Knoxville, where he entered after being discharged from service. He trained only a short while in the States before being sent to the European Theater and six months from the time he left Franklin he was wounded in Germany and spent three years in hospitals trying to recover. Word reached them he was wounded in action, for which he was later awarded the Purple Heart, but they knew nothing more until he called them from New York City, where he had been flown by plane and was sent to Memphis for hospitalization. Before he was discharged, he also received treatment and operations at White Sulphur Springs, Virginia, Daytona Beach, Florida, and Kalamazoo, Michigan. He is also planning to enter the insurance field.

Leaving the farm in 1945, and it was then when his brother, John, took over, Roy and his family came back to Franklin, bought a house on Columbia Avenue and for four years and five months, he was with the post office as city carrier, trudging eleven miles a day, carrying letters, papers, and magazines to those along his route. The worst catastrophe he suffered during this time were run-ins with pet dogs and he would come off with bites on his shins.

Mr. and Mrs. Barker are members of the Church of Christ, and both take an active part in the work. He likes to hunt quail and squirrels, goes in for football games and horse shows, never missing an opportunity to attend one.

The new circuit court clerk is looking forward with much pleasure to the next four years' work in the courthouse where he will not only be associated with other county officials but will come in contact with the citizens of Williamson County whom he hopes to know better and to serve them to the best of his ability. He may make mistakes, for who doesn't, but as time goes on and he becomes better acquainted with the duties of the office he will be able to handle every matter, coming under his jurisdiction with accuracy and speed.

As he goes quietly about his duties of life, Mr. Barker carries with him a pleasant smile, a helping hand, and a word of encouragement for the faint-hearted. Burwood honors and respects one of her splendid sons, as does all of Williamson County.

Home of John W. and Blanche Lavender Barker on Barker Road, south of Burwood

BOYD RIDLEY CRITZ

JANE OWEN

The Review-Appeal, December 30, 1944

Boyd Ridley Critz (1875-1947)

For the past forty years, Boyd Ridley Critz has lived on a farm of five hundred acres near West Harpeth, owned by W.T. Berry of Nashville. Few people know that Mr. Critz is not the owner for he is just as careful to keep the land in a splendid state of production by crop rotation and fertilization as if it were his. The owner at that time made a contract with him and, though the land has changed hands, the original contract stands without any alterations.

Though he has already celebrated his 72nd birthday, he is still actively engaged in raising his allotment of tobacco, which is now seven acres, also corn, wheat, barley, rye, and oats. In former years he was a great millet grower and was one of the farmers in that community who put West Harpeth Railroad station on the map as a millet shipping point. He formerly operated a good-sized dairy, but after his son, Boyd Ridley, Jr., left home, and help was so uncertain, he stopped. He says in years gone by, he kept colored families on his farm as long as twenty years at a time, and now they do well if they finish out a year's contract. He finds white tenants are also transient but at present has two families on the place who have been with him for several years.

Due to the labor situation, Mr. Critz has more pasture than in former years, grazing cattle, sheep, and hogs. When asked what breed of sheep he has, he answered, "Just sheep. But I raise spotted Poland China hogs for they are a paying stock, producing poundage on the least feed and that is what counts." He uses mules for cultivating, having ten or twelve busy most of the time, but has ordered a tractor to cultivate next year's crop, for labor at the present prices makes it too expensive to put a hand behind a mule.

He has never known any life except that on a farm and considers cultivating land as much of a calling as any other profession. It takes skill and management to make it a success and no lackadaisical, slipshod methods can be applied any more than in banking, mercantile business, or law practice. He was born at the old home place within six miles of where he now lives, one of eight children of the late Tom and Julia Ridley Critz, and here five of the family, John, Tom, Lillie Mai, Juliette, and Sallie Ridley Critz, live and with them is their aunt, Miss Sallie Ridley, who has been a second mother to them, having lived in the home since before they were born. They grew up knowing that when parental justice was about to be meted out, if they could only reach Aunt Sallie's protecting arms, they had hopes of escaping, for no one had the will to resist her kind, reproving expression and it usually wound up with, "Well, I'll let you off this time, but next time …" and the parents left the sentence unfinished. Today she is the special charge of each of them, for years she has slowed her step, speech, and sight but has never dampened the affection the family has for her.

Speaking of depression, Mr. Critz said, "I was brought up under a depression and the hard way at that. I remember selling corn at 90 cents a barrel delivered at Thompson Station depot. Hogs often sold for two cents a pound and we thought we were getting rich at that. A ten-cent piece looked as big as a ten-dollar bill does now. There were no eight-hour days then. We went to the field before the day and came back after dark. Dinner was the only meal eaten when there was no lighted lamp on the table. Sometimes we had less at the end of the year than was on hand at the beginning except that we had eaten and had something—but little at that—to wear. I bought forty acres of ground for $250, paying for it with that 90-cent corn in ten years. When the Democrats came into power twelve years ago, I owed every bank and almost every man I knew, and I hated to come to town. Now I owe no man anything, can look them in the eye and I have money in the bank. The farmer has had a chance to make good if he only tries."

Mr. Critz received his early education in a little school near the Critz home, but later went to Thompson Station where several teachers then conducted a flourishing school. He married Mable Creath, the wedding taking place in the home of her sister, Mrs. John B. Ridley, and they went to keeping house on the Bob Kittrell farm on Buckner Road. The next year they went to the C.K. McLemore farm and then to the place where they now live. The original house was a two-story brick built over a century ago and known as the Jack Watson place [C.D.Berry]. Mr. Critz found an old account book in the cellar dating back 123 years, containing items of whiskey made on the place and stowed in the cellar by the owner for his private use.

The Thomas L. and Juliet Critz family on Critz Lane. Juliet and Boyd Ridley on bottom.

Twenty-two years ago, a cyclone tore away the upper story and part of the first floor. No one was at home at the time except Mrs. Critz and the two smaller children, as the older ones were at West Harpeth School. After the cyclone passed, Will Ladd, a neighbor, with other helpers rescued Mrs. Critz and the children who were penned in the house but unharmed. Two Negro boys were in a cabin in the yard at the time. One was blown down into the field and was unharmed. The other was found in the Critz house with no recollection of how he got there. As all the outside doors were closed it still remains an unsolved problem. The cabin was blown away with no vestige of it left.

When the house was remodeled, it was made into six rooms, all on the same floor. It has since been electrified along with the cabins and barns. They have a Frigidaire and other electrical conveniences, but Mrs. Critz prefers her wood range for cooking purposes. The water supply comes from a bored well in the yard. When the boring machine reached fifty feet the water began to rise freely. A rope has been lowered to the depth of 300 feet yet no bottom has ever been found. Threshers have used from it without lowering the waterline. Civil engineers, who have visited the well, say water pockets of this nature in the earth's formation are rare.

Mr. Critz is a Democrat and a member of the Farm Bureau. He served as school commissioner in the Fourth District for several terms many years ago. He has had to serve on the Grand Jury but is thankful he has never been called on a murder trial.

Bethel Methodist Church, which stood near the school, was blown away the same day the Critz home was partially demolished and was never rebuilt. Here the family had attended services and after that, they transferred to Thompson Station Church, which Mr. Critz's grandfather, John Boyd Ridley, was active in helping build. In fact, when the day set for the dedication services neared and there still remained a debt of $500, he gave his personal check for the amount. Among the stained glass memorial windows in the beautiful edifice are two to the memory of this grandfather and his wife, Mack Fitzgerald Ridley, and to Mr. Critz's parents, Thomas L. and Julia Ridley Critz, placed there by the family. Here Mr. Critz is a member of the Stewards and superintendent of the Sunday School. His wife is a member of the Woman's Society of Christian Service and their four children were fed and nurtured on the faith of their father in its Sunday School.

The Critz children graduated from Franklin High School. Ruth married Robert Stewart and they with their high school daughter, Jean, now live in New York City, but for several years made their home in Chester, Virginia. Boyd Ridley, Jr., and his wife, the former Marion Archer, of Richmond, Virginia, and their sons, Boyd Ridley, III, and Trainer Archer, live in Clinton, Iowa, where he works for Dupont. Irene lives in Nashville where she holds a responsible position and comes home nearly every weekend for she is a great home lover. Frances is a member of the personnel of the Williamson County Extension Service, wears a happy smile, and makes all who enter feel welcome.

Mr. Critz is three inches short of six feet, his broad shoulders carry well his 185 pounds, and his gray hair lends an air of distinction to his well-preserved features. He says he has always had splendid health and attributes his good start in childhood responsible for it. Not only did he have the care of his parents and his Aunt Sallie, but his black mammy, Aunt Mary, and her husband, Uncle Pete, who saw that the children were well fed and made them walk according to their standards of rights and never failed to administer the switch when they thought it necessary, although they were right there to take the children's part when the parents thought the punishment should be meted out. He is thankful for all this training in his boyhood for he believes the old saying "men and nations can only be reformed in their youth; they become incorrigible as they grow old."

WILLIAM COLEMAN JONES

The Review-Appeal, July 23, 1936

W.C. Jones

Within the bounds of Williamson County are many industries, each in its own way adding to the up-building and fame of this locality. Most of the trades or callings may have more or less competition but little as one may realize there are only two commercial meat packers in the county, W.C. Jones and Cannon Brothers, who live within a stone's throw of each other on the Carter's Creek Road. Each is independent of the other and both are doing a thriving business.

Mr. Jones inherited his skill in this art from his father, "By George" Jones, who for several years packed hogs with a neighbor, Robert A. Bailey, selling mostly to Columbia and Nashville concerns.

Mr. Jones completed his educational activities in the Wall and Mooney School in 1889 and on leaving there accepted a position as clerk for John Atwood. Three years later at the death of his brother, he returned to the farm and entered business with his father until his death several years later and, since that time, has gone it alone.

Formerly Mr. Jones killed 500 to 800 hogs a year; now he averages something less than 300. He buys shoats three to four months old and fattens them, and again he buys them ready to slaughter. He is prepared to take care of 600 hogs in packing season, employing about twenty men at this time. He does not use artificial smoking. He uses hickory wood and sound sawdust, and no better hams go on the market than the ones he cures.

He sells through brokers to Atlanta, Birmingham, Nashville, Memphis, and other cities. He has individual customers in Birmingham to whom he has sent hams since 1908. Many times, he has calls for his famous hams from Los Angeles and other Pacific ports. His smoked sausages go every year to points in Canada, New York City, Boston, and other eastern markets. Nothing is sold "green" except the "bones" which have to be gotten rid of promptly. The chittlings, another by-product, are sold on commission. Mr. Jones says lard is the most difficult product to handle. Sausage and ham are his best profits.

Until 1905, Mr. Jones stuffed his sausage by hand—a very slow and tedious process. As he only received ten cents per pound for it smoked, he felt it a losing proposition to make much sausage at this rate. About this time, he learned of a lard press and sausage stuffer, as a combination machine, that revolutionized this part of the work as it could stuff 2000 pounds per day. He immediately quit the hand stuffing entirely. Soon he purchased additional ones and now at hog killing he has three machines going full tilt and the supply is used up long before the day is done, so just how many they can stuff has to be estimated for he never yet has had enough meat killed at one time to give them a tryout. No busier place can be imagined than Mr. Jones's slaughter pen and workhouses on a crisp winter's day.

At one time many years ago, he killed 500 hogs and lost 6500 pounds of meat. The morning he killed, the ground was frozen hard but the wind was in the south. He did not have ice in abundance in those days and was not prepared for ice packing. For the past several years, he packs in ice whether cold or otherwise. He says he learned his lesson, though, and never kills unless the wind is out of the north. He finds in his business as everyone else does that all is not profit. One winter he packed 500 hogs and lacked $250 of getting cost on them. But being the man he is, he took it as his part, charged it up to profit and loss, took the bit between his teeth, pulled on the traces a little harder and the next time he was more fortunate.

Mr. Jones says the days back before good roads and motor trucks were when he really had a tough break. In freezing weather, he would leave home before night with five mules hitched to a wagon filled to its capacity with bacon, taking to Nashville. He would walk most of the way to keep up circulation and get to Market by daylight, dispose of his load, and spend the day returning home over frozen rough roads. Now he puts his meat on a truck in the morning, sends it in and by noon the man is back home ready for another load. He says it is only by comparison that he is able to appreciate and enjoy the modern conveniences. The person who has been reared with every modern convenience can by no stretch of the imagination realize the privations of the days of thirty-five or forty years ago.

Cynthia Cannon Jones with daughter India Coleman Jones Mizell

The original tract of land of 518 acres had a double log house on it when Tom and India Jones came from Maury County with their interesting family of six children to make their home here when the subject of this sketch was five years old. He and his sister, Mrs. Robert P. Pope, of Mobile, Alabama, are the only ones left. The old house was destroyed by fire in 1892. This was replaced by a two-story frame of impressive architecture.

It is today one of the most imposing in appearance as well as one of the best-kept places in the county. Strangers passing along the thoroughfare slow down their motors to admire it. Mr. and Mrs. Jones's hobby is to keep everything in and outside the house in perfect condition. They have one child, India Jones Mizelle, wife of Robert Mizelle and mother of a winsome granddaughter, Lucy Merrell Mizelle.

Mr. Jones says 13 is his lucky number. He married on April 13, 1898. There were 13 people taking part in his wedding, 13 candles were burning at the altar, and there were a number of other 13s that he failed to recall.

W.C. and Cynthia Cannon Jones and Jim Cannon

PERCY NEAL LAVENDER

JANE OWEN

The Review-Appeal, March 20, 1952

Percy Neal Lavender

When passing the Franklin Post Office grounds, with its perfectly trimmed grass, hedge, and shrubs, did you ever stop to think it is not just a "happen so?" It is the result of the clippers and lawnmowers in the hands of the energetic superintendent of the grounds and building, Percy N. Lavender. He takes as much pride in seeing that the brass trimmings and windows of the building gleam with cleanliness as he does that not one blade of grass stands higher than another on the lawn

For the past seventeen years, he has been on the job daily and is not looking forward to retirement, for he says he likes his work too well to turn it over to another. At sundown, it is one of his favorite duties to lower the flag, which flies every day except Sunday. He says in all this time he has never allowed it to touch the ground and, as the life of one is only about four months, this makes more than a half-hundred different ones he has lowered. When he began work there, the late Chapman Anderson was postmaster, succeeded later by the present incumbent, John A. Jordan.

Born at Burwood, he was the youngest of seven children, two daughters and five sons of Gus and Cornelia Ann Shaw Lavender. He has not the faintest memory of his father for he was only a year old when Mr. Lavender caught his arm in a cotton gin at Thompson Station and died from the injury. His grandfather, John A. Shaw, of Scots-Irish blood and possessing a stern disposition, came to his daughter's aid and helped her with her responsibility. They never thought for a minute of disobeying either grandparent for they loved them devotedly. The grandfather always wanted a bowl of clabber by his plate at breakfast, and as baby Percy's highchair was next to his, he was taught to like it also. He says even today when he sees it, his mind reverts to the days when his grandfather taught him to use his spoon so that he would not get more on his clothes than in his mouth.

Another pleasant memory of childhood was the sticks of peppermint candy his grandfather kept for them in the drawer. They were given one stick a day, but it had to be given to them, never being allowed to help themselves. He liked to ride with his grandfather on his trips to the store. When they came to a certain steep rise in the road, they both got out and pushed while Dolly, the family mare, pulled the buggy. This almost became a ritual with them, so seriously did they undertake the ordeal.

Cornelia Shaw Lavender
(1840-1926)

When Percy reached the age of seven, his mother took her family to Nashville where the eldest son, Charlie, secured work and the children attended school. One of his brothers, Riley, stayed on with his grandparents. As soon as school closed, Percy would join them for the vacation months and would spend as many weekends as he could. After Charlie's death, the mother returned to the old home at Burwood.

When his grandfather died in 1895, followed by his wife three years later, he said he felt as if the very joy of living had passed away. His mother lived until 1926.

Shortly before his grandparents died, they held a family reunion, having present their six children and their families. The large yard was full of grandchildren but there was plenty of room left for two long tables which were laden with everything from barbecue, boiled ham, and fried chicken to pies and cakes in abundance. Mr. Lavender says he does not remember to have eaten as much at any one time as he did that day.

The old log house of his ancestors, where his grandparents finished their earthly careers, was blown away in a cyclone about 1918. Not far away was the home of his brother, Riley, which was completely demolished. When his brother regained consciousness, he was in the yard sitting in a paneless window frame with a large rock in his lap. A nail had pierced one jaw and he was bleeding profusely. But the part to him that was most pleasing was the fact that other members of his family miraculously suffered no harm. When he decided to rebuild, he chose the site of the old log house for his new home. It was there he had spent the greater part of his life and expects to round out his days there.

Mr. Lavender says the Lavender and Barker families have intermarried so that when relationships are being traced, a pencil and paper are required to decipher the accuracy of the kinship. His mother's younger sister married a Barker, then the two daughters, Blanche and Lottie, and son, Riley, married brothers, and a sister in this same Barker family. No wonder it is a puzzle for the children and grandchildren to figure out whether they are cousins, uncles, aunts, nieces, or nephews.

Another brother, Claude, lives in Nashville. Alvin, who made his home near Thompson Station for many years, moved to Columbia where his four sons, James, Russell, Jack, and Bill, might have a better chance for a high school education. It was there he died and where his wife and their oldest son continued to make their home. In 1909, Mr. Lavender married Miss Hattie Stanley. Having no children of their own, they adopted an eight-month-old baby whom they named Virginia Ward Lavender, and on whom they lavished their affection. She is now Mrs. Al Johnson of New Orleans. Her son, Tommie, spent much of his childhood in the home of his foster grandparents. They lived on a farm in Burwood, but Mr. Lavender worked much of the time in Franklin. For seven years, he was connected with the firm of Brittain and Fristoe. In 1933, when he went to work at the post office, they bought a home in Franklin on North Fifth Avenue, and it was there that Mrs. Lavender died. His nephew, Blythe Lavender, and his family went to live with him.

In 1945, Mr. Lavender married Mrs. Rachel Fitzgerald Parman, of a family long prominent in Williamson County, living in the Berry's Chapel neighborhood. They sold the city property and purchased the old Fitzgerald place of 293 acres and made their home there for three years. Mr. Lavender found the two jobs of farming and his post office duties too much for him, so they sold the farm and bought two adjoining houses on South Margin Street, living in one and renting the other.

Percy and Rachel Lavender

Mrs. Lavender is a perfect housekeeper and does not know what the proverbial "spring cleaning" means, for not enough dust ever accumulates to fill a tablespoon. She is a great lover of African violets, and her large collection is greatly admired as they are constantly in bloom. Mr. Lavender says she is a splendid cook, with the only trouble being it keeps him hustling to provide the groceries. She is also well-versed in sewing and says she has enough country left in her to believe the sweetest music is that of a hen cackling. She has two bedrooms furnished entirely with antiques and other pieces scattered about the house. They are all family relics.

Both are members of the Church of Christ. Mr. Lavender attends the Men's Bible Class and his wife the class taught by Mrs. R.H. Cook. They are good neighbors and have many friends. Mrs. Lavender's hobbies are her home and flowers, while Mr. Lavender divides his interest between that of his yard and the post office grounds. He never likes to see anything out of place and is not satisfied until his landscaping is as near perfect as it can be made. When the crepe myrtle shrubs, in pink, white, and red, are in bloom on the post office grounds, they are the envy of all who see them and are often commented upon by tourists passing through. A canna bed, with equally as many colors, is always greatly admired. To Mr. Lavender, flowers are the emblems of friendship and there is nothing he appreciates more than a loyal friend.

Siblings of Gus and Cornelia Lavender: Blanche Barker,
Alvin, Lottie Barker, Percy , Riley, Claude Lavender

The Barker-Lavender family of Burwood, Summer 1919

Front row: Annie Lou Barker, James A. Lavender, Cornelia Barker, Christine Barker, Robbie Lee Barker, Polly Barker, Russell Lavender, Aline Lavender;

2nd row: Riley Lavender, Jack Lavender, Percy Lavender, Virginia Lavender, Blanche Barker, Margaret Barker, Lottie Lee Barker, Ruth Barker, Cornelia Ann Shaw Lavender, Alvin Lavender, Bill Lavender, Claude Lavender, Thelma Lavender;

3rd row: Blythe Lavender, Pearl Lavender, Hattie Lavender, John Barker, Houston Barker, Margaret Lavender, Bessie Mai Lavender, Minnie Lavender, John L. Barker, Colley Lavender;

4th row: Glen Lavender and Roy Barker.

JOHN T. LAWRENCE, "RED"

JANE OWEN

The Review-Appeal, July 6, 1950

John T. Lawrence, the 23-year-old refrigerator serviceman at Sewell Electric Company, says he went back a few generations to inherit his red hair, but his wife claims he did not get the temper that usually accompanies it, for he has, according to her version of the matter, an even, serene disposition even under adverse circumstances. But he does have the freckles that go with the hair and gives him the nickname of "Red" which often follows one with his markings. He claims he would rather have this one than "Freckles."

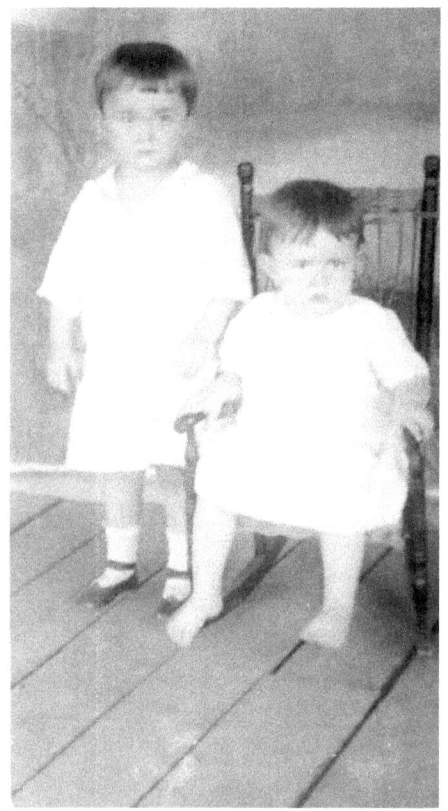

Sister Virginia Lawrence and John "Red" Lawrence

Being the youngest of six children of C.W. and Minnie Tomlinson Lawrence, he, as were his sisters and brothers, was born and reared at Burwood, where at the age of six he entered school with Miss Mary Lou Cannon as his teacher. When he reached the third grade, he found Miss Ruth Alexander as his guide along the path of learning and the next time he met up with her was when he went to work for her husband, Robert E. Sewell. They have much fun talking about those days at Burwood when he was usually the butt of every joke.

He remained in Burwood School until reaching the sixth grade when his sister, just older than him, was ready for high school at Spring Hill, so he had to transfer to go with her. Here he remained until his parents moved to Triune and he continued his education at Franklin High. Soon the Navy needed his services to help win World War II.

As a boy, John, or rather, Red, worked on the farm with his father and brothers. One day, when he was so small that he could hardly sit on the wagon and guide the team while the others gathered corn, he drove too close to a gully. The wagon overturned and he and the corn landed in the ravine. When he was rescued, the worst injury was that to his dignity, for after finding he was unhurt, his father and brothers broke into side-splitting laughter which raised that Irish temper inherited from the same sources as was his red hair.

Being the youngest of a family has its disadvantages as well as advantages. When company came, the women would always say, "Why, this is the baby and my, isn't he growing! Come kiss me, honey," and, after they left, the brothers would tease him, using the same style, tone, and caressing manner as did the visitors. This was also a strain on his temper and led to where he left the house when he saw company arriving and remained away until they left, even it if meant doing without his lunch. But his sisters, Josephine and Virginia usually saw to it that he did not go hungry. Josephine married Robert Inman and lives in Franklin on North Fifth Avenue, and Virginia is the wife of Kenneth Martin, of Nashville. Nathan and Charles are unmarried and are at home with their parents who live on Critz Road and are still farming, while the other brother, Herschel, and his Texas wife live in Decatur, Alabama.

Red says he has nothing but the kindest regards for the number 13. It did cause him some concern when he was sworn into the Navy soon after his 18th birthday on the 13th of the month, but after 13 months and 13 days when he received his discharge, he changed his mind and has since considered it his lucky number. He trained at Bainbridge, Maryland, and was stationed at Quonset, Rhode Island. He was fortunate in not having time to go across as hostilities ceased. He does not look back on his training with any regrets; the worst he had to endure was homesickness and this was made more bearable by the presence of other Williamson County boys, Fleming Williams, Jr., Oscar Simpson, and Claude Southall. Then he had another break in getting to come home every three months.

Upon returning, he was presented with his high school diploma by Prof. Daly Thompson for completion of his high school work while in the service. He went to Nashville for a course in refrigeration at the Auto Diesel College. Completing this in two months, he had on-the-job training at Franklin Supply Company where he worked with Robert Sewell, who later went into business, and Red went with him. Here he installs grocery store and home refrigeration. In making trips to private homes for installing or repairing, he has on several occasions been bitten by house dogs but looks at it from a philosophical standpoint. The dog has been trained to look out for the safety of the family and cannot discriminate between an intruder and a friend on first acquaintance. For this reason, he admires rather than blames the little beast who is doing what he considers his duty.

The worst trouble Red has encountered since coming to Franklin was the big flood a few years ago when the Harpeth River certainly put on an act. He says he never dreamed the time would come when he would enter the Williamson County Locker in a canoe, but this he did. He found the deep freeze floating around and his job was to get the motors out as quickly as possible to make it ready for use as soon as the water subsided. Several crews were at work in the business houses in that section, workman and owners working together, taking everything good-naturedly, knowing no one was to blame for the great disaster and the situation was out of their hands. All they could do was make the best of a bad situation and work to keep down the damage as much as possible. Sometimes when he passes the service station and tells those with him that he has seen water up to the globe on the pump, they look at him as if they are sure he is out of his mind.

In October 1944, Red married Eunice Gunnells, of Spring Hill, who was at the time secretary for Modern Motors. He said when he walked down the aisle at the Methodist Church after Rev. Frank A. Calhoun had heard them promise to love and honor, the sea of faces scared him worse than when he looked out on the ocean with no land visible in any direction. He and Eunice had attended school together at Spring Hill. He often refereed games when she played and she says he was always nice to her. But after they were married, her team was playing Hillsboro and he was serving as referee. He called her down and this did not please her any too much. "But," she said, "when we reached home, I got even with him good and plenty. It was my time to call him down. I did not get anywhere with it for he just laughed. Now, who can get any satisfaction out of being angry if the other person laughs as if it were a big joke?"

Red and Eunice live on North Third Avenue and when work hours are over, he makes for home where he has a great time playing with his small son, Charles Thomas. Though only a few weeks old, his dad has already supplied him with a mitt, baseball, and other ball equipment. Young as he is, he shows definite signs of being left-handed and the proud dad said, "With his red hair and a southpaw, no telling where he will go in the athletic world. One thing sure, he shows no sign of being a sissy."

In the Harpeth Valley Baseball League, Red is a member of the Harpeth team, which has won eight straight games with ten more to go. He also likes to fish in the nearby streams and lakes. Squirrel hunting is another favorite in the sport line. He always goes alone as talking notifies the little animals that danger is near, and they hide out. He is a member of the Williamson County Sportsmen's Club and enjoys meeting with other enthusiasts. He is also a member of the John E. Stephens Post, American Legion.

On Sunday, when not playing ball, he and his wife and son spend the day with either his or her parents for there is no time to visit during the week. Though he is on the job from 7:30 in the morning to 5:30 in the evening, this does not take care of the out-of-hours calls, anywhere, from dark to midnight and sometime later.

Red is interested in his work and says there are no nicer men to work with than Robert Sewell and his brother, J.M. They are 4-square and the three have the same measuring rod: the Golden Rule. When employer and employee speak as highly of each other as these do and the praise rings so clearly of sincerity, there must be mutual respect and understanding back of it. Such seems the case with Robert. E. Sewell and John T. Lawrence, a team that is hard to find and cannot be surpassed.

Sewell Electric Company workmen: Boyd Robinson, J.M. Sewell, Hugh Cunnington, Fulton Johnson, Wallace Lampley, John "Red" Lawrence, and Bob Sewell.

A friend and Red Lawrence serving their country

COLONEL HARDY MURFREE

ELVA MAYO DARBY

Williamson County Historical Society Journal, No. 8, Fall 1977

Col. Hardy Murfree

Lieutenant Colonel Hardy Murfree was an officer of distinguished North Carolina ancestry in the Continental Army who settled in Tennessee in 1807 and became a large landholder, and for whom the town of Murfreesboro, Tennessee, was named.

In October of 1798, Ezekiel White of Bertie County, North Carolina, a private in the Continental line, sold 274 acres of land in Davidson (now Rutherford) County, Tennessee, on the waters of Stone's River, (a tract granted to him on March 7, 1786, as a Revolutionary War soldier) to Lt. Col. Hardy Murfree, of Hertford County, North Carolina, under whom he had served during the Revolution. Colonel Murfree had been an officer in the Revolution and prominent in the political affairs of the state thereafter serving in both the legislature and the Constitutional Convention.

Colonel Murfree was born in Hertford County, North Carolina, on June 5, 1752, the son of William and Mary Murfree. He was married on February 17, 1780, to Sarah Brickell, daughter of Matthias and Rachel Noailles Brickell, of Hertford County. Hardy and Sarah Murfree were the parents of ten children.

Soon after the close of the Revolutionary War Colonel Murfree visited Tennessee and began buying tracts of land in the present Williamson, Rutherford, and Bedford Counties. He received over 6,000 acres of land for his own services in the war, and through purchases of the warrant, grants, and other soldiers, such as that of Ezekiel

White's, the purchase price of that being $100, he eventually owned over 40,000 acres of land in Tennessee.

After the death of his wife in 1802, Hardy Murfree remained at his home in Murfreesboro, North Carolina, (named for his parents) for five years, and then, in 1807, he moved to Tennessee and settled on his plantation at "Murfree's Fork," a branch of the West Harpeth River in Williamson County.

While he was still living in North Carolina, in 1804, Colonel Murfree registered the land which he bought from Ezekiel White. The fact that neither the original grant of 1786 nor the transfer to Murfree of 1798 was recorded in Tennessee until 1804 is indicative that the land was not actually occupied at some later date.

Colonel Murfree died in Williamson County, Tennessee, near Burwood, on April 6, 1809, on the plantation where he settled and where some of his children were living, at the time of his death.

The town of Murfreesboro, Tennessee, was named for Colonel Hardy Murfree at the request of his friend, Captain William Lytle. A legislative act had specified that the site for the Rutherford County seat be named Cannonsburg, in honor of Newton Cannon of Williamson County, later a governor. However, Captain Lytle, who had donated 60 acres upon which to erect a courthouse, suggested that the town be named for his friend, Colonel Hardy Murfree, who had recently died. His request was granted, and the legislature passed another act naming the town Murfreesborough, the spelling of which changed after the Civil War.

In addition to his vast holdings of land and properties, Colonel Murfree left posterity with something far more valuable. His great-granddaughter was Mary Noailles Murfree, known for years in literary circles by her pseudonym of Charles Egbert Craddock, who was responsible for the authorship of some twenty-five books over her long writing career. Her work centered around the rugged mountain people of Tennessee. She was the daughter of William Murfree, a lawyer who had plantations in Tennessee and Mississippi.

When Colonel Murfree died intestate in 1809 his land holdings were so extensive that the Tennessee legislative passed an act, in 1812, empowering the Court of Williamson County to appoint seven commissioners to make an equitable distribution of his lands among the several heirs. In its report to the Court, on December 14, 1814, the Commissioners included the Ezekiel White tract in the considerable portions allotted to one of Murfree's daughters, Sarah Hardy, who had shortly before married Dr. James Maney. Also listed in the Tax Book I, Williamson County, 1800-1813, to Hardy Murfree are: 5,000 acres, Continental line near the crossing [of the Duck Ridge]; 6,400 acres, Murfree's Fork of the West Harpeth; 768 acres, Stewart Creek; and 960 acres, Harpeth.

Colonel Hardy Murfree's grave is in the family cemetery on the Jim Cannon farm in the fourth district, near Burwood. This land was originally a land grant to Colonel Murfree for his services in the Revolution. He was buried grandly with Masonic honors, hundreds attended the interment, and Judge Felix Grundy of Nashville delivered an eloquent address. That burial was talked about for more than a quarter of a century afterward — "so grand and imposing the ceremonies, so great the number that witnessed it."

[Children of Hardy Murfree: William Maney, Fanny M. Dickinson, Mary M. Hilliard, Mathias B. Murfree, Sallie M. Maney, Martha M. Maney, Salley B. Murfree, and Elizabeth Murfree.]

The Col. Hardy Murfree Cemetery was recently cleaned as an Eagle Scout Project.

A.G. OVERBEY

JANE OWEN

The Review-Appeal, February 9, 1939

Albert Glen Overbey

Five miles southwest of Franklin on the Carter's Creek Pike at a sharp turn in the road is located the general mercantile store of A.G. (Glen) Overbey, whose motto is "You get full value for your money when you trade with us," and he lives up to it. He also advocates "Home Trading Insures Home Prosperity," for he is a hundred percent Williamson Countian although he was born at Lyle's Station in Hickman County where he lived until his parents moved here when he was twelve years old. He and Governor Prentice Cooper were born on the same day, September 28, 1895.

He says he was named for his uncle, Albert Beasley, and a Mr. Glen, who was paymaster for the N.C. and St. L., where his father was getting his living as he was operating a store at Lyle at that time and his main revenue came through the railway workmen.

In Hickman County, the Overbey name dates back to the early part of the last century. His great-great-grandfather, Daniel Overbey, who married Emily Tyler, a kinswoman of President John Tyler, was a trapper. He left North Carolina in 1807, came to Sumner County, and in the autumn of 1814, moved his family to Lick Creek where buffaloes, deer, and other wild animals were plentiful. His great-grandfather, Daniel Overbey, Jr., was also a trapper and farmed on the side, and since then, the Overbey men have mainly been men of the soil.

One of his great-great-uncles, Garrett Turman, was a Revolutionary soldier and was at one time held prisoner for six months by the Indians. His grandfather, Garrett

Turman Overbey, married Emily Moss and had eight children. His father, T.F. Overbey being next to the youngest and has in his possession a wagon hammer picked up by his great-grandmother, Emily Tyler Overbey, on the trail as she came over from North Carolina.

T.F. married Etta Beasley Overbey, the eldest of nine children and they have five girls and three boys. Beasley elected to farm and lives near his father. Glen is the merchant and William teaches shop and coaches at Franklin High. Eunice teaches home economics in San Bernardino, CA, and Emma had the same work in Franklin High until she married Milton Hunter, of Franklin, and now they live in Lexington. Mary is a home demonstration agent and lives in Jasper, Arkansas. Annie is with the Social Security Board in Nashville and Dorothy is a freshman at U.T., having finished last year at Franklin High School.

Glen attended school at Forest Hill and later at Battle Ground Academy where he played football. As guard, he helped win hard-fought games over their old rivals, Branham and Hughes at Spring Hill, Massey at Pulaski, Montgomery Bell and Wallace of Nashville. He put more time on athletics than books. He says from the rapid rate that he, "Baby" Jones, and Jim Cannon rode their horses into town, leaving a trail of dust in their wake, it would seem they were anxious to reach the "hill," as the school grounds were called, and apply themselves to their studies, but not so. It was only a race.

Beverly and Beasley Overbey, Jr., neighbor Lula Layne and Glen Overbey on the store porch.

After leaving school, he opened the store where he is now located in 1916, selling everything from a jelly glass and spool of thread to machinery. He buys country produce and sends it by truck to the Nashville markets.

In May 1918, he was drafted for the World War and was in training at Camp Pike, near Little Rock, Arkansas, with the 87th division. He sailed on August 12, 1918, from Montreal, Canada, with Company K, 126th Infantry, 32nd division, made up mainly of Wisconsin and Michigan National Guards. They were 28 days going over, having been held up three days at Halifax by submarine dangers. They landed at Southampton, England, and crossed the English Channel to Cherbourg, France.

He saw service in Argonne Forest with the Army of Occupation and was at the front for forty-two days. He was never wounded though there were over seven thousand casualties, either killed or wounded, leaving very few of the original men in his division. He was the only Franklin man in his company, having only twelve or fifteen Tennesseans in it. Clayton Arnold, of Thompson Station, was in the same division but a different regiment and they never met.

His division, the 32nd, was one of three to serve in the Bridge Head Sector in Germany. They crossed the Rhine on December 11, 1918 and remained until May 1919. He says he only saw the good side of the enemy and was treated kindly by all Germans encountered. His company was in a little town called Jametz, near Longwy, a railroad center, when the joyful news came that hostilities had ceased. They sailed for home from Brest, France, landed eight days later in New York City, and were sent to Fort Oglethorpe, Georgia, to be discharged. His father had charge of his business while he was gone. He came back and took up where he left off.

Fighting was no new thing in the Overbey family as Glen's grandfather Overbey served four years in Company G, 48th Tennessee Infantry in the Confederate Army, and was in many of the major battles.

Being asked in what line he excels, Glen's answer was, "Well, I guess it must be as a chitterling eating champion. I don't know how many pounds I can eat at a time, but I never miss one of these suppers when given by Dr. Nolen, 'Possum' Prowell, Henry Matt Cotton, or Charley Fox and I reckon their wives can pretty well tell you how many I eat." A friend hearing him said, "I have never found anything wrong with your steak-eating capacity."

As a citizen, he is highly respected, and the Fourth District claims him as one of the best Democrats in its borders. He takes an active part in every election and is usually on the winning side. He is a director in the Harpeth National Bank, a member of the John E. Stephens Post, American Legion, and the Church of Christ, worshipping at Southall with the rest of the family. He is known for his generosity, great devotion to his family, judge of great produce, and how much a nickel can buy. He does not smoke but can chew as much tobacco in a day as anybody; is a great reader, leaning toward historical and political books; cares very little for the radio and picture shows but enjoys a good game of football and makes a fine sideline rooter.

Polly McCampbell, Glen Overbey, and Vernon Beard

T.F. OVERBEY

JANE OWEN

T.F. Overbey family: 1st row: William, Annie, Eunice, Mary, Twins Beverly and Beasely, Jr., and Dorothy Overbey; 2nd row: T.F. and Etta Overbey, Eph Tatum, Glen, Emma and Milton Hunter, Aldea and Beasley Overbey.

The Review-Appeal, January 11, 1945

Mr. and Mrs. T.F. Overbey live on their farm of 742 acres just past Forest Hill School on the Carter's Creek Road, which they bought from the Thomas F. Perkins heirs in 1907 and moved there the following year. The original Perkins house burned and had been replaced by a frame cottage. After the present owners took possession, they moved this house to another location and in 1914, built the present imposing dwelling of nine rooms, large halls, spacious attic and basement with concrete front and back porches equipped with electricity and running water.

It was here on Sunday, December 31, this happy couple celebrated their golden wedding anniversary, keeping open house from three to six o'clock, with many relatives and friends calling, despite the inclement weather, to wish them continued happiness. Both were proudly wearing wristwatches, gifts from their eight children, all of whom were present except Eunice, whose school work as a home economics teacher in San Bernardino, California, forced her to leave a day or so before the celebration in order that she might be at her post on time. The three sons, Glen, a merchant near home; Beasley, farmer and trader; and William, teacher of manual arts in the Chattanooga Public School System, were busy greeting the guests as they arrived, while Jane, wife of Milton Hunter, of Lexington; Anne, who works in Nashville; Mary, of Marion, Ark.; and Dorothy, of Roan Oak, Alabama, both home demonstration agents, were busy as bees along with Beasley's wife, making every guest feel at home and seeing that they were served in the dining room. Beasley's twins, Beverly and Beasley, Jr., were inviting each visitor to sign the register.

Mr. Overbey was in a pensive mood when visited a few days later while talking with a guest concerning his long useful life spent in doing good.

"I was born," he said, "May 17, 1870, on Lick Creek, one of six children of Turman and Emily Moss Overbey, and am the only member of the family living. I was reared on a farm with work as my daily companion, but I am glad my parents taught me to know that labor is honorable and I have passed it on to my children.

"My wife, the oldest child of John and Emma Cowan Beasley, who also lived on Lick Creek, and I were married in her home. Elder James Litton rode a mule ten miles to perform the ceremony. Several were here Sunday who were present that day and two of them, Mrs. Henry Skelley, of Triune, and Mrs. C. C. Skelley, took part. We went to the home of my parents for the wedding supper, and it was the second time my wife ever rode in a buggy, having gone everywhere on horseback or in the family wagon. All I remember about the supper was the long table was full of good things to eat.

"We lived at Lyle Station in the home of my brother, John, for three months until my house was completed. Here we lived for seven years, and our first three children were born. My brothers, John and W.W., and I were in business together. W.W. ran the store, John the sawmill, and I took part in both but mostly driving the log wagon, superintending the felling of trees, and was busy all the time from early to late. With my wife's help, we put aside part of every dollar we made, and at the end of the seven years, we paid $6,000 cash for a farm of 300 acres on Lick Creek near Primm, where another child was added to the family. Much of the land was rough but I ran a sawmill and the large poplar forest was converted into lumber and although I sold the place for only $6200, I made a big profit in the deal on the lumber.

Forest Hill, the home of T.F. Overbey, was built in 1910, after the original house by that name, burned. It remains today on Carter's Creek Pike in front of the famous Beaver Spring.

"My next move was five miles nearer this way but still on Lick Creek, where the land was not much better, but I again made a good profit on lumber and the family went up another notch as again a baby daughter brought added cheer to the circle. It was from this place we moved to our present location and here the three youngest children were born.

"One day while we were living at our first place on Lick Creek, a deaf and dumb [mute] boy came to our home asking as best he could by signs for something to eat, indicating he wanted to work for it. We took him in and he has never left us. Eph is as one of the family, spoiling all the children as they came along and adding to it with the two grandchildren. Tho he can neither read nor write, he readily understands signs and they rarely have to be repeated for he is always anxious to do every job just as it should be. He was never able to let us know how he became a mute, whether by birth or a lick on the head.

"My sons, Glen and Beasley, and I operate our three farms of 1,100 acres, and Beasley trades on the side. We have eight families on our places and have never had any trouble keeping help. We raise wheat, oats, barley, rye, corn, tobacco, and cover crops. We have a large tobacco barn and have already disposed of part of our crop on the Franklin markets. We use tractors and mules for cultivation. I prefer the eleven mules and my mare, but the boys think tractors are better.

"In my dairy barn are thirty cows milked by hand night and morning, and the milk is picked up at the door by a truck. As soon as conditions permit, I shall install an electric milking machine. Only enough hogs are raised to supply the family's needs. I have about 75 sheep but the goats multiply so rapidly I can't keep track of them. I only know they are numerous. My wife has splendid luck with her flock of Plymouth Rocks, but the eggs and chickens are consumed at home.

"I bought my first buggy soon after we were married. Many years ago, the children, wishing to keep up with the times, wanted me to buy an automobile. Beasley and I rode into town to look at one Ben Christian had for sale. It seemed to be what the boy wanted so I gave Ben a check for $500 and he sent a demonstrator to take us home and to give Beasley his first lesson. When we reached home, I got out, Beasley went back with the man to Franklin and drove home alone.

"William is a genius when it comes to making furniture. In our home are many articles of his labor and they are works of art, a credit to any cabinet maker. He made his mother both a cherry and a walnut corner cupboard, a walnut banquet table with eight ladderback chairs, several chests of drawers, a four-poster bed, a number of tables including drop-leaf models, rocking chairs, and other things. He has furnished the twins' playhouse with all kinds of furniture. Another very fine thing that he did was install an electric elevator in Beasley's barn to stow hay, a device that saves both time and labor.

Albert Beasley, Daisy Sewell, Laura Davis, Etta Overbey, Lucy Bizwell, and Earlie Beasley, children of Emma Cowan and John Beasley

"While all my family have passed on and I miss them, yet I get much pleasure from my wife's brothers and sisters. Albert, Barney, and Ernest Beasley are mighty fine Williamson County farmers and Earnie is a merchant in Centerville. Three of her sisters, Mrs. R.E. Sewell, Mrs. W.H. Bizwell, and Mrs. Burton Davis live in Franklin, and another, Mrs. Andy Warf, makes her home at Hillsboro. I like to see them get together and hear them talk.

"While I have worked hard, time has been most kind to me. I have passed my 74th year and my wife is 71, and we have been spared all of our children who are a credit to us. We made our contributions to World War I when Glen spent a year in France and, I am glad to say, came home sound and well.

"Since our early youth, my wife and I have been members of the Church of Christ and all our children are too. We go to Berea at Southall where I have served as treasurer for many years. The only guide a man needs is the Bible and I have taken it as mine and endeavored to follow it."

When Mr. Overbey ceased speaking, the guest looked over at Mrs. Overbey, who sat quietly talking to Aleda, Beasley's wife. When asked if she too had found life full of joy, she smiled sweetly and said, "Yes, very, but sometimes a bit humdrum for from the time Glen entered school as a small boy until William completed four years of teaching in Franklin High School and went to Chattanooga, I had packed school lunches for a period of 32 years without a break for my children. You know that can get a bit monotonous. But it has always been a pleasure to add to the happiness of my family."

In their son-in-law, Milton Hunter, and daughter-in-law, Aleda, Beasley's wife, they have found two more children. Aleda's daughter, Evelyn Cunningham, by a former marriage, has also found a place in the heart of each, and when she married Pfc. Jack Custer, he was also received as a member.

Time has dealt kindly with both Mr. and Mrs. Overbey. Neither is very gray, are well preserved, happy in their home, and looking forward to reaping a glorious reward for the deeds done while serving their Maker all the days of their lives.

Beasley Overbey at the Forest Hill Spring House in 1964

MYRTLE RIGGIN RAGSDALE

JANE OWEN

The Review-Appeal, April 26, 1945

Myrtle Riggin Ragsdale
(1886-1968)

Every town, village, and countryside has its "angel of mercy" who is always at hand when emergencies arise to give much valuable assistance when it is most needed, not selecting the persons where probably future remuneration is possible, but to the high, low, and those termed the "middle class."

Such has been the life of Mrs. J. S. Ragsdale, who lives in Lynhurst, a suburb of Franklin, built at the extreme end of West Main Street and along Carter's Creek Road. Here the inhabitants are real neighbors, ready and willing to help each other. When one gets sick or suffers an accident, Mrs. Ragsdale is the first to be summoned and never fails to respond promptly.

She was born, reared, and educated at Burwood where were also her parents, Robert and Sarah Jones Riggin, and her brother, Will Riggin, is a farmer. Her sister, Mrs. Tom Huff, makes her home in Mt. Pleasant. Another sister, Mrs. C.H. Ormes, died several years ago.

When Mrs. Ragsdale, who was named Myrtle, was four years old, her father died. Her mother took her children and went to live with her father, D.F. Jones, known by his friends as "Dock" and here they grew up. Mrs. Riggin, being of an independent nature, accepted nothing more than shelter and food from her father, and this she earned for she did all the work about the house with the children's assistance. On the sideline, she wove, spun, quilted, and knitted for her family and for neighbors. She raised large flocks of chickens, turkeys, and geese. As her mother had also passed away, she took her brother, the late Sam H. Jones, under her protective care until he was grown. One of their major blessings was good health. They never had any broken bones. Tonsils, adenoids, and appendices had not been discovered so the doctor's bills were light. Mrs. Ragsdale never forgot all the trials her mother had to endure and tried to repay her in later life, taking her into the Ragsdale home where she died in 1936 at the age of 81, tenderly loved and cared for by the entire family.

In 1903, Mr. and Mrs. Ragsdale were married. They drove to Thompson Station where, in the presence of his sisters and a cousin, the vows were taken in the Methodist Church parsonage. She was only seventeen and the groom was just past his twenty-first birthday. They went immediately to housekeeping at Burwood where Mr. Ragsdale was also born and reared. She kept the three-room house clean and attractive. The lack of furniture did not bother them for they added piece by piece just what they wanted. Having been taught by her mother to sew, cook, and other household arts, she did not seem so young and certainly not inexperienced.

Soon after Mrs. Ragsdale passed her twenty-first birthday, her elder son, Mack, was born, and about three years later, Albert put in his appearance. They grew up in the home of their grandfather where their mother was reared, for Mr. and Mrs. Ragsdale had found it necessary to leave their little cottage they had learned to love so well and move to the homeplace to help with the care of her aged grandfather since the strain of the hard years was telling on her mother and assistance was needed.

Everbright

Having learned the carpenter's trade, Mr. Ragsdale came to Franklin where he would stay all week, working with the late Pete Vaughn, going home for the weekends. Mrs. Ragsdale, finding extra time on her hands, began sewing for her neighbors. After the death of the grandfather, Mr. and Mrs. Ragsdale with her mother and their two sons moved to Franklin where Mr. Ragsdale could be at home and more convenient to his work. They first lived in old Everbright, a house of twenty rooms, which they occupied with Mr. and Mrs. John Elmore, and the two Elmore boys with Mack and Albert made a lively and happy foursome. Before buying their present home, they lived two years at Myles Manor before it was made into a clubhouse. It also possessed many rooms, and it was a relief to move into a smaller home.

The two Ragsdale boys were always together. As they grew up, Mack would get a job and take Albert along to help. Whatever the older undertook the younger was sure it would turn out all right. They both graduated from Franklin High School and got jobs at North Drugstore, Mack as a clerk and Albert as a laundry collector. When the time came to marry, they both selected Franklin girls with whom they had been classmates from the time they entered first grade until they graduated. Mack married Evelyn Potts, daughter of Mr. and Mrs. H.J. Potts, and built a brick home on Battlefield Drive, Nashville, where they both worked until he volunteered for the Navy. Albert married Elizabeth Lewis, daughter of Mrs. W.T. Lewis, and the late Mr. Lewis. They also built a brick home on Battle Ground Heights, Franklin. He was a foreman for S.E. Farnsworth and Company where he likewise volunteered for the Navy.

Grandmother Sarah Jones Riggin with Mack and Albert Ragsdale.

For the first time in his life, Albert made a move ahead of his older brother as he volunteered first and entered training in October 1942, at Norfolk, Virginia, was sent overseas the following February, and is now in Guam as chief carpenter's mate. Mack's training began the month following his brother's leaving for foreign service, receiving it at Camp Peary, Virginia, sailing in February 1944, for duty in the Pacific the day his father died of a heart attack. He did not know of his loss for several weeks. He is now chief storekeeper in the supply department on Tinian Island.

Their good luck kept up for on July 4, 1944, the brothers met quite by accident on the Marshall Islands and had a pleasant two weeks together before their paths again parted.

Undaunted, Mrs. Ragsdale carries on, living alone in her one-story frame cottage, raising a brood of one hundred chickens and many beautiful flowers. She keeps up her sewing for she does not like idle moments. Many is the baby who finds itself wearing its first clothes which are the product of her needle. Girls graduating from high school and bridges also have looked their loveliest in dresses she made. Many a loved one is laid to rest wearing a robe or winding sheet that often she sat up all night to have ready at the appointed hour. In times of sickness, she is ready to do what she can to help with the household chores. Mothers who cannot afford hospitalization find Mrs. Ragsdale ready to receive the newborn baby from the doctor's hands and she knows just what to do with it. Accidents occurring in the home, a runner is sent posthaste or a telephone call will start her on the way to help alleviate the suffering. Then when death is an unwelcome visitor, it is she who closes the sightless eyes, comforts the broken-hearted, and ministers to the family needs.

In speaking of her daughter-in-law, Mrs. Ragsdale said, "I remind myself of Naomi with her daughters-in-law, Ruth and Orpah of Bible days, only neither of mine turned back. They never fail to remember me and often I visit in their homes for a week at a time if my duties do not keep me at home. I think of daughters without the added in-laws."

The many handmade articles in Mrs. Ragsdale's home are a wonder to see – crocheted bedspreads, table runners, doilies, luncheon sets, and many other pieces; quilts of various and intricate patterns; embroidered pillow slips; hemstitched sheets; all these and others put away for my children when they need them.

Albert Ragsdale

Elizabeth Lewis Ragsdale

Mrs. Ragsdale, a member of the Methodist Church, was asked if she had a motto, and she answered in her deliberate manner, "Well, no. I just move along and do the best I can. My married life was a happy one for I had a good, kind, considerate husband and two as good, obedient, industrious sons as ever grew up. They have always been a credit to us and never gave their father or me any cause to worry. I have not made any changes since their father died. I am only waiting until they return to tell me what to do and, whatever one says, the other will agree to."

While Mrs. Ragsdale has been a constant worker, she has not craved riches, realizing, "It is good to have money and the things that money can buy, but it is good, too, to check up once in a while and make sure you haven't lost the things that money cannot buy."

WILLIAM HAMILTON SEDBERRY

BILL WOOLSEY

The Nashville Tennessean Magazine, July 11, 1948

William H. Sedberry, Sr.

Time is a notoriously long-suffering goddess, but William Hamilton Sedberry, Sr., inventor, fisherman, hunter, marksman, and taxidermist of Williamson County, must occasionally try her patience. He refuses to take her seriously.

With mortals, particularly sportsmen who bring him fish and fowl to mount for their yawning mantels, he is similarly elusive. A master of what show business people call the throwaway line, he pacifies them with a jocularity about the gray hair they have acquired since bringing him their game. "How old are you?" he recently asked a Nashville man who had come to collect a large-mouthed bass on a trophy board. He didn't wait for an answer but continued. "You'll be a little older before that bass is ready." Then he begins to talk about fishing or hunting with them. His dark, quizzical eyes brighten and his thin, rather tired, face becomes animated. Invariably, the customer goes away mollified.

The corollary of Sedberry's cavalier attitude toward the passage of time is that his old red-brick farmhouse, so screened by trees that a motorist on the West Harpeth Road passes it unaware, has become a sort of a wildlife mausoleum where the dry, odorless inanimate skins of hawks, ducks, deer, bear, fish, and owls are stacked on the floor, on tables, and hung from the ceiling. There is even the green feathered hull of somebody's pet parrot awaiting Sedberry's skillful restoration.

Persons who know him well frequently speculate as to what successes Sedberry might have enjoyed in the fields other than taxidermy where the sun of his interest shone brightly but briefly. Once he perfected a fishing rod improvement, mailed a model to a manufacturer, and never heard another word about it, although his modification was widely used. He intends to be more careful with a new invention, an automatic choke to focus bullet pattern, and has patented the device.

The Sedberry home atop a knoll

Ten years ago, his talent as a marksman was acknowledged when he lost by only one shot in the run-off for the state outdoor trapshooting title. He decided the sport was too expensive and dropped out of competition.

Some years before, he traveled 14 southwestern states demonstrating a stock feed grinder, but he severed his connection with the manufacturers before the grinder achieved commercial success and made several fortunes for its sponsors, one of whom was his brother.

His father's chance at material gain as a novelist suffered a considerable setback, too, around the turn of the century, when the publishers of the senior Sedberry's first book abruptly went bankrupt. The book, *Under the Flag of the Cross*, dealt with a hypothetical Caucasian-Mongolian clash (the title was the publishers' idea, not his father's. Sedberry says) and there are still a few copies on the bookshelves of persons acquainted with the father, J. Hamilton Sedberry, who continued to keep a general store at Thompson Station, Tennessee, and even wrote two more novels, historical fiction, neither of which got into print.

Inflation, or the higher price plateau, or whatever you choose to call, it spurred Sedberry to a spate of intensive taxidermy this summer in an effort to complete jobs that were contracted during an era of lower costs. From now on he expects to charge about $18 for mounting a fish and about $14 for mounting large birds, say the size of a great blue heron. He is also eager to concentrate his work, heretofore scattered around the house, in a clapboard shop building which he built some time ago but as yet has not utilized.

Sedberry is 55, slight, and rather rumpled-looking. He was born at Thompson Station in the same big stone house in which he and his wife lived until about twenty years ago when they moved into their present home. The latter abode is chiefly distinguished, from the exterior, by its aged appearance, but the interior is distinctly more prepossessing. Apparently, all unfinished souvenirs of the hunt have been barred from the square, comfortably furnished living room (one suspects Mrs. Sedberry here), and the huge rattlesnake, the mole, and the several birds, on display are respectably stitched, glued, and mounted in lifelike poses.

Mrs. Sedberry is regarded by their friends as an almost phenomenally imperturbable hostess, undisturbed by even so much as a dozen extra quests at dinner, and as a most understanding wife, not given to worrying about desiccated eagles, hanging from the ceiling.

Seated: Dolly, Carline, Billy, Sr.; Standing, Billy, Jr., Barbara, Zulieme, and Jimmy Sedberry

The Sedberrys have two sons and three daughters. The oldest girl, 20-year-old Barbara Faye, works in Franklin; the younger girls, Jesse Zullieme and Carline, 13 and 9 years old, live at home. One son, William Sedberry, Jr., is a farmer, and the other, James Franklin Sedberry, is in the Marine Corps. None of them, their father has indicated, takes much of an interest in taxidermy.

Sedberry, himself, got interested in what is now his chief occupation as a boy of tender years. It seems plain that he found his métier, quickly, under the guidance of an older man, for he recently discovered an eagle he had stuffed during his apprentice days glaring balefully from the window of a Franklin bank and still in good condition. "Just needs cleaning up a little," he said.

He progressed rapidly in his career and in his zeal took up the study of painting, too, the better to simulate the colors of life upon the chill, gutted bodies of trophy fish. For some years he hunted and mounted specimens for state exhibits of birds and animals.

"I had to quit it, though," Sedberry explained the other day. "It was taking me too long to find the specimens. Even though all they wanted was some common variety of bird when I went out to look for it that bird would be just as hard to find as if it was a rare one."

Another talent that he has pretty much put to pasture these days is his technique with fishing flies which once he made in considerable quantity for the sporting goods department of a Nashville retail store. He can and does create a wide variety of flies but for his own use, he prefers any one of three: Red Squirrel, Gray Squirrel, and Guinea.

As is inevitable for a man with such varied abilities and interests, Sedberry is remembered for different accomplishments by different persons. But the two small boys whom he once took on a tour of his taxidermy exhibits probably carried away the most appealing recollection of his perennial humor. As they passed an old gentleman asleep in a chair somewhere about the Sedberry house, their host noted that the sleeper's lower plate had slipped out of his mouth. Turning to the boys, Sedberry cautioned them solemnly, "Don't touch that one.' He pointed toward the old gentleman. "I haven't finished with him yet."

Frances Dolly Sedberry

James Hamilton Sedberry
(1863-1931)

William H. Sedberry, Sr.,

Zullieme Johnson Sedberry

NOTABLE HOMES OF THE FOURTH DISTRICT

James and Fannie Hassell's log cabin

W.C. Pope – R.H. Barker – Polly Duncan home

FAIRVIEW

VIRGINIA MCDANIEL BOWMAN

Home of Brown Kinnard

Fairview was built in 1850 for Claiborne H. and Elizabeth Fleming Kinnard, located on Carter's Creek Pike at the West Harpeth River Bridge.

The land on which Fairview is located was originally part of the land grant to Edward Swanson, Williamson County's first settler and one of the founders of Nashville who visited the Cumberland country with James Robertson before the "founding" expedition late in 1779 and early 1780. Brown Kinnard, the present owner, holds in his possession a deed from Edward Swanson to his grandfather, Claiborne Holmes Kinnard. [*Editor's note: the deed was signed by James Swanson, son of Edward Swanson, not Swanson himself.*]

The house was built in 1850 by Claiborne H. Kinnard (1813-1863) who married Elizabeth Fleming (1818-1884), the daughter of William and Mixey Thompson Fleming, in 1834. It was remodeled in 1898 by his son, Claiborne H. Kinnard, Jr., who had married Rebecca Campbell, the daughter of John and Rebecca Campbell in 1882. During the renovation, at that time the nursery, bathrooms, and porches were added. When visitors comment on the wide porches that almost completely surround the fourteen-room frame house. Mr. Kinnard laughingly remarks that his father must have had a "porch fit" when he remodeled the original structure.

Fairview takes its name from the beautiful views spread out around it in every direction. The story is told that when Rebekah (Mrs. John R. Lionberger), the eldest child of Claiborne H. Kinnard, Jr., was a little girl, she heard a guest remark to her mother that the view from the house was beautiful. The child rushed out to see what the guests had seen!

Dr. Claiborne Holmes Kinnard

Much of the furniture in the house today is that used by the parents of the present owner when they started keeping house in 1882. Trees, shrubs, lawns, and flowers reflect the zealous maintenance and love each generation has lavished on the place. The old cedars were put out when the house was built over a hundred twenty years ago. The present mistress of Fairview states that she finds the outstanding charm of the house today to be the 'good living" that it reflects for all its years.

Nothing has been overlooked to make it comfortable and livable. Its ingenious owners found ways to provide conveniences not yet available in their time. For instance, the first windmill in this section of the country was installed by Claiborne H. Kinnard, Jr. to bring water from a nearby spring. The same spring continued to serve the home (via an electric pump) until the summer of 1970 when a public water line was made available to this part of the county. Long before bathrooms were in every home there was one at Fairview. Brown Kinnard remembers sitting as a little boy on the edge of the marble lavatory in the dressing room and washing his feet in the basin.

There are marks left upon the place by each generation that show it has been a place for "living" and full enjoyment of the surroundings. The flower garden established by Mrs. Claiborne H. Kinnard, Jr. more than forty years ago still exists and has many flowers blooming that were planted by her.

Only recently a workman dug up the foundation of a pen that Brown Kinnard built thirty years ago to house some pet foxes for his son, Brown, Jr. Other pets which it is recalled were collected and cared for, in addition to the usual cats and dogs, included squirrels, buzzards, and skunks. Mr. Kinnard said that his older brother, Claiborne Holmes Kinnard, III, improvised a way to keep squirrels in captivity and yet not deny them completely of their natural way of living. He built a pen at the base of a large tree and constructed a runway up the tree and into a barrel that had been placed high above.

Brown and Cynthia Kinnard

Carolyn, Brown, Ida, and Brown Kinnard

A search of the storage room recently revealed a doll cookstove—a replica of the old wood-burning kitchen range. Rebekah Lionberger remembers that she "cooked" on this stove as a child but does not recall that it was purchased for her. So, it is unknown just how many generations have enjoyed this toy which is in perfect condition and carefully preserved for the present generation of children.

A windowpane in the kitchen still carries the crude inscription "BCK", reflecting the earliest efforts of Brown Kinnard, Jr. to write his name in glass with his mother's diamond ring. These "scratches" are enjoyed rather than resented as they represent the child's effort to prove that a diamond will cut glass.

Claiborne Holmes Kinnard [Sr.] who purchased the land from Edward Swanson, is buried in a small plot surrounded by an iron fence just outside the yard of the residence.

Text: Bowman, Virginia McDaniel. *Historic Williamson County: Old Homes and Sites*. c1971. Republished by Sovran Bank, 1989.

THE COLLINS - LAYNE HOME

John Collins family of the Forest Hill Community

John and Elizabeth Thweatt Collins and family lived next door to Overbey's Store in Forest Hill. The house was built in 1899 and demolished in 1965. Lula P. Collins Layne is the child in her mother's lap. Mrs. Lula P. Layne (1898-1990) reared her children, Harry, Jim, Edward, and Elizabeth, here.

Ernest, Harry, George, Leroy Collins, sons of John and Elizabeth Collins

Harry Layne, Robert Green, Jim Layne, and Ed Layne, sons of Lula P. Layne and a nephew

THE LAMB - LAWRENCE HOME

The Drury Lamb-John W. Lawrence home, front view, is located near Lawrence Grove Baptist Church.

The Drury Lamb-John W. Lawrence home, back view

A cemetery located near this log home may reveal more about the house. The oldest couple buried there is James Watson (1795-1879) and Sally N. Watson (1805-1887). Drury Lamb (1810-1887) and Elizabeth Lamb (1823-1879) were living here in 1878. John W. Lawrence (1854-1902) and Josephine Lawrence (1862-1923) were most likely the next owners. C.W. "Jack" Lawrence and Minnie Tomlinson Lawrence reared their family here.

We noted in the local servicemen of World War II section that this couple furnished three serviceman- Charles "Woodie" Lawrence, Nathan Lawrence, and John T. "Red" Lawrence. Their granddaughter, Janice Inman Duff has supplied these photos plus one of her Aunt Dora Lawrence and her mother, Josephine Lawrence Inman, and Uncle Herschel P. Lawrence.

Herschel P. Lawrence

Dora Lawrence

Robert and Josephine Lawrence Inman

Jack Lawrence's children: Woodie, Pat, Josephine, Nathan, and Virginia before J.T.

C.W. and Minnie Lawrence

The Lawrence family band: Nathan, Woodie, Red; Back row: Josephine, Herschel, and Virginia.

JOHN WILSON LAWRENCE (1854-1902) AND JOSEPHINE LAWRENCE (1862-1923), MARRIED IN 1881

Children:

    Charles W. "Jack" 1881-1952

    Eddie E. Lawrence 1882-1971

    Ollie E. Lawrence 1886-1976

    Henry T. Lawrence 1887-1960

    Walter E. Lawrence 1888-1980

    Elizabeth Lawrence 1890-1950 married G.V. Elmore

    Willie Lawrence 1896-1986

    Dora Lawrence 1905-1965

CHARLES WILSON (1881-1952) AND MINNIE TOMLINSON LAWRENCE (1881-1969), MARRIED IN MAY 1913

Children:

    Josephine Lawrence (1914-2006) married Robert Inman (1909-1988) in January 1933

    Nathan Burch Lawrence (1915-1996) never married

    Herschel Patton Lawrence (1918-2007) married Willie Merle O'Neill in December 1947

    Charles Woodard Lawrence (1921-1983) never married

    Virginia Pearl Lawrence (1923-2017) married Kenneth Martin in September 1945

    John Thomas "Red" Lawrence 1927-2007 married Eunice Maxine Gunnels in October 1947, and Audrey Merl Hawley on June 9, 1993.

THE W.P. THWEATT HOME

Sons of William Howard and Mary Allen Thweatt: Pleasant Samuel, William Peter, and John Henry

W.P. Thweatt and his family lived in this one-and-a-half-story frame house and worked as tenant farmers for Thomas F. Perkins at Forest Hill Farm on Carter's Creek Pike. This house, with its tall brick chimneys and decorative millwork under the cornice and on the porch, was located on West Harpeth Road. It burned in the 1940s.

THE WILLOWS

VIRGINIA MCDANIEL BOWMAN

The Willows, home of John and Jane Reese Watson, later Dewees and Sue Berry is located on West Harpeth Road.

This beautiful home, known originally as The Willows, was built by John Watson (1778-1851) who married Jane Reese in 1808. Mr. Watson was a planter of considerable influence and wealth who came to Williamson County early in 1800 and settled at West Harpeth. An inventory of his estate in 1851 listed one hundred thirteen slaves by name, an enormous amount of personal property which included handsome furnishings for the house and "two pleasure carriages" among other items. After Mrs. Watson's death, the property was to pass to Thomas J. Watson (1829-1875). In 1855, Thomas Watson married Susan Catherine Puryear (1831-1907), the daughter of Mordecai and Sarah Reese Puryear.

The Willows

John Watson 1773-1851

Jane Reese Watson
1787-1855

The Willows derived its name from the beautiful willow trees formerly leading up to the front entrance which faced the old West Harpeth Road. Later this road was moved about one-quarter mile behind the house. There is still evidence of the old roadbed, much of which is below ground level with stonewall sides.

The house was originally a two-story brick structure with a large front porch, probably also two-story. Later two one-story wings were added in front with a porch connecting them. Among the distinguishing features of the house are the floor-length windows many of which have the original sashes containing six panes above and nine below.

The walls rose from handmade bricks fashioned on the place from the bluish-red soil and laid in Flemish bond. There were tall chimneys flanking either end of the house and one in the center. There was a beautiful curved stairway in the entrance hall. The original floors were all ash while those in the added wings were of blue poplar. The east wing floor was replaced with long-leaf pine following a fire. The wall between the two east rooms was removed when the wing was added to make double parlors. There is evidence that the original living room had fireplaces at each end; mention is also made of a "children's wing."

Jane Watson (Bradley) and Thomas Watson 1829-1875

In early days water was brought from the "Good Spring" or "Knob Spring" back in the hills in front of the house by means of a cedar trough hollowed out of solid cedar trees. It is also possible to see the remains of a mile racetrack right in front of the house. John Watson had many friends among the prominent turfmen of his day when horse racing was a gentlemen's sport. Horseshoes and pieces of iron were found under a shade tree in front of the house near the track indicate the site of a smithy in days past.

The Willows was purchased in 1892 by C. Dewees Berry, an attorney of Nashville, Tennessee, at a Chancery Court sale. Mr. Berry began the study of law in the office of Judge David Campbell of Franklin and was well known in his profession.

For almost one-half century thereafter, Valley View Farm, as it was then called, was the home of Mr. and Mrs. Boyd Ridley Critz. After the death of C. Dewees Berry in 1911, his son, William Tyler Berry, pursued an active interest in the farm up to the time of his death in 1937. Following his death his widow, the former Mary Washington Tillman, and her son, Dewees, maintained the warm relationship that had existed with the Critz family.

Bethel Methodist Church was destroyed on April 22, 1920.

Many Williamson Countians remember happy times at the "Critz Place," as it was locally known. Miss Irene Critz of Franklin, a daughter of Mr. and Mrs. Critz, vividly recalls the cyclone that struck in 1920 and took off the second story of the house. "My sister Ruth and I had gone on the train to high school in Franklin," she remembered. "Mother had kept the younger children, Boyd Ridley and Juliet, at home because it was such a terrible rainy day. My father had gone to Nashville on the train for a business appointment with Mr. Dewees Berry. My baby sister, Frances had not quite gone down for her morning nap. My brother, Boyd Ridley, came running in and said, "Mama, come look at the big ball of fire coming over the hill." Mother went out and realized the danger. Boyd Ridley said, "We'd better run back to the house," but Mother said calmly, "No, we'll walk." She picked up the baby out of her bed and gathered the children in the room in the southwest corner, and stood there. The next thing she knew the big, thick front door was knocked down. Looking up, she could see the sky. Across the middle of the back part of the house (the two-story part), the upper story was completely gone with only one floor, over the dining room, left. Every chicken house and shed was blown away. A small cabin near the old smokehouse was also blown away. Only one person was hurt, a young boy on the farm. Mother bound up his head and sent him over to Dr. Greer's by mule, the only transportation available, and he dressed his wound."

West Harpeth School was spared from the cyclone and later moved to Thompson's Station School. Today, it may be found at Homestead Manor.

For the next three months, the Critz family lived in tents in the front yard. Three tents sufficed with one used for a living room and two for bedrooms. Two "rooms" made out of tin and wood were used for the dining room and kitchen. School was almost out for the summer when the house was rebuilt, this time with only one story.

Many people recall this tornado or cyclone that occurred on April 22, 1920. In addition to private homes, barns, and other property, it destroyed two historic churches—Bethel [Methodist Church] at West Harpeth, and Douglass [Methodist] at the corner of Lewisburg Pike and Henpeck Lane. There was an interesting parallel between the two old churches. Both had one-room frame schoolhouses almost in their yards and, although both of the sturdy brick buildings were destroyed, the small schools were spared.

Miss Ethel Edgmon and her students started to Douglass [Methodist] Church, but the ferocity of the storm prevented their leaving the school. "Miss Beulah" Pollard and part of her pupils made it from West Harpeth School to Bethel Church but were forced almost immediately to climb out a window when the building started falling in. She and the children then made their way to a tenant house by clinging to a fence. People often speak of the curious yellow lighting, dark overcast skies, and heavy rain in the West Harpeth community before the storm hit that morning. One resident expressed the emotions of many of his neighbors when, at the height of the storm while his cabin was vibrating with the terrible wind, he called out in the middle of a fervent prayer, "Lord, you is done heard me, but You ain't listening now!"

In 1952, C. Dewees Berry, III, the son of William Tyler and Mary Tillman Berry, an attorney like his grandfather, moved his family into The Willows. Once again, the house has undergone changes to suit a more modern way of living, yet it still retains the charm and atmosphere of an old house. Almost every room has a door to the outside. A kitchen wing was added when the old outside kitchen (and one-time smokehouse) was joined to the main dwelling. This addition has been converted into an office.

C. Dewees and Sue Douglas Berry

In digging around the yard, the Berrys have found much evidence of life in years past in bits of china, metal utensils, and old crockery. One of the children found an 1869 nickel, and when the outdoor kitchen was remodeled, remnants of tiny tea sets and china doll heads recalled childish laughter and tea parties of a day long gone.

The place has been well cared for all along. From 1948 until 1951, Mr. and Mrs. Kenneth Blackburn, now of Leiper's Fork, and their children, Montie and Elwin, lived at Valley View Farm and managed the property. The A.C. Hughes family has lived on the place in a neighboring house and managed the farm until 1960.

In November of 1909, the first C. Dewees Berry wrote to the Alumni Secretary of Yale University where he had graduated in 1868: "I have a mind to retire to my farm, a fine one in an adjoining county, and enjoy rural life for the balance of my days. I am looking forward to a country life." He died before his dream could come true, but his grandson, the present owner, has fulfilled the same dream for himself, his wife, and their family of five children, all of whom—Dewees, Douglas, Will, Mary Susan, and Amanda—love the place in the manner its heritage so richly deserves.

Text: Bowman, Virginia McDaniel. *Historic Williamson County: Old Homes and Sites*. c1971. Republished by Sovran Bank, 1989.

THE SAMUEL P. CANNON HOME

The Samuel Perkins Cannon home overlooks the Col. Hardy Murfree
cemetery and Murfree's Fork Creek, which flows through the 775-acre farm.

In 1842, Samuel Perkins of Triune bought part of the Col. Hardy Murfree homeplace located on Murfree's Fork from William Law Murfree, grandson of Col. Hardy Murfree. Perkins divided the large tract between his son Thomas F. Perkins, and his daughters, Leigh Perkins Allison, wife of William Allison, and Susan Agatha Perkins Cannon, wife of William Perkins Cannon. T.F. Perkins received Forest Hill Farm, a 1300-acre farm, later owned by Frank Overbey. The Allisons received the farm of 930 acres on the west side of Carter's Creek Pike, later known as the James Allison-W.C. Jones-Bill Cherry Farm. The Cannons received the farm of 775 acres on the east of Carter's Creek Pike, from West Harpeth Road to the Thompson Station Road. The sixth generation currently owns the Cannon Farm.

In recent years, the Edgar Brown Cannon family has enjoyed living in their mid-19th century home. The exact date that the house was built cannot be determined. However, the two front rooms are brick, followed by an ell-framed addition. The fertile farm has produced many hogs and cattle over the years, plus tons of tobacco on its 15-acre allotment.

William Perkins Cannon, son of Gov. Newton Cannon

Samuel Perkins Cannon

Wilmoth Pointer Cannon and James H. Cannon

Jim and Sara Cannon

Mary and Brown Cannon

Brown Cannon

THE RIDLEY-BEASLEY-CHURCH HOME

The Ridley-Beasley-Church-Cannon house is unoccupied.

The Ridley-Beasley-Church home is unoccupied and located on the east side of the Brown Cannon farm, northeast of Thompson Station Road West. In 1869, W.M. Beasley bought this home from R.F. Ridley. The main kitchen area and adjoining room are made of logs. In 1889, George Abram and Savantha Church bought it from the Beasleys. The Brown Cannon family now owns it.

Abram George, Odell, Savantha, Abram Baker Church

A.B., Mary, Abe, Reba, and Willie Church

Unoccupied for years, the old house has lost its front porch and log room on the back, and yet it still stands.

THE AKIN-BOYD-DODD HOME

Akin-Boyd-Dodd Home at the foot of the Duck River Ridge on Carter's Creek Pike.

The Akin-Boyd-Dodd house was built in 1872 by William Akin and his wife Mary Terrell Akin. At their deaths, it was inherited by their daughter Cora Akin Boyd. Zan and Louise Dodd bought the house from Mrs. Boyd in about 1922 and lived there until 1972.

The family of Zan and Louise Dodd: Bill, Jenny, Rebecca, Jane, Emily, and Calvin Dodd

Calvin Washington Dodd (1859-1926)
Ida Beasley Dodd (1862-1928)

Zan Dodd and Louise Shaw Dodd

The family of C.W. and Ida Beasley Dodd—Ruby Riggin and Carl Dodd, Adron Dodd, Tish Dodd Lavender, Gertrude Dodd Sparkman, Ruth Sparkman Dodd, Louise Shaw Dodd, Zan Dodd.

THE VACHEL BARNHILL HOME

The home of Vachel I. Barnhill on Thompson Station Road is no longer standing.

Laura Bradford Barnhill (1903-1996) and her chicken house

Seated: Carl, Curtis, Hobert; Standing: Cully, Reese, Jeane, L.D., Ester, V.I., Marie, and Laura Bradford Barnhill

V.I. Barnhill and Dora E. Rainey Barnhill

V.I. Barnhill (1885-1964) on the left with Oscar Green in the center, 1946.

THE ASHWORTH HOME

This home was formerly owned by Josephus Ashworth. The house has two log rooms, a kitchen, and a dog-trot. It is thought to be built between 1878-1888 and added onto in later years by Fate Ashworth. The house and 91 acres were later owned by Kerry Edwards.

There is the story that the James Gang stayed here once. It seems, as the story goes, that they came ... very tired and hungry. They were given food and rest and treated well. After their rest, they are said to have left a mule as payment and told if they did not return it could be kept as payment. They were never seen again and only years later did it become known who these strangers were.

At left: Josephus Ashworth (1845-1914) Co. D, Cooper's Cavalry CSA

Front row: Nannie Ashworth Hawkins, Perlina Locke Ashworth, Mahala A. Riggin, and Wilson Ashworth; Back row: James, Walter, Charles, Bolton, and Fate Ashworth.

Ruby Riggin Dodd

THE POPE-LAVENDER-HUFF HOME

The Pope-Lavender-Huff home on Evergreen Road is one of the four Pope homes in the neighborhood.

The three Pope sisters were charming examples of the last of the Old South in the Burwood community. Edith Drake Pope (1869-1947) made a name for herself as business secretary (1893-1913) and editor (1914-1932) of the *Confederate Veteran* for the magazine's entire 40-year history. She was a leading light in the promotion of "The Lost Cause." Miss Carrie Pope (1872-1961) was the last of the Pope sisters. Coley and Mary Lavender were the next to call this home. Later, Charlie Huff lived here.

Coley and Mary Parson Lavender

Edith D. Pope graduated from the Tennessee Female College in Franklin, Tennessee, in 1888. Around 1890, she moved to Nashville, Tennessee, and from 1892 to 1913 she was the secretary of Sumner Archibald Cunningham, editor of the *Confederate Veteran* magazine. After Cunningham died in 1913, Edith D. Pope became editor of the *Confederate Veteran*; and remained so until the magazine ended, in 1932. She was a member of the Tennessee Women's Press and Author's Club, a member of Nashville Chapter No. 1, United Daughters of the Confederacy (U.D.C.), a member of the Confederate Memorial Literary Society, a member of the Women's Historical Association, and a member of the Association for the Preservation of Virginia Antiquities.

In 1934, she returned to her family home in Burwood, Williamson County, Tennessee. Never married, she lived with her sisters (who also never married) Mary Elizabeth Pope (1861-1944) and Carrie Campbell Pope (1872-1961). The Pope sisters were the daughters of William Campbell Pope (1833-1910), who served as a private in Company E, Forty-fourth Tennessee Infantry Regiment, C.S.A., and Mary Caroline Drake Pope (1839-1911). A biography of Edith D. Pope was published under the title of Edith D. Pope and Her Nashville Friends: Guardians of the Lost Cause in the Confederate Veteran, by John A. Simpson (Knoxville: The University of Tennessee Press, 2003).

Mary, Coley, Jr., and Coley Lavender

THE SPARKMAN-JOHNSON HOME

Gus Sparkman's home

Gus Sparkman (1853-1944) owned a good farm north of Burwood. At his death, his daughter, Missie Sparkman Gatlin, Mrs. Willis Gatlin, (1894-1976), and his second wife, Mintie McKee Sparkman (1874-1955) inherited the farm for their lifetime. At their deaths, the farm would belong to the Leiper's Fork Primitive Baptist Church. The Sparkman farm was sold at auction to Douglas and Pat Johnson.

The Sparkman-Johnson Home

Gus Sparkman-Douglas Johnson house

The Gus Sparkman-Willis Gatlin-Douglas Johnson House is located at 5342 Carter's Creek Pike. It was probably built in the mid-19th century. In 1976, Douglas and Pat Jones Johnson bought the house and reared their children, Theresa, Cindy, and Chris here. A beautiful catfish pond was built behind the house where all fishermen, regardless of their skill, were assured a full stringer.

Douglas and Pat Jones Johnson with Chris, Cindy, and Teresa Jones

THE JOHNSON-MORROW-DODD-HUFF HOME

The home of Hiram Johnson-Robert Morrow-Adron Dodd-Robert Huff, Jr., once stood on Carter's Creek Pike and Johnson Hollow.

Nannie and Robert G. Huff, Jr.

Clarence Adron and Ruth Dodd family: Ruth, C.A., Edward Dee, Hugh, J.C., C.A., Jr., Brown, Rose Xena, Ruth Zane, and Otis Dodd

Hiram Johnson, Martha Robinson, William "Judge," unknown, back row: Elizabeth Marlin Johnson, unknown, Ophelia Johnson, Callie Rader Johnson, granddaughter Estella Johnson Baker, son Eugene Johnson

THE BURNETT HOME

Mary Campbell Burnett

This is the home of Col. Joseph Burnett (1800-1849) who served as postmaster in this place for Carter's Creek Post Office from 1837 to 1848. The Beers Map of 1878 indicates the place as Cottage Home, owned by W.W. Burnett. A Civil War map indicates it was known as Old Burnett's Tavern. His granddaughter, Miss Mary Campbell Burnett, a beloved Franklin Elementary teacher, was the last of this family to call this home. Sadly, after years of being unoccupied, the home was taken down in 2023. The Burnett cemetery is located on the hill to the west.

The Burnett Home

During demolition in 2023, the original log room was discovered.

The right side was the original log room.

THE JACOBS, SATTERFIELD, PRINCE, STANLEY, BROOKS HOME

The Jacobs-Satterfield-Prince-Stanley-Brooks Home is located north of the Maury-Williamson County line on Carter's Creek Pike. It is believed the house may have served as a way-station for travelers on the Carter's Creek Pike. On the hill behind the house, the Jacobs-Beasley-Satterfield Cemetery may be found. Interred here are Emily McKee Beasley (1825-1902) and her husband, John J. Beasley (1815-1873), Joseph R. Jacobs (1807-1870) and his wife, Louise Jacobs (1812-1875). The Beers 1878 map shows that H. Jacobs was living here at the time. Also, buried here are Joseph Satterfield and his daughters, Emily Jane Satterfield, and Mary E. Satterfield Southall, wife of J.R. Southall. The Allen Prince family moved here in the mid-1920s. Their daughter, Stella Prince, and her husband, Howard Stanley, worked as nurse and office manager for Dr. Harry Guffee in Franklin. The Stanleys had one daughter, Myrtle Marie, who with her husband, Bobby Brooks, calls this home today.

Emily McKee Beasley

Stella Prince Stanley

The Allen and Maude Prince family—James and Tom Prince; Hugh, Stella, Grandmother Thompson, and Joe Prince

Allen S. Prince (1896-1973) and Maude Thompson Prince (1897-1966)

THE BARKER-PLEMONS HOME

The George Hightower Barker – John W. Barker – Hop Plemons House on Barker Road stands abandoned as if waiting for someone to rescue it from the elements. The house stands behind the gravestones of James Lee Plemons and Molly Ann Plemons. Earlier tenants here were the families of George Hightower Barker and John W. Barker for whom the road is named.

Rebecca Lucretia Dodson (1839-1915) and
George Hightower Barker (1838-1907)

John W. Barker (1873-1952) and
Blanch Lavender Barker (1876-1974)

Hop Plemons (1910-1994) and Myrtle Osborne Plemons
(1920-1976)

THE POPE-BARKER-DUNCAN HOME

The home of W.C. Pope, R.H. Barker, Sr., Herman and Polly Barker Duncan sits on the bank of Murfree's Fork Creek near the village of Burwood.

The Pope-Barker-Duncan Home

Knox Norman, Eva Barker, Herman Duncan, Hilda Barker, L.B. Grigsby

R.H. Barker, Sr.

Lottie Lee Lavender Barker (1885-1963)

Neil Barker

Robert H. Barker and Lottie Lee Lavender Barker

R.H. Barker, Jr., FHS senior

Ruth Barker, 1931

Annie Lou Barker and Polly Barker Duncan

Robbie Barker Norman

EASTVIEW

VIRGINIA MCDANIEL BOWMAN

Eastview, home of Rev. John Pope, Henderson Helm, and Leonard B. Grigsby

The Reverend John Pope was paying taxes on property in Williamson County as early as 1805. Over the years he increased his holdings until by 1828 he had 2,261 acres. Most of the land lay on the "headwaters of Murfree's Fork of West Harpeth" and was derived from grants to James Robertson, Martin Armstrong, Benjamin Carter, and Daniel Anderson. This property extended as far as the law allowed settlers to go without infringing on land that had not yet been treated for by the Indians. The Pope estate was bounded on two sides by the Indian Boundary Line; to the north, his closest neighbor

Eastview

was Colonel Harding Murfree. At the time, John Pope settled in what was then a remote section of the county, there were few inhabitants before him.

John Pope (1762-1829) was born in Granville County, North Carolina, the son of John and Elizabeth Jeffries Pope. Large landowners in that area, the Popes were meticulous record keepers. Many of their deeds, receipts, and record books, some dating to 1704, have been preserved.

Upon his arrival in Williamson County, Reverend Pope selected as the site of his home a knoll in the long valley which spread out in front of the site with Duck River Ridge on one side of the valley and the hills of the area on the other. Here he built a two-story log house in 1806. Although framed over and devoid of its slave cabins and detached kitchen, the residence stands today basically the same as when it was built. The sprawling estate was, of necessity, self-sustaining and was complete down to the distillery.

The fact the house has survived one hundred and sixty-five years is proof that John Pope used the best materials available in his home. One interesting feature was a secret enclosure cut in the paneling on the right side of the entrance hall. Here the historic and valuable papers of the Pope family were kept. The old batten doors remain in most instances, but the broad plank floorboards have been covered with hardwood. Many of the walnut and cherry furnishings of the original home were made by a slave carpenter and have been passed down through the years to the present generation.

The Pope Family Cemetery, located south of the house, was recently cleaned by a crew from the sheriff's office.

On November 23, 1780, John Pope married Ann Whitaker, the daughter of Richard and Elizabeth Cary Whitaker, in Granville County, North Carolina. By her, he had five sons and two daughters. His wife died at the age of thirty-seven shortly after the birth of the youngest child Elizabeth in 1797. In February of 1798, John Pope married Ann Lucas (1774-1836) who bore him seven more children, the last five of whom were born after the Popes came to Williamson County in 1806. Here they spent the remainder of their lives and were laid to rest in the family burying ground beyond the garden. The first to be buried there was Reverend Pope in

1829. Since then, over forty graves have been added to the plot—wife, sons, daughters, in-laws, and grandchildren. The last burial—that of a grandson—took place in 1910.

On September 4, 1818, John Pope deeded the one-half acre on which Pope's Chapel was built. From that year until 1910, when it was destroyed by a tornado, the building served as both a meeting house and school. The Reverend Pope meticulously set down in writing the specifications by which the church was to be built and appointed Samuel Akin, John Moore, and James Patton as trustees. It was to be "accessible to all ministers of the Gospel of a Godly and moral character of any sect or denomination so long as they did not interfere with each other's appointments.

The building was to be thirty-six feet long and thirty feet wide framed and weatherboarded with good poplar and covered with shingles of heart poplar or chestnut. The floor was to be laid "good and square joint" with seats provided for the congregation. Two doors, several windows, stone or brick chimneys, and a plain pulpit were to complete the sturdy structure. Both school and church were to have free access to a large spring close by. The road running in front of the Pope home bears the name of Pope's Chapel Road to the present day in honor of its donor.

Before the church was built, Pope's Campground, where the early settlers met in a beech grove to hold religious services, was widely known. John Pope was not a regularly ordained Methodist minister but was a lay preacher of the Protestant Methodist Church and as such was bitterly opposed to bishops and missions. Before churches were erected, he preached in the surrounding homes one of which was the Swanson house where the family, to relieve the harshness of frontier life, frequently entertained with parties and dancing. After Reverend Pope preached against such sinful activities the good times abruptly ended.

John Pope's grandfather by the same name had been a member of the courts of Edgecombe and Halifax Counties. He died while serving as a member of the House from Edgecombe County in 1745. He was a member of the Colonial Assembly and was on the committee to arrange a rent roll for "His Majestie." He was a planter of note, Justice of the Peace, sheriff, tax collector, and vestryman of St. John's Church of Edgecombe Parish. He, too, had donated land and built a church near Oxford, North Carolina, known as Pope's Chapel. It is not surprising, therefore, that as soon as his grandson had cleared land and harvested a few crops at his new home he built a meetinghouse and school where his family and neighbors could worship and educate their children for he put great emphasis on both religion and education.

The community that developed in this area was first known as Williamsburg, and later Shaw. The present name of Burwood was suggested by a grandson of Reverend

Pope, James Drake Pope, who took the name from Mrs. Humphry Ward's novel, *Robert Elsmere*.

As the Pope children reached maturity, their father gave each a farm near him except for those who moved to his extensive holding in the "Western District." His sons Thomas Anderson and John Whitaker Pope were progenitors of the families who continued to live in this county. There are none of the name left, but among the female descendants is Mrs. Louise Shannon Dedman of Franklin who owns many of the Pope papers and the family Bible taken from the secret enclosure in the paneling.

Descendants of Pope's slaves, Joe and Leslie Pope with Joe's great-grandchildren, Damali and Ormari Pope

The last Popes by name in Williamson County passed out of existence with the death of Misses Mary, Edith, and Carrie Pope who spent their lives on their ancestral lands. Other family homes were scattered up and down what is now Evergreen, Cayce Springs, and West Harpeth Roads.

In 1811 John Pope and two of his eldest sons made a trip back to North Carolina to settle the estate of his bachelor brother, Osborne Pope. They brought back the slaves John Pope had inherited from his estate with the written specification that "old Bandy" was not to be separated from her children. Every indication points to strong ties of affection between the Popes and their servants through the generations. They were taught the Bible, were treated medically as receipts show, and many of their marriages carry the signature of "Parson Pope." Descendants of those slaves, many of whom still lived in the same vicinity, bear the Pope name.

The homeplace, located at the intersection of Evergreen and Pope's Chapel Roads, continued [as] the home of Mrs. Pope until she died in 1836 at which time it was to have gone to a son who died unmarried before that date. It was owned for many years by Colonel Helm, and at his death passed into other hands. An outstanding landmark in Williamson County, it is now owned and occupied by Mr. and Mrs. Leonard Grigsby.

Text: Bowman, Virginia McDaniel. *Historic Williamson County: Old Homes and Sites*. c1971.

Annie Lou Barker and Leonard B. Grigsby made their home at Eastview.

Jack and Judy Grigsby

THE KATE NORMAN LAWRENCE KYLE HOME

The humble home of Kate Norman Lawrence Kyle is located at the foot of Sugar Ridge on Pope's Chapel Road.

Kate Norman Lawrence Kyle (1893-1987), wife of Henry Thomas Lawrence

Ray Lawrence (1917-1964) and Paul Lawrence

Paul Lawrence (1919-2010)

THE POPE-MARTIN-PEWITT HOME

VIRGINIA MCDANIEL BOWMAN

The Pope-Martin House remains a landmark on Evergreen Road.

This house, the oldest portion of which is log, was originally the home of Thomas Anderson and Rebecca Jane Campbell Pope [now known as the Pope-Martin House]. Located on Evergreen Road, it was built on land given to them by his father, the Reverend John Pope. Thomas and Rebecca Pope had a number of children among whom was a son, William Augustus, killed in a skirmish at Thompson Station on April 15, 1862.

Jacob Martin (1828-1897)

When this property passed from Pope hands, it became the home of a neighbor, Jacob Thomas Martin. The Martin family had come to this county around 1818 and settled in the vicinity of Cayce Springs. In 1814, William Kerr bought 48 acres that included these famous mineral springs from James Giddens. Mr. Kerr had married Katie Ross who, after bearing him eleven children, died in 1826. On July 5th of that year, William Kerr sold the land, including the springs, on Murfree's Fork to William and Shadrack Cayce. Mr. Kerr later married Mary Gray Crafton, a widow from Kentucky, who bore him seven more children. He moved to Fountain Creek in Maury County where the old Kerr house still stands near Campbell Station and Shane cemetery.

The Cayces developed the springs into a widely known resort. People came from miles around to drink the water and enjoy the social life the spot afforded. Cabins and a hotel were built back from the bluffs over whose face the healing waters flowed in heavy streams to empty into Murfree's Creek just over the Maury County line. The resort flourished until around 1890 when the hotel burned, and it continued as a favorite place for picnics and campgrounds for many years. Its memory is kept alive by the use of its name on a county roadway.

On October 2, 1853, Jacob Thomas Martin (1828-1897) married Susan Drake (1836-1908), the daughter of James Love and Caroline McCarty Drake, whose home was in a valley east of the Drake-Martin-Neely cemetery on Cayce Springs Road. The Popes, Neelys, Drakes, Martins, Baughs, Critz, and other prominent names in that vicinity, intermarried time and again. They were all large landowners and early settlers of what was then a remote section of Williamson County.

During the war, Jake Martin commanded Baker's Company of Holman's Cavalry Battalion which was organized on August 16, 1862, at Thompson Station. He was acting Major of G Company which was merged into the Eleventh Tennessee Cavalry by Forrest, but he was never promoted to that rank.

Since he was thoroughly acquainted with this territory, Captain Martin was in command of an advance party sent into Tennessee ahead of Hood's Army in 1864. In October of that year, he and some twenty-five men captured a troop train of Federal soldiers and threw it off the tracks in front of the Ewell farm at Spring Hill. The captured soldiers were either exchanged or paroled since there were too few

Confederates to guard them. Infuriated and chagrined over this coup accomplished in the face of overwhelming odds, the Federals burned the Drake house where the Martins were then living in retaliation. It was the only house in the neighborhood destroyed.

Miss Olive Martin (1879-1967)

The Martin family later moved to the Thomas Anderson Pope place. Captain Martin covered the log portion with clapboards and built the dining area and the back bedroom section around 1880. Jacob and Susan Martin were the parents of a large number of children. Mr. Douglas Martin, who died in 1962, and his twin sister, Miss Olive, who died in 1967, were the last of the family to live here. The place remained throughout the years a well-loved and substantial country home. A greenhouse provided fresh flowers all year round. These were brought into the house to shed their fragrance over the rooms filled with long treasured family pieces.

The property went out of the Martin family when it was sold at auction on May 17, 1967. It has been carefully and beautifully restored by Mr. and Mrs. J.L. Read who are presently residing here.

[Editor's note: As of this writing, the owners are Tony and Sue Pewitt, who lovingly restored the home.]

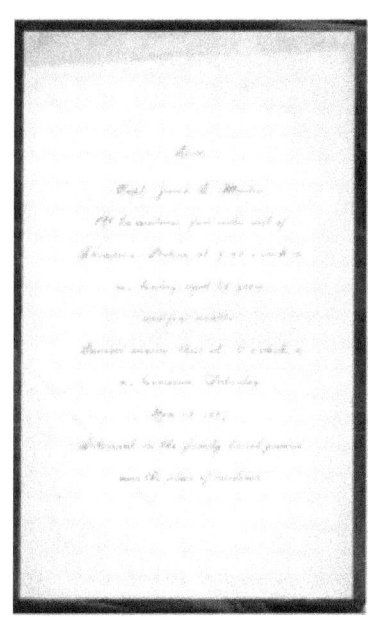

Capt. Jacob Martin's death

Text: Bowman, Virginia McDaniel. *Historic Williamson County: Old Homes and Sites.* c1971.

THE POPE-SOUTHALL HOME

An unidentified man and Oliver Southall, on right, with the Pope-Southall home in the background.

The Pope-Southall house is the only Pope home no longer standing. Sadly, it burned. Gustavus and Rebecca Southall reared their family here consisting of three sons, Oliver, Tom, and Dayton, and two daughters, Maude (Mrs. Glen Sparkman) and Willie Mai (Mrs. A.B. Church). Gustavus Southall (1861-1925) and Rebecca Anderson Southall (1872-1956)

Gustavus and Rebecca Southall

Maude Southall and Glen Sparkman

The Pope-Southall home on Cayce Springs Road with Rebecca Southall Harris in front.

THE MCRAE, SHAW, LAVENDER, BARKER HOME

McRae-Shaw-Lavender-Barker Home

The McRae-Shaw-Lavender-Barker Home is located in the heart of Burwood, next to the old Short Store and across the road from the old Shaw Store.

Neil and Hilda Barker, WWII

Nancy, Sandy, Hilda, and Neil Barker

THE CRITZ-LAZENBY HOME

Today, the home of Mrs. Alex Lazenby

The Joseph Critz House is a two-story brick central passage plan antebellum residence constructed ca. 1835. The house was built in an ell plan and despite added porticos and changes to the main entrance, its basic form and arrangement are evident.

Joseph Critz, Sr. came to Tennessee in the late 1820s and by the mid-1830s had constructed this two-story brick residence in the Thompson Station area. The house was a typical design of the period, with its main facade laid in Flemish bond and built in a central passage plan. Critz died in the late 1830s, and the property was inherited by his son, Joseph Critz, Jr.

The Critz-Lazenby Home

He owned several hundred acres by the 1850s and was listed in 1859 as owning eight slaves, and 250 acres of land. His son, John M. Critz, who occupied the house in the 1870s, sold it to D.B. Jones in 1882. The house was sold again in 1904 to the Will Short family, who lived here until the 1940s.

Daphne and Alex Lazenby owners of the Joseph Critz House since 1961.

The original portico configuration on the main façade is unknown and there are no ghosts of previous porticos visible. The entranceway was also altered and has double doors with large single-light sidelights. Windows are a combination of original and replacement but have original frame lintels. Today the main facade consists of a one-story frame portico which was added in 1961.

Windows on the rear façade have jack arching instead of lintels. Doors on the side and rear facades are original five-panel frame design. The entry porch on the east façade was added in 1961.

The interior retains its central hall design and has original fluted door moldings, bull's eye corner blocks, simple Greek Revival-design mantels with Doric pilasters, and a staircase with a round newel post and square balusters.

National Register Properties: Williamson County, Tennessee / compiled and edited from the original Williamson County National Register, Hillsboro Press, 1995. The Joseph Critz House became a National Register of Historic Places property in 1988.

THE SHAW-HUFF-JOHNSON HOME

The W.A. Shaw-R.G. Huff, Sr.-Harold Johnson Home

William A. Shaw and Delilah Lavender Shaw (1843-1919)

W.A. Shaw (1838-1929) served in Co B Holman's Tennessee Cavalry Battalion CSA and was the first postmaster of Shaw, Tennessee. The home was located south of Shaw's Store. Later, the R.G. Huff, Sr. family lived here. Harold and Martha Johnson lived here with their family – Mike, Monica, Raymond, and Jonathan.

The Shaw-Huff-Johnson Home

Martha Woodard and Harold Johnson

The Robert and Hattie Huff Family – Robert G. Huff, Sr., Hattie Stovall Huff, 2nd row; Ann York, Agnes Caldwell, Virginia Nichols, Dorothy McLemore, 3rd row; Glen, Robert, Jr., Milton "Mutt," and Ken

HILLTOP MANOR

VIRGINIA MCDANIEL BOWMAN

Hilltop Manor – home of John Neely, ca. 1808

Although much altered from its original appearance, this fine old brick house has been a landmark in the Thompson Station area for over a century and a half.

Williamson County was still in its infancy when John Neely, along with his family and his three brothers and their families, cut a trail from Virginia over the mountains to Tennessee. John Neely was the son of James Neely, originally from Philadelphia and later Botetourt County, Virginia, and Jane Grymes Neely of Northampton, Burlington

County, New Jersey. He married Susanna Evans, the daughter of Daniel and Rhoda Griffith Evans, sometime after 1770. By 1791 he owned almost 2,000 acres "on the north side of the Roanoke (River)" in Virginia where apparently all of his children were born.

They arrived in Williamson County early in 1806 since John Neely bought town lots 85 and 95 in February of that year. In 1808 he made a permanent settlement on land bought from James Robertson in the West Harpeth area where he built this brick house on a rise overlooking the rich meadows and forests spread out below. His children were James, Rhoda, Jane, John H., William, Sophia, and Charles Lynch who married into the Sanders, Drake, Neely, Woldridge, Priest, and Welles families and are the progenitors of numerous descendants in Williamson County today.

John Neely died in 1818. Both he and his wife were buried in a rock-walled cemetery, and their graves were well-marked with inscribed tombstones. However, much to the regret of the present generation, no trace of the graveyard can be found.

Sarah Wells Neely (1799-1880) wife of Charles Lynch Neely

The Neely land on the waters of the West Harpeth River was sold in tracts by the Neely heirs over a period of time to John Fitzgerald (1778-1858). The house in its prime had a columned portico across the front. The sloping yard was sowed in bluegrass and was beautifully landscaped with flowering shrubs and immense shade trees. The bricks that went into the house were made by the Neely slaves in a kiln in the garden. The inner walls were strongly braced and further strengthened with thick wooden pegs. The floorboards of ash and poplar were eight and ten inches wide. The land drops steeply away on the northeast side of a twenty-acre meadow where a racetrack was formerly located.

John and Ellender (1780-1844) Fitzgerald had two sons, John and Bird, and three daughters, Elizabeth Dodson, Polly Dodson, and Nancy Bowden, mentioned in his will. After dividing out his property in a fair way, John Fitzgerald directed that his sons were to take good care of "five old and favorite slaves" and treat them kindly while they lived.

The other twenty-five slaves were allotted to the children by families; the home tract he left to the sons, John (1816-1884), and Bird (1803-1873).

Mary Jackson (1828-1880), the daughter of Bird and Julia Fitzgerald, married John B. Ridley (1818-1882). The Ridleys never lived here after their marriage but are buried with the Fitzgeralds in the cemetery in a woodlot off West Harpeth Road.

When the Dodsons lived here, the boys would ride their ponies upstairs and stand at the open windows. More than one passer-by drove his team in a ditch while gazing at the unexpected sight of ponies' heads thrust out the upper windows of the fine old house.

William H. Sedberry
(1892-1969)

Located on the Sedberry Road leading from West Harpeth to Thompson Station, the property was bought from the Fitzgerald heirs in 1926 by William Hamilton and Frances (Dolly) Green Sedberry. At this time William Hamilton, Jr. their eldest child, was two years old. The other four children—Barbara Faye, James Franklin, Jessie Zulieme, and Frances Carline—were born in this house.

Noted for his excellent work and realistic touch, Mr. Sedberry was a taxidermist of world renown. After his death in 1969, the place was bought at auction by William, Jr. (Billy) who already owned the adjoining property which had been the home place of his wife, the former Ann Adair. The house is now being completely renovated and in the near future will be the home of Mr. and Mrs. William Sedberry, Jr., and their three children – Barbara Marie, Frances Yvonne, and William III – who make the third generation of the Sedberry family to reside here.

Text: Bowman, Virginia McDaniel. Historic Williamson County: Old Homes and Sites. c1971, republished by Sovran Bank, 1989.

THE CAIN POLK HOME

Johnson Hollow – Cain Polk's house

What a gathering of Sycamore and Johnson Hollow Folks! Nelson Polk, Gene Johnson, Wiley Johnson, John Ragsdale, Tom Polk, Estella Johnson, Ruby Riggin Dodd, Mahala and Will Riggin. The house belonged to Cain Polk and later Farris Huff.

Another generation, maybe fifty years later – Albert and Clyde Andrews, Cain Polk, Bob Johnson, Lilia Polk Waddey, John Oakley Johnson, Florence Polk, Millie Polk Johnson.

Front: Elsie Johnson, Anna Johnson, Millie Polk Johnson, and Hazel Pentecost; standing: Annie Jones, Kate Byrd, and Era Andrews

THE BYRD-VENABLE-HUFF HOME

Byrd-Venable-Huff house

This home was bought by Tom Byrd in the early 1900s and sold to Jim Venable in the midtwenties. Pictured here are members of the Venable family—Bob Venable, Lawrence Hicks, Mattie Venable, Jim Venable, and Susan "Sook" Venable.

Rev. Lawrence Hicks

Bob and Lizzie Mae Venable and
Lawrence Hicks

Farris Huff's home was taken by I-840

THE SAM AND IDA HAY JOHNSON HOME

Sam and Ida Hay Johnson's homeplace on Bear Creek Road

Sam Johnson (1869-1947)

Ida Hay Johnson (1871-1964)

The family of Sam and Ida Hay Johnson. Standing: Emma, Ruth, Vernon, Frank, and Eva; Sitting: Ada and Alice Johnson.

THE HELM-AKIN HOME

Fielding Helm and Timothy Terrell Akin home

Located just south of the village, on the left, was the Fielding Helm house that is thought to have been built between 1840 and 1850. The partial log house was later owned by Timothy Terrell Akin and passed to his grandson, Greg Akin. Passing along Carter's Creek Pike today, you will not recognize the T.T. Akin farmhouse.

Lera (1897-1985) and Timothy Terrell Akin, Jr. (1894-1944)

Marion, Lera and Ted Akin

THE SPARKMAN - DODD HOME

This log home covered with weatherboarding was the original home of Calvin Sparkman, thought to have been built in the 1830s. It was later known as the Millard Akin Place, which was sold it to Carl and Ruby Dodd in 1925. In recent years, the new owners, Bitsy and Henry Headden, have remodeled the inside for modern convenience and replaced the old siding.

THE AKIN-HUTCHERSON-NORMAN HOME

The Millard F. Akin-Lewis Hutcherson-Richard Norman Home

The James Bruce Akin home, called "Breezy Hill," just one-half mile from the village of Burwood, became a landmark for those traveling on Carter's Creek Pike. Built in 1885, the up-right and wing house was a popular and spacious design. Millard F. Akin (1858-1934) and Lula Boyd Akin (1869-1948) reared their family in this house, consisting of two girls, Joella and Ruth, and two boys, J.B. and Robert.

The James Bruce Akin family, 1903.

Those present included: James Bruce, Jim, Mamie, Cam, Maggie, Cammie, Mat, Mittie, Ollie Mai, Raleigh Pope, Madison, Sam, Ida, Ora, Mann, Vance, Bob, Lena, Robbie, Ethel, Ewell Clark, John, Dora, Kattie Hattie, Millard, Lula, E.B. and Joella.

The James Bruce Akin family in front of Breezy Hill

THE AKIN-RAGSDALE HOME

This was originally the home of William T. Akin and later, the home of his daughter, Lilia Mai Akin Ragsdale.

THE AKIN-TOMLINSON HOME

The Samuel Akin-Thomas Tomlinson house

Thomas J. and Louise Harper Tomlinson (1866-1921), parents of Thomas Tomlinson.

Samuel Akin, one the earliest settlers in Burwood, was born in 1771 in South Carolina. In 1793, he married Dorcas Starr who was also born in 1771.

It is unknown when they came to Davidson County, Tennessee, but, in 1801, Samuel Akin, then living in Davidson County, bought from "Thrasher" McCollum 60 acres of land for $100. This tract was located on the headwaters of Murfree's Fork of the West Harpeth River. In 1811, he purchased 127 acres for $330 from Benjamin Carter, who had received a very large grant of land in Williamson and Maury Counties for his services in the Revolutionary War. In 1831, Akin bought from John Pope 25 more acres for $800, giving him a total of 212 acres. The above information was obtained from old deeds registered in the Williamson County Register of Deeds. The Samuel Akin place was a mile south of the present village of Burwood.

His will, a specific document written a short time before his death on February 11, 1844, is also recorded at the courthouse.

Samuel and Dorcas Starr Akin had 12 children, five sons and seven daughters. Dorcas Akin died in 1850, at which time only two sons survived, John Akin and Arthur Stewart Akin. By the terms of Samuel Akin's will, his land was to be divided equally between these two sons – John Akin and Tim Akin.

Samuel Akin was one of the first trustees of Pope's Chapel Church, the forerunner of the present Burwood United Methodist Church.

Many descendants of Samuel and Dorcas Starr Akin still live in Williamson County.

The following genealogy may explain why: Samuel Akin was born on December 30, 1771, in South Carolina and died in Williamson County on February 11, 1844. His wife, Dorcas Starr was born in 1771 and died September 11, 1850. They married on January 24, 1793, before coming to Middle Tennessee. They are buried in the Spring Hill Cemetery.

Their children were as follows:

Matilda Starr Akin (1793-1835) married Michael Robinson in 1808.

Edith Akin (1795-1833) married James M. Alexander in 1815.

William M. Akin (1797-)

Samuel W. Akin (1799-1844) married Eliza C. Alexander in 1822.

Polly Vance Akin (1800-1823) married Duncan Campbell in 1818.

John Akin (1803-1864) married Adeline Craig in 1824.

Betsey Akin (1804-1881)

Rebecca Akin (1807-1881) married W.B. Nesbett in 1829.

James Akin (1809-1830)

Dorcas Akin (1811-1850) married William Ferguson

Nellie Akin (1813-1866) married Nathan Meacham in 1837.

Arthur Stewart Akin (1818-1878) married Nancy J. Mayes in 1842

Thomas and Lucille Tomlinson enjoyed living here for many years.

Thomas and Lucille Sparkman Tomlinson on 5th Avenue South in Franklin.

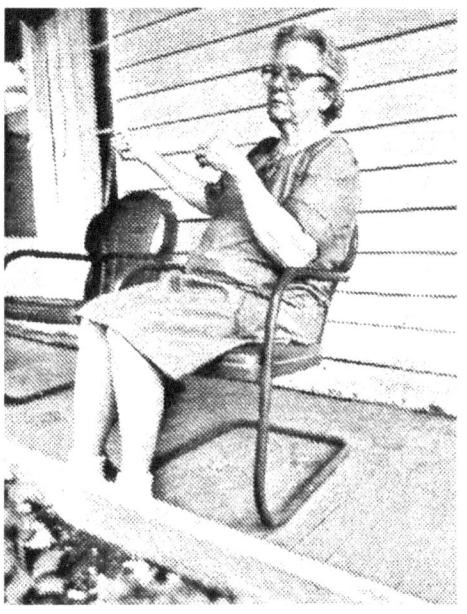

Lucile Sparkman Tomlinson on the porch of the Dodd-Tomlinson House.

Lucille Sparkman Tomlinson, Billy Barnhill, Lester, Thomas, Jerry Tomlinson, Bessie Mai Barnhill, Henry Porter Sparkman, L.D. and Neil Barnhill

Ollie Sparkman, Sr.

THE BEASLEY-HUNT-SPARKMAN HOME

Ella, Eveline and J.B. Hunt in from their home

The Pope-Beasley-Sparkman family has lived in this house on Carter's Creek Pike near the Maury County line for decades. Within the weatherboarded house, featuring a pedimented porch with Greek Revival elements; is a log house built about 1830. The walls have poplar paneling and wainscoting along with detailed mantels.

The Beasley-Hunt-Sparkman Home

Willie Beasley (Mrs. Ridley Jones) and Eveline Hunt Beasley (Mrs. N.C. Beasley) stand in front of the same house fourteen years later.

Ollie Sparkman, Jr., Joe Sparkman, and Alice Evelyn Jones Sparkman enjoy the home today.

Zachariah W. Beasley (1849-1925) and SamElla Beasley (1851-1926)

Ollie Sparkman, Jr. and Joe Sparkman

Willie Beasley and Ridley Jones

Newton Cannon Beasley and Evie Hunt Beasley

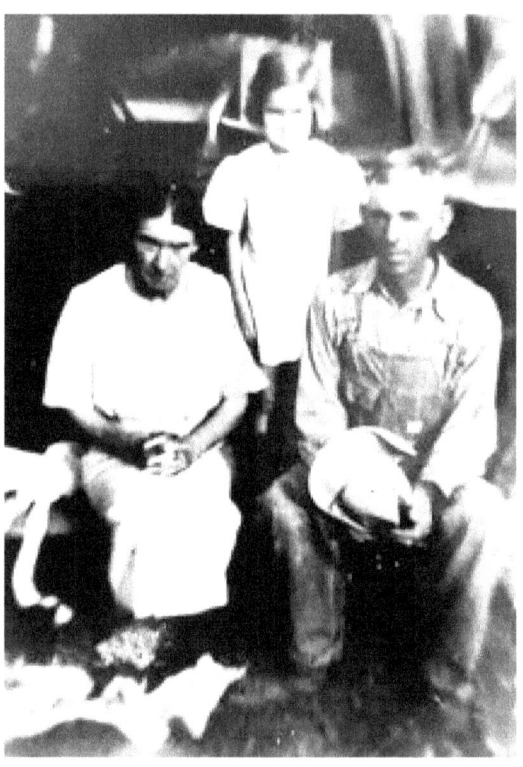
Evie Hunt Beasley, Alice Evelyn Jones, and Newton Cannon Beasley

THE SI AND POLLY MCCAMPBELL HOME

Home of Si and Polly Huff McCampbell on Carter's Creek Pike

Arthur "Si" McCampbell (1922-2004) and Polly Huff McCampbell (1921-2010)

Polly Huff and Arthur "Si" McCampbell on their Wedding Day

Polly Huff and Arthur "Si" McCampbell with Suzanne and Deborah

THE STEPHENS-GARLAND HOME

The home of A.H. and Nannie Fitzgerald Stephens-Dewey and Melissa Garland is located on Thompson Station Road West. Ezekiel Chaney (1791-1863) is buried on the hill behind the house, which indicates this site has been a home place since the early 19th century. The house was built for the A.H. Stephens family in the late 19th century. Dewey and Melissa Garland have enjoyed living with its history for many years.

Dewey and Melissa Garland

Bessie with Nannie Page, Ollie, Sally, Louise, Nannie Fitzgerald, and A.H. Stephens stand in front of their home.

TIDBITS

Doug and Herschel Harmon at play in the woodyard.

CAYCE SPRINGS, SUMMER RESORT OF THE FOURTH DISTRICT

RICK WARWICK

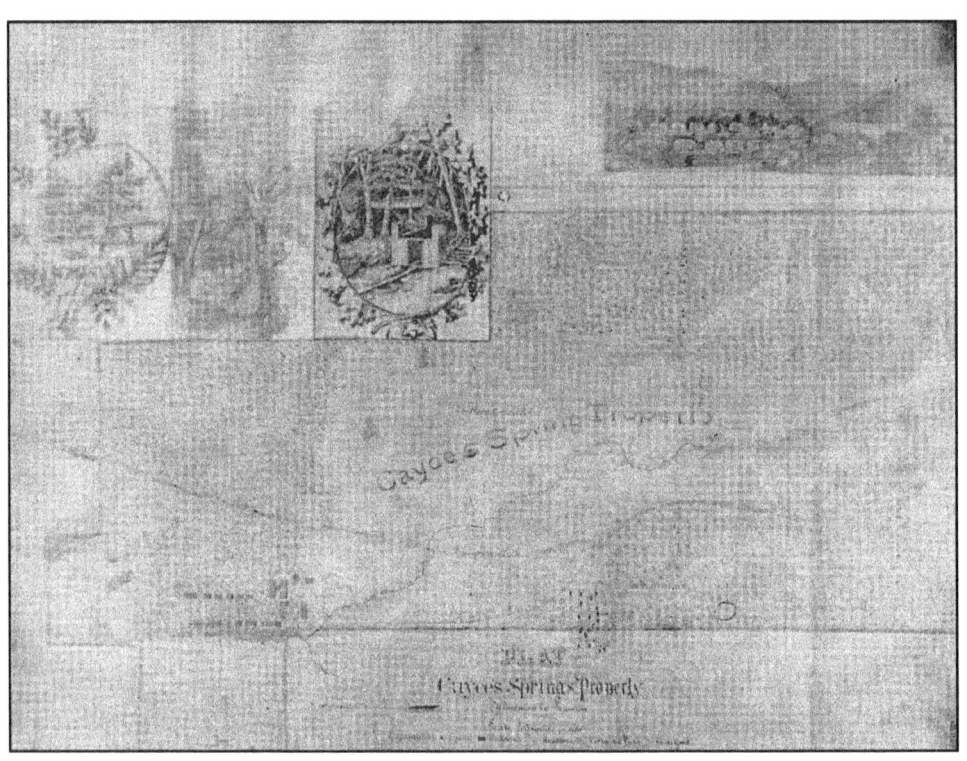

Medicinal Springs

The Western Balance, February 3, 1827

Located on Cayce Springs Road, now extinct

William Cayce, having become the owner and proprietor of these springs (formerly known as Kerr's) in Williamson County, about 10 miles southwest of Franklin, respectfully informs the public that he has made the requisite preparations, and can now accommodate any number of visitors in the greatest comfort and may find it beneficial to their health to honor the springs with their attendance. To the invalid, to the sick, to those in pursuit of pleasure or health and change of scene and air, and who would purchase all on very low terms, he recommends a resort of those springs. The quality of the waters are so well-known and highly appreciated by all who have had an opportunity of tasting their superior medicinal effects, that he considers it unnecessary to remark particularly about them.

The following are his charges:

Boarding per month – $10
Boarding per week – $3
Boarding servants, domestics – $1.50
Single meals – 25 cents
Horses per week (pasture) – 37.5 cents
Horse – single feed – 12.5 cents

By virtue of a deed of trust being dated January 1829, executed to me by Wm. Cayce, I shall on Friday, the 16th of this month, at the house of said Wm. Cayce sell to the highest bidder for cash an undivided half of the tract of land containing 48 acres on which said Wm. Cayce now lives lying on the waters of Murfree's Creek bounded by John Pope, Wm. & J.W. Pope, Dr. Barnett. A number of different kinds of livestock; a variety of household tables and kitchen furniture, a set of smith's tools, and other articles. On the above-mentioned, tract of land is the noted Mineral Springs, known by the appellation of Cayce Springs.

Cayce Springs root cellar

Dinner at Sulphur Springs … On Wednesday the 25th, a dinner will be furnished by the subscriber, at the Sulphur Springs, 9 miles from Franklin. The price for each person partaking will be 50 cents. July 1831

May 18, 1832, Sulphur Springs

The subscriber wishes to inform his friends and the public that his establishment at the place generally known as Cayce Springs is now fitted up in complete repair and well-fitted for the accommodations of visitors ... John B. Anderson.

December 10, 1835

Dr. Newman Cayce of Lawrence Co., Tenn. To Joseph Yates. He sells his half of an undivided tract of land which includes the Mineral Springs for $250.00.

Western Weekly Review, October 1840

Joseph Yates sold to Henry H. King a tract of land containing about 48 acres, for the sum of $1,000 the land known as Cayce Springs. Sometime later King purchased another tract of land from James Drake containing 58 1/2 acres for the sum of $885. The land in the 4th district bounded by Tatum, Wiggins, Critz, and William Stephens. King, being embarrassed by circumstances, and about to move to the state of Mississippi, had sold nearly all his personal property. He still owed Joseph Yates about $800 on the 48 acres so Yates took two tracts of land at about $2,700. King moved to Mississippi in December 1839, where he now lives. Yates had possession of the land several years before his sale and at that time endeavored to make the Springs a watering place and to provide accommodations for visitors. When Yates sold the land there was a comfortable dwelling and necessary outhouses.

One of the cabins at Cayce Springs Resort

In 1837 and 1838, King hired John W. Pope to make repairs to the dwelling house by adding a room on one side and a piazza on the other side. In early 1838, Pope had a contract to furnish the material and put up 20 cabins near the dwelling house at $30 to $35 apiece. "Not a log cabin, but a sanctuary of Western forest life; rough frame about 14-foot square, weatherboarded to be sure, but no fireside, and were to be completed previous to July 1838, the watering season for that year. Pope had finished 6 of the cabins by July and afterwards completed 6 more. On July 1, 1839, Pope commenced a suit against King for payment. Sometimes after the suit was filed, John Pope died, and the suit was revised in the name of his administrator on April 8, 1840. A bill was filed and obtained attachment against the property of King as a non-resident and a lien was obtained on 13 acres of land.

July 30, 1841, Joseph Yates sold a tract of land in the 4th district containing 106.4 acres to William Cayce for the sum of $2,000. William Cayce to John M. Cayce in January 1873, $5,000 for a tract of land in the 4th district known as Cayce Springs containing 106.4 acres. John M. Cayce from William Cayce September 1873 for $1,000 to John M. Cayce trustee for his wife, Virginia Cayce, and their children, land in 4th District containing 7 acres. Virginia was the daughter of Matthew Cayce.

In the early 1880s, the Cayce Resort Hotel burned. The cabins remained for a long time and picnics were often held by the springs. Only one cabin remains today and has been moved to the barn area of the Ray and Pat Logan property. John M. Cayce later sold the land containing 113 acres to J. Brice Martin, a relative of Cayce's, and then moved to Mississippi. In 1909, N. Douglas Martin and wife Hattie bought the property from his brother J. Brice Martin. Douglas Martin built the big house that now stands on this land and lived there until the early 1940s when he sold to Jonas Amos the area containing 133 acres for $14,000. Mr. Amos kept the property for a very short time selling it in July 1945 to Raymond Logan for $15,000. Later, Mr. Logan bought 52 ½ acres from Walter and Sadie Burns making the property 185 1/2 acres. Mr. Logan, his wife Allie, and one child William Raymond lived in that house and farmed it until he retired in 1965. His son continues to farm there today and lives on the farm with his wife Patricia, his children, and grandchildren.

The Cayce Springs are no longer visible, William Logan having dug a pond that contained them … but they still seep out from the dam.

Information supplied by: Louise Lynch, John W. Johnson, and Pat Logan in 1986

RIDE-A-THON

RICK WARWICK

Ride-a-Thon Staged in Williamson

THOMPSON'S STATION, TENN, OCT. 26

Jimmy Huff, Jimmy Johnson, Bud Osborne, Frank Bruer, Coley Lavender, Marion Akin, Farris Huff, Riley Lavender, Charles Dunn, Fred Kinnard, Kenneth Adair, and Faye Ferguson

Nashville Banner, October 28, 1940

Ride-a-thon, popular Middle Tennessee recreations in the saddle, were introduced in Williamson County at Burwood Saturday when seventy-five riders followed Director-General Ollie Sparkman over a twelve-mile trail that traversed the south section of the county in a west-to-east direction.

So pleased were the neophyte saddle-sitters at the pleasure and social aspect of their initial ride that it was unanimously voted at the noon luncheon rest period to make the rural trek an annual affair, and the 100 horse enthusiasts present predicted that the second Ride-a-thon on the last Saturday of next October would be close to the century mark in number.

Leaving the Burwood School at 10 o'clock, the riders headed west out the ridge road up into the hill section of south Williamson County to the Boston community, from whence they made their return by way of the picturesque Johnson Hollow Road to the starting point where the Burwood P.T.A. served the luncheon under the direction of Mrs. Allen Prince, chairman.

At the noon stop, Gilbert M. Orr of Columbia addressed the devotees of the saddle and related the brief but colorful history of the Tennessee Ride-at-thon, a brain-child of Dr. Willis B. Boyd of Cookeville. He told his listeners of the number of horses in the United States, and their value in dollars and cents, as well as their worth for pleasure riding over trials throughout America and of their medium for affording exhibition entertainment in the show ring. He said there was a growing demand for the Tennessee Walking Horses and made a plea for more meticulous breeding with closer attention to the bloodlines of the produce.

The Burwood Ride-a-thon introduced a new feature to these outings in the saddle when a cash prize was given for the best couple riders on horses and the best couple on ponies. The former was won by Mr. and Mrs. George Shaw of Mt. Pleasant, and the latter to Anderson Buckner of Thompson Station and William Brittain of Franklin.

Cliff Sparkman and J.C. Dodd, juvenile equitation experts of Burwood, received "honorable mention" in the show ring for their twelve-mile ride on two oversized "walking mules" of the sugar type. The judging was by R.V. Akin and Percy Lavender of Burwood and Hughes Brooks of Theta.

The afternoon ride was east toward Thompson Station with a brief pause at Cayce Spring, thence to the Spring Hill Road and back to the schoolhouse, Sparkman said as he added that Burwood had joined the "ride-a-thon fraternity" of Middle Tennessee which now has thirty full-fledged chapters and approximately 1,500 duly-initiated members.

Burwood Ride-A-Thon

By Gilbert M. Orr

Burwood Ride-A-Thon, 1988

Nashville Banner, October 16, 1942

The Community of Burwood—Browsing around last Saturday morning in search of a source for data on old homes in Middle Tennessee, we trekked out to Thompson Station in Williamson County. it was a lovely, bright, and warm day, a day that only the month of October can give.

We were slowly going along a narrow country lane doubting the correctness of our meanderings in trying to find the home of Mr. Douglas Martin. Up the road, we spotted a lone rider on horseback. As the rider came across the crest of a small hill in the bend of the lane, we could tell that the person up was a woman. It proved to be lovely Mary Lavender of Burwood. She was seeking a group of riders somewhere back to the north of us. We learned it was a ride-a-thon that had left the Burwood, Williamson County community and that it was 100 percent "hossy". She told was where Mr. Martin lived.

Not finding Mr. Martin at home, we slowly rode over to the old Martin home where we found Miss Olive Martin and Jake Martin. For sheer beauty and peace of surroundings, this Martin home is tops. Situated upon a slight elevation which is reached through a private driveway bordered by giant pecan trees is the snow-white low, rambling house that has stood for more than a hundred years. These are great locusts, the lawn of bluegrass. A screened-in front is inviting.

Miss Olive, as gracious a lady as one can meet, came out and chatted the while that we were waiting for her brother, Douglas. A mockingbird was singing from the perch atop of a big pecan tree. His song, Miss Olive said, had been continuous since daylight. Some squirrels scampered about the lawn and shyly stopped in the forks of trees to take in the situation. Her garden was ablaze with autumnal flowers of many colors. A hand came in off the farm riding a mule. He was singing as the hybrid slowly went along. Peace—that's the word for this home of the Martins.

OTHER RIDERS – Deciding to go back to the home of Douglas Martin, which is only half a mile away, we started backtracking along this narrow road. There we met Buster Curry and Wayne Hardison up on two good walkers. We were invited to lunch at Burwood at noon.

Looking up the road ahead of us we saw the ride-a-thon coming across a high place near a great hill that had a rare picture of beauty painted on its trees that were turning gold and red and brown. We stopped and the riders single-filed past us. There were 60 on horseback, men, women, and children. At the rear were Mrs. Glenn Lavender and Mrs. Jim Ball, each of whom was driving a pony to low-flung buggies and each of whom had two passengers.

Horse-drawn wagons also make the Ride-A-Thon more fun.

THE BURWOOD P.T.A. LUNCH

Teachers Polly Duncan, Mrs. Hatcher, Gladys Whitley, Annie Lou Grigsby, Charles Dunn. Riders: Charles Wall, Faye Ferguson, Kenneth Adair, L.B. Grigsby, holding Jon Duncan, Riley Lavender, Leroy Barnhill, Clyde Fitzgerald, Farris Huff

There were flocks of youngsters and many oldsters too.

NOONDAY PROGRAM—Wayne Hardison, of whom there is none other just like him, was master of ceremonies. He presided, after the feast, with much dignity and enough fun to make it go. Joe Prince in the uniform of our Uncle Sam and home on a furlough, wouldn't talk when called for a speech. Wayne passed the buck, and we made the gathering a short talk on the horse's place in the economic setup of the country today. They were kind and courteous enough to listen in rapt attention.

Prizes were awarded that had been offered, that for the oldest couple riders going to Mr. and Mrs. J.R. Lavender of Burwood, who didn't give their ages, but they could still sit a horse. The youngest couple riders were Eloise Priest, 9, and Dorothy Huff, 11, both members of two families who have long lived in this community. The prize for the one having the most members of their family for lunch went to Mrs. Allen Prince who counted five present- she had two other boys in the service who were absent.

OUT OF DOORS AGAIN

There was one more prize to be awarded. It was for the best couple of riders. Thirty-four riders competed, 17 couples of on Tennessee Walking Horses, not of the shoe type but the kind that have the "free and easy" gaits.

It was Miss Rachel Hill, cousin of Steve Hill of Beech Grove, and John A. McMeen who copped the top honors in the saddle. They rode well and looked good up on their mounts.

As we left Burwood Schoolhouse, a baseball game was in progress—we didn't learn who played or who won, but that didn't matter for they were having a lot of fun batting the ole apple all over the lot.

Why this column – we were impressed with the wholesomeness of this day. The 60 members of the ride-a-thon indulged in a clean and healthful sport. They lived a lot along the 12 miles of their rustic trail where nature furnished the beauty of a landscape that comes only to Middle Tennessee in October.

The village elders – Fate Ashworth, Will Akin, Riley Lavender, and Will Riggin

Burwood Ride-A-Thon 1954

BY GORDON H. TURNER

Ride-A-Thon reached Joe Pope Road and Cayce Springs intersection in 2006.

Nashville Tennessean, October 22, 1954

The 14th annual community ride-a-thon took place here not long ago, and what a day for the folks down in southeast Williamson County!

Strictly a local festival, nearly everybody has some part in it. Participants or spectators can choose their favorite phantom from horseback riding, baseball, baby showing, guessing contests, barbecue eating, talkfests, or the colorful local version or horse shows.

Launched by P.T.A.—The ride-a-thon began as a P.T.A. sponsored project in 1940. Back then 60 to 75 riders made the 10-mile circuit from the school campus and in two or three hours were back for a picnic lunch served by the women and there wasn't much else to do.

As time went on riders decreased until this year only 30 made the rounds. But now everybody else comes to enjoy added attractions, and home demonstration clubbers, teachers, and others are drafted to help run the show.

As president of both the P.T.A. and home demonstration club, Mrs. Herman Duncan invited me to share the 1954 ride-a-thon's fun, food, and fellowship. I once rode horseback a lot but not having been up on a horse in a decade, and with much work planned for the next day, I declined the ride. I arrived, however, in time to watch riders come in on their walking and roping horses, ponies, Texas nags, and even plug mules!

Led by Riley Lavender—From the start, every ride-a-thon has been led by Riley Lavender, now 77, and each time the route is changed. He described this year's leisurely ride as going up George Johnson Hill, then by Sycamore and Boston, and back by Rand and Beech Hill. The youngest "solo" rider was Betty Huff, 9, but 5-year-old Jon Duncan rode behind Leonard Grigsby the whole round. There has never been a mishap, Lavender said. But more showers this time than ever before drove participants to barns along the way.

Ride-a-thon proper ended, the dinner bell rang in the school cafeteria, and for an hour or so folks had plates heaped with barbecue, trimmings, and homemade pies by Mesdames James Huff, Lula Layne, Thomas Tomlinson, O.B. Petway, Pete Davis, J.C. Ragsdale, C.A. Raine, Tom Johnson, LB. Grigsby, Lera Akin, L.B. Pewitt, and H.T. Duncan. Sitting with me to eat were W.J. and Mahala Ashworth Riggin (longest married couple here—58 years), Mrs. Duncan, and Charles F. Dunn, principal of the 125-pupil school.

And was the afternoon a big'un! Must have been because dozens of oldsters also had fun looking and taking part in activities. A thrill came when "Uncle Will Noland" drove up in his mule-drawn "hack" and took for a ride over the campus; A.L. Ashworth, 84, W.J. Riggin, 78, Mrs. Riggin, 80, and Mrs. Callie Huff and Mrs., Myrtle Riggin Ragsdale.

Baseball played—Baseball games were played by the boys' and girls' teams of Burwood and Thompson Station schools. While the local coeds (Wilma Jones, Barbara Rainey, Martha Williams, Ann Ray, Judy Johnson, June and Susie McGee, Patsy Barker, and Ann Lavender) were "in town" I shot their picture which they are going to hang in the school office.

The "horse show" was a dilly, ring-mastered by Frank Bruer of Nashville, whose wife is the former Bessie Ashworth, daughter of A.L. Ashworth, long a prominent farmer here. Riders of winning mounts got pies, sugar, or cash for prizes. I also shot pictures of the "littlest" campus rider, 3-year-old Dianne, daughter of the Haywood Johnsons, and a three-generation set of riders—A.L. Ashworth, 84, Mrs. Frank Bruer, and Vicki Bruer, 5.

I missed out on extra field events for schoolsters but was entranced by other thrills and hearing old citizens recite local history. Mrs. Farris Huff, one of the few to ride in all 14 ride-a-thons, won the quilt whose sale added $100 to P.T.A. funds. And on another campus corner, 86-year-old W.J. (Uncle Will) Akin joined Ashworth, Riggin, and Lavender to voice solutions to the world's problems, and one could tell from their gestures and animated conversation that they are far from being on the shelf!

I asked Uncle Will, whose wife is deceased, if he lived with some of his children. "No sir, they live with me," he beamed.

Among tiny babies whose mothers, with others, watched ride-a-thon activities from the school's entrance hall, were one-month-old Franklin, Jr., son of Franklin Neil and Hilda Stokes Barker, and Harold Wayne, four-month-old son of Harold and Dorris Wall Huff.

Fiesta's Winning Riders, Mounts – From among 30 participants in the recent community ride-a-thon here, these riders and their mounts won out in the afternoon horse show. Riders are James Huff, best walking horse; Jimmy Johnson, best rider under 12; Bud Osburn, ugliest horse (old gray mule); Marion Akin, prettiest horse (a strawberry roan mare owned by James Huff); Riley Lavender, best rider over 12 (now 77), he had led every ride-a-thon procession; and Kenneth Adair and Faye Ferguson, the best couple of riders. Judges were Frank Bruer, Coley Lavender, Leonard Grigsby, Farris Huff, and Ted Akin.

Ride-A-Thon 1956 – Will Nolen, Will Riggin, Mahala Riggin, Fate Ashworth, Myrt Ragsdale, and Callie Huff

THE HAWK BROTHERS VS. LIONEL JOHNSON

RICK WARWICK

The killing of Lionel Johnson by Fred and Charles Hawk at Lavender's Store on February 10, 1913 is still talked about in Burwood a hundred and twenty years later. We will explore the tragic event from period newspaper reports.

SHOT NINE TIMES

The Nashville Tennessean, February 11, 1913

FRANKLIN, Tenn., Feb. 10 – (Special) – Lionel Johnson, aged 22, was shot and instantly killed this morning at about 10:30 in Lavender's store, at Burwood, a village in the western part of this county, by Fred and Charlie Hawk, brothers, aged 30 and 25, respectively, sons of Sam Hawk. The slain man, a son of Elisha Johnson, and the Hawks, live three miles apart. The tragedy has created intense excitement in the neighborhood; and the sheriff and posse, accompanied by bloodhounds, this afternoon were in search of the brothers.

It seems that for some time there has been a bad feeling between young Johnson and the Hawks which culminated in a fight last Saturday at Burwood between Johnson and the elder Hawk, who is 59 years old, in which Hawk was severely handled.

This morning Johnson was seated near the stove in Lavender's store when the Hawk brothers entered. The shooting immediately began. At its beginning, Johnson grappled with one of the brothers, but their aim was rapid and deadly, and he soon fell dead, pierced, it is said by nine bullets. While the shooting was in progress, Constable Tom Byrd, brother-in-law of Johnson, tried to enter the store but is said to have been kept at bay by one of the brothers. Byrd was unarmed. After emptying their pistols, the brothers reloaded and left the scene. Eleven empty shells were counted on the floor of the store.

Sheriff Nevils was notified and went to the scene of the trouble. Bloodhounds from Nashville were ordered by telephone and were carried there late in the evening. The exact whereabouts of the Hawk brothers were not known, but it was surmised that they were near home.

The search with bloodhounds proved unfruitful because of a rainstorm that washed away the tracks of the fleeing brothers. The sheriff and deputies searched every house in the neighborhood to no avail. Family lore in the James and Sallie Hawk Sparkman family of the Boston community maintains that the brothers took refuge in the attic of the Sparkman home. Sallie Sparkman being an aunt of the brothers, most likely provided aid and comfort to her nephews.

NO TIDINGS FROM HAWK BROTHERS

Nashville Banner, February 26, 1913

Fred Hawk   Charles Hawk

"Reward of $200 offered for Arrest and Conviction of Williamson Countians"

Franklin, Tenn. February 24—The accompanying photographs are those of Fred and Charley Hawk, charged with killing Lionel Johnson at Burwood, in this county, on February 10, and for which a reward of $50 each has been offered for their arrest and delivery to the Sheriff of Williamson County. An additional $100 is offered on conviction making a total reward of $200 for arrest and conviction.

It has been over two weeks since the tragedy occurred and no tidings of their whereabouts have been received since the day of the killing, despite the fact that officers from here and Nashville have been on the hunt since.

Fred Hawk is described as being about six feet tall, 32 years old, weighs 165 pounds, has dark hair, and has a Roman nose. Charley Hawk is about 23 years old, weighs about 150 pounds, and has dark hair and a large nose.

Sheriff Nevils believes that they have made their way to West Tennessee, as it is understood they have relatives in that part of the state.

The Hawk Brothers vs. Lionel Johnson

FATHER OF HAWK BOYS UNDER PEACE BOND

Nashville Banner, March 12, 1913

FRANKLIN, Tenn., March 12—Sam Hawk, father of Fred and Charlie Hawk, who shot and killed Lionel Johnson at Lavender's Store at Burwood about a month ago, was arrested and placed under a peace bond at the instigation of Elisha Johnson, father of Lionel Johnson, Tuesday. He was brought to Franklin and later made a bond for $500 which he was required to give. It is claimed by Johnson that Hawk had made several threats about him and had told several parties that if Johnson raised the amount of reward for the capture of his sons there would be further trouble. After being arrested Tuesday Hawk stoutly denied having made the statements attributed to him and was somewhat wrought up over the affair.

FRED AND CHAS HAWK IN JAIL

Nashville Banner, July 12, 1913

Charged with Murder of L. Johnson on February 10, near Burwood
  Arrest on Train
  "Deputy Sheriff Bob Dalton and Constable William Goad of Maury County Effect Capture"
  Had Walked to Waverly

FRANKLIN, Tenn.,—July 12—Fred and Charley Hawk, charged with the murder of Lionel Johnson at Lavender's Store, near Burwood, on February 10, were lodged in jail here this morning. A reward aggregating $200 offered by the state and by Elisha Johnson, Lionel's father, has been outstanding. Their capture was effected by Deputy Sheriff Bob Dalton and Constable William Goad of Maury County on a train beyond Waverly Friday night.

The Hawks declare that until this week they have not been more than a mile or two from their home. Tuesday night they left home on a tramp to Waverly, where they planned to take a train and go to Fulton, Ky. The officers got wind of the fact and coming to Nashville caught the train which the Hawks boarded at Waverly and were arrested. They offered no resistance.

The killing of Johnson at the time it occurred caused considerable excitement in the part of the county in which the parties lived. For two years there had been bad feelings between Johnson and the Hawks. Sometime before the tragedy they had an encounter and Johnson was worsted. On Saturday before the killing on Monday, Johnson met one of the Hawks family at Burwood and gave him a beating. On the day of the killing, Johnson, with a half dozen loiterers, was at the store. It is charged that the Hawks brothers suddenly appeared on the scene with pistols and began shooting. Johnson was hit by nine bullets and was killed almost instantly.

STATEMENT BY FRED HAWK

The Nashville Tennessean, July 13, 1913

Sallie Hawk and James Matt Sparkman of the Boston Community

FRANKLIN, Tenn., – "So far as the arrest was concerned," said Fred, "the evening papers is about correct." We had started to make our way to Fulton, Ky., where we have a sister living. It was our intentions to stay with her for about a year until the excitement had died down, and then, give up. But someone tipped the officers to our movements. I won't call any names, but I have a good idea who that somebody is. All I shall have to say about the trouble will be said at the trial.

Shortly after the young Hawks' arrival in Franklin, they asked to be allowed to go to the bank. Their request was granted, and they placed $300, all they had on deposit, subject to their checks.

According to the accepted version of the killing, Lionel Johnson, a young farmer, 22 years of age, had had some trouble with Sam Hawk, father of Fred and Charles. At one time during the trouble, it is said, the Hawks' father and sons had administered a severe beating to Johnson. Johnson later met the elder Hawk and, after having added insult to injury whipped the old man. This turn of affairs is said to have made the Hawk boys very angry, and they resolved to kill Johnson.

Though he had been warned and begged to leave town, Johnson was in Lavender's store when the Hawk boys came in. He is said to have made no effort to escape. After driving out the dozen or more people in the store, it is alleged the Hawk boys turned on Johnson and emptied their revolvers at him, nine shots taking effect and killing him, and it is evident that they kept very closely confined. Until Friday they had not dared to make an attempt to leave the state, the officers being too hot on their trail. According to

Fred, at one time he 'could have spit in a deputy sheriff's eye. He says that Sheriff R.H. Neville did everything he could to catch him and his brother, reports to the contrary notwithstanding, but that "he didn't have a chance to get us."

The Maury County officers had been tipped off to the proposed exodus of the alleged murderers, they being told that the boys would take the train at Waverly Friday night. Going to Nashville, the officers boarded the train ahead of them and hid in a toilet, making the arrest a few minutes after the fugitives boarded the train at Waverly. No attempt to resist was made, the officers taking their men completely by surprise.

Officers Dalton and Goad will receive the $200 reward offered by Gov. Hooper and the relatives of Johnson.

HAWK BROTHERS ON TRIAL AT FRANKLIN

Nashville Banner, March 3, 1914

Franklin, Tenn., March 3 —the case of the State against Fred and Charley Hawk, who shot and killed Lionel Johnson at Lavender's store at Burwood last February, was called in the Circuit Court here Monday afternoon, one of the largest crowds seen in the courtroom in many a day being present. The case promises to be one of the most hotly contested ones that has come up in some years. A brilliant array of legal talent has been retained by both sides. Attorney-General John L. Neely, for the state, is being assisted by J.C. Eggleston and W.J. Smith, and for the defense, Henderson & Henderson, McCorkle & White, and Faw & Crockett. When court adjourned for the day eight jurymen had been secured.

It is understood that a large number of witnesses for both sides will be examined, and the case will more than likely consume the best part of two weeks by the time it goes to the jury.

BURWOOD AND BEYOND

MURDER IN THE FIRST DEGREE

The Nashville Tennessean, March 11, 1914

Judge Douglas W. Wikle

Franklin, Tenn., March 10—The trial of Fred and Charley Hawk charged with the murder of their neighbor, Lionel Johnson, on February 10, 1913, in a store at Burwood, this morning. At 9 o'clock Judge Wikle called the Jury into court. They have had the case since 6 o'clock the evening before when at the expiration of his honor's charge they were locked up for the night. When asked this morning if they had reached a verdict the foreman replied, "Not exactly," and the jury retired to their room. In a short while they notified the court that they were ready to report and filed into the large room where for a week, hundreds from all parts of the county had witnessed the legal battle now approaching its climax. When again asked if they had reached a verdict the foreman replied in the affirmative, and handed, in a written verdict of murder in the first degree with mitigating circumstances. At the announcement of the verdict, the younger brother paled, but the older made no manifestation of feeling. The prisoners were remanded to jail and the crowd dispatched. Motions for a new trial, it is understood, will be at once entered.

THE END OF THE STORY

Fred and Charley Hawk served four years in the Tennessee State Prison in Nashville. Fred joined the U.S. Army in 1918 and died in 1954. Charlie bought a house in Franklin in 1920. No record of Charlie's death has been found.

Home of Samuel Hawk on Bear Creek Road

Fred and Charles grandparents, Jerry Hawk (1812-1893) and Mary Jane Beasley Hawk (1831-1897), parents of Martha Ann Baxter, Mary Jane Gooch, Sam Hawk, Elizabeth Sparkman, Sallie Sparkman, and Emma Skelley.

The home of James Matt Sparkman and Sallie Hawk Sparkman provided the Hawk Brothers refuge.

BURWOOD'S BASEBALL TEAMS OF 1947

Baseball was considered the "National Sport" in the 20th Century in the United States. Local teams were pitted against other community teams for a great weekend experience. Burwood prided itself on having a good, talented team. As seen in this photograph, Manager Robert H. Huff, Sr. was not against bringing in players from Franklin to "strengthen" the Burwood team. Take note: A.C. Mealer and Billy Lynch lived in Hillsboro, Gerald Hood at Harpeth, and Bobby Gentry in Franklin.

1st row: Si McCampbell, Billy Zan Dodd, Arvis Thompson, Jimmy Akin, Robert Huff, Jr., Gerald "Mama" Johnson, A.C. Mealer, Bobby Sullivan; in Front: Bat boy, Gene Johnson;

2nd row: Gerald Hood, Billy Lynch, Glen Huff, Ken Huff, Bobby Gentry, and R.G. Huff, Sr., manager in 1947.

Burwood's Baseball Teams of 1947

Burwood boys baseball team

Bobby Sullivan, Kenneth Huff, Dewey Latta, Billy Dodd, Bill Zan Dodd, Marion Akin, Edward D. Dodd, and Claude Southall

FOURTH DISTRICT FOLKS
A PHOTOGRAPH ALBUM

Ruby Riggin Dodd

NAMES AND DATES FEATURED IN FAMILIAR FACES

Names of people pictured or mentioned in this section are recorded below with birth and death dates, when known. Women's names are generally listed under their marital surnames. Refer to the general index for names and page numbers for all sections of the book.

Akin, Cammie S. (1879-1945)
Akin, James Bruce (1835-1920)
Akin, James N. (1871-1960)
Akin, Lera Mai Thweatt (1897-1985)
Akin, Lula Shaw (1869-1948)
Akin, Mansfield "Man" (1876-1964)
Akin, Timothy Terrill (1894-1944)
Andrews, Albert Jackson (1872-1951)
Andrews, Audra Harris
Andrews, Bessie (1904-1983)
Andrews, Frances Polk (1873-1921)
Andrews, Glover Clyde (1924-1991)
Andrews, J.T. (1929-2008)
Andrews, Jessie Coates (1918-1966)
Andrews, Joe Carl (1930-1998)
Andrews, John Bolin (1904-1970)
Andrews, Margaret Johnson (1926-)
Andrews, Robert
Andrews, Ronnie
Andrews, Snow Hassell (1898-1930)
Andrews, Walter Howard (1914-1966)
Baker, Estella Johnson (1893-1974)
Barker, Blanche (1876-)
Barker, Ellen Dodson (1815-)
Barker, Eula Sparkman (1882-1911)
Barker, Eva (1913-2004)
Barker, Fannie Hughes (1869-1916)
Barker, Frank (1875-1923)
Barker, Hilda (1924-2016)
Barker, John L. (1906-1990)
Barker, Lottie Lee (1885-1963)
Barker, Mary Lou
Barker, Nell (1907-2002)
Barker, Neil (1924-2006)
Barker, R.H. (1920-2015)

Barnhill, Bessie Mai Sparkman (1915-2001)
Barnhill, Hobert (1913-2004)
Barnhill, L.D. (1908-2006)
Beasley, Andrews Craig (1827-1915)
Beasley, Sara Andrews (1848-1918)
Beasley, Willie Mai (1901-1985)
Burke, Dot Jennette (1931-2010)
Byrd, Clay (1941-2009)
Byrd, Leta Hughes (1915-1994)
Byrd, Louise Crane (1944-)
Byrd, Thomas (1915-1990)
Byrd, Thomas J., Jr. (1925-2009)
Caldwell, Aline (1947-)
Caldwell, Irene (1947-)
Cameron, Jessie Grigsby Huff (1911-2008)
Campbell, Bettie (1847-1926)
Campbell, Charles (1899-1969)
Campbell, Ezekiel (1843-1921)
Campbell, Lula E.
Capley, Ike (1910-1972)
Capley, J.T. (1907-1992)
Capshaw, Carolyn (Johnson) (1937-)
Capshaw, Lera Atkins Polk (1909-1994)
Capshaw, Lettie (1908-1988)
Cash, Betsy Mai Johnson
Clark, Bob (1936-1960)
Clark, Ida May Akin (1862-1927)
Clark, Sam M. (1859-1946)
Cannon, Brown
Crowson, Prentiss (1876-1964)
Dodd, Billy (1926-2000)
Dodd, Bobby
Dodd, Esther Barnhill (1926-2016)
Duncan, Polly Barker (1910-2004)
Elliott, Dorothy Jones (1929-2020)

Fentress, Lera Mai (1911-1987)
Fentress, Melvin (1906-1970)
Fewell, Gary
Fitzgerald, Clyde (1885-1975)
Fitzgerald, Gertrude (1889-1981)
Fry, John Wesley (1882-1952)
Fry, Margaret (1878-1973)
Garland, Bobby (1950-1991)
Garland, Cornelia Ann (1944-)
Garland, Daniel (1948-)
Garland, Dewey (1946-)
Garland, James (1918-1975)
Garland, Kathleen Johnson (1912-1983)
Garland, Lois (1942-)
Garland, Reda Mai (1939-2022)
Garland, Zenith (1941-)
Geasley, Fred (1916-1994)
Geasley, Kathleen
Geasley, Lena Andrews (1922-2004)
Geasley, Louise
Geasley, Mildred
Geasley, Wilma
Gray, Alexander W. (1816-1883)
Gray, Bill
Gray, Cecil (1908-1989)
Gray, James W. (1821-1894)
Gray, Jewell Burnett
Gray, John Black (1852-1928)
Gray, Joseph A. (1855-1929)
Gray, Lena (1899-1983)
Gray, Loulie Russell (1859-1932)
Gray, Will (1865-1949)
Gray, Willie (1904-1978)
Grigsby, Annie Lou Barker (1907-1977)
Grigsby, Glen
Grigsby, Jack (1938-2019)
Grigsby, Leonard (1916-1992)
Grigsby, Ollie (1870-1958)
Grissom, Anita Harris
Haley, Claudine (1952-)
Haley, Dallas Johnson (1927-1999)
Haley, Dorris (1932-1995)
Haley, June (1959-)
Haley, Ronnie (1954-)
Hargrove, Bertha (1906-1983)
Hargrove, Cora Gray (1906-1988)
Hargrove, D.P. (1872-1955)
Hargrove, Florence Polk (1874-1953)
Harris, Bob (1885-1973)
Harris, Bryant
Harris, Charlie
Harris, Fred
Harris, Henry
Harris, LouAnna Gordon (1898-1971)
Harris, Myrtle
Harris, Rebecca Southall

Hassell, Annie or Anna A. Polk (1875-1951)
Hassell, Autry (1917-2011)
Hassell, Catherine Coats (1844-1929)
Hassell, Georgie Rainey (1918-1971)
Hassell, James W. (1810-1898)
Hassell, John T. (1870-1957)
Hassell, W.J. (1836-1910)
Hayes, Jim (1941-2019)
Hayes, Judy Grigsby
Huff, Aught (1875-1954)
Huff, Betty (Garcia) (1946-)
Huff, James (1904-1956)
Huff, Jessie (1911-2008)
Huff, Ken (1927-2014)
Huff, Lou McClain (1928-1992)
Huff, Martha Harris (1852-1903)
Huff, Rennie
Huff, Robert G., Jr. (1918-1984)
Huff, Robert G., Sr. (1891-1973)
Huff, Robert Park (1901-1993)
Huff, Sam (1848-1918)
Inman, John Wesley (1859-1941)
Inman, Wesley Samuel (1824-1891)
Jennette, Ben (1890-1964)
Jennette, Claudie
Jennette, Doris
Jennette, Jesse (1916-1983)
Jennette, Joseph (1861-1939)
Jennette, Nannie Myrt (Huff) (1919-1998)
Jennette, Percy (1897-1980)
Jennette, Porter (1899-1996)
Jennette, Richard H. (1858-1948)
Jennette, Sarah Polk (1873-1942)
Jennette, Turner (1889-1960)
Jennette, Louella (1893-1963)
Johnson, Abram (1919-1972)
Johnson, Allen Wayne (1933-1977)
Johnson, Annie Lela Jones (1895-1971)
Johnson, Arthur Byrd (1931-)
Johnson, Barbara (Barker) (1942-)
Johnson, Barkley (1910-1984)
Johnson, Barnett (1902-1969)
Johnson, Bernice (1908-1985)
Johnson, Bessie Leola Chandler (1896-1992)
Johnson, Brenda
Johnson, Byrd (1853-1897)
Johnson, Carl (1907-1987)
Johnson, Charles Green (1836-1925)
Johnson, Claude (1885-1951)
Johnson, Cola Jennette (1916-2011)
Johnson, Columbus (1879-1924)
Johnson, Cub (1900-1984)
Johnson, Dianne (1950-2019)
Johnson, Elton (1925-1974)
Johnson, Emery James (1896-1958)
Johnson, Emmalee

Johnson, Eugene
Johnson, Eva (1900-1977)
Johnson, Floyd (1895-1952)
Johnson, George (1865-1929)
Johnson, Gertie (1900-1968)
Johnson, Harold (1934-2005)
Johnson, Hayward (1902-1969)
Johnson, Hazel (1924-2019)
Johnson, Herbert (1932-2003)
Johnson, Hiram (1846-1906)
Johnson, Ida Mai (1921-2006)
Johnson, James Edward (1921-1982)
Johnson, Jean (1942-2023)
Johnson, Jennie Ragsdale (1870-1958)
Johnson, Joe
Johnson, Joe Carl (1907-1987)
Johnson, John
Johnson, John Ben (1915-1998)
Johnson, John M. (1817-1900)
Johnson, John Oakley (1898-1978)
Johnson, Johnny Fulton (1932-2018)
Johnson, Judy (Sweeney) 1940-2021)
Johnson, Kate Holt (1865-1929)
Johnson, Kathryn (1927-2016)
Johnson, James Edward
Johnson, Lela Snow Jones (1925-2008)
Johnson, Lemuel Byrd (1867-1947)
Johnson, Leslie B. (1896-1964)
Johnson, Lewis (1826-1895)
Johnson, Linda (Allums) (1947-)
Johnson, Lodus Neil (1931-2008)
Johnson, Lorne (1938-1952)
Johnson, Lucille (1915-2010)
Johnson, Ken (1948-1959)
Johnson, Mae (Frost) (1924-1997)
Johnson, Mahala Ragsdale (1812-1906)
Johnson, Malachi (1875-1950)
Johnson, Malachi, Jr. (1917-)
Johnson, Mallie Lena (1874-1934)
Johnson, Margaret
Johnson, Martha (1927-2016)
Johnson, Martha Robinson (1846-1906)
Johnson, Martha Woodward
Johnson, Matilda Elizabeth Marlin (1873-1947)
Johnson, Mike
Johnson, Mildred (1925-2008)
Johnson, Milton "Buster" (1930-2014)
Johnson, Nannie Marion Inman (1857-1943)
Johnson, Neil (1945-2008)
Johnson, Oakley (1910-1984)
Johnson, Ollie Hassell (1886-1959)
Johnson, Opal (Primm) (1927-2008)
Johnson, Ophelia Sophronia (1876-1946)
Johnson, Peewee
Johnson, Rhoda Merritt (1827-1900)
Johnson, Robert (1873-1959)

Johnson, Rollie Gordon (1897-1969)
Johnson, Rosie Lee (1903-1991)
Johnson, Sallie Holt (1838-)
Johnson, Seth (1899-1921)
Johnson, Susan Byrd (1900-1986)
Johnson, Tommy Carroll (1944-2010)
Johnson, Vivian Gray
Johnson, Vuna Jennette (1895-1975)
Johnson, Wiley Blount (1871-1954)
Johnson, William (1920-1998)
Johnson, Wilma (Heithcock) (1934-2015)
Jones, Alice
Jones, Annie Williams (1889-1948)
Jones, Bill (1915-1996)
Jones, Pvt. Clifton (1890-1918)
Jones, Clifton (1918-1970)
Jones, Dorothy (Elliott) (1929-2020)
Jones, Dot (1907-1988)
Jones, Elsie (1889-1971)
Jones, Emery
Jones, Grace Andrews (1917-2002)
Jones, Herbert (1916-2002)
Jones, James Bruce or J.B. (1927-2013)
Jones, James Taylor ((1886-1975)
Jones, Larry (1947-)
Jones, Lela (1929-1940)
Jones, Leslie Burton (1898-1984)
Jones, Mary
Jones, Mary Alice (Potts) (1922-2007)
Jones, Mildred (Candler) (1939-1985)
Jones, Oneda Rainey (1928-2018)
Jones, Ophelia Merritt (1869-1948)
Jones, Patsy (Johnson) (1945-)
Jones, Richard (1940-2013)
Jones, Ridley (1902-1991)
Jones, Ruby (1913-1949)
Jones, Taylor (1857-1938)
Jones, Tim (1955-)
Jones, Wiley Franklin (1882-1956)
Jones, Willie Mai Beasley (1901-1985)
Jones, Wilma (Davis) (1941-)
Inman, Avie (1897-1988)
Inman, John Wesley (1859-1941)
Kelly, Beal
Kelly, Beulah (1887-1981)
Kelly, Nora (1885-1967)
Kelly, Susie (1859-1935)
Kelly, Vallie (1883-1955)
Kelly, William A. "Bill" (1860-1930)
King, Silva Harris Osborne (1925-2012)
Langford, Dean Johnson (1935-2015)
Langford, Leigh (1932-2014)
Langford, Leonard (1905-1980)
Langford, Louise (Jones) (1911-1989)
Langford, Steve (1940-2020)
Langford, Wayne (1934-1973)

Langford, Wiley (1943-2014)
Lavender, Alvin (1882-1945)
Lavender, Blythe
Lavender, Glen (1902-1992)
Lavender, Pearl
Lavender, Riley (1878-1962)
Lillie, Mary Louise (Glasgow)
Lockridge, Dixie Shaw (1908-1989)
Logan, Allie Lavender (1900-1980)
Logan, Amanda
Logan, Pat Gray
Logan, Ray (1941-2013)
Logan, Raymond (1896-1986)
Logan, Sherry Still
Logan, Tandy
Marlin, Ever Lena (1890-1987)
Marlin, Joseph Bonaparte (1839-1921)
Marlin, William Samuel (1866-1952)
Martin, Benton (1934-2020)
Martin, Grace (1909-1990)
Martin, Ray
McKee, Luther (1909-1974)
McKee, Virginia Andrews (1923-2014)
Merritt, Wiley Blount (1831-1912)
Morrow, John P. (1876-1959)
Morrow, May (1876-1963)
Morrow, Ola Clark (1889-1920)
Nix, Rebecca Brown (1820-1900)
Oakley, John (1898-1978)
Osborne, Angie
Osborne, Betsy
Osborne, Bill (1923-2006)
Osborne, Bud (1941-2006)
Osborne, Copperhead
Osborne, Dawn
Osborne, Effie Lee (1920-2006)
Osborne, Faye
Osborne, Fulton (1907-1955)
Osborne, Harvey
Osborne, Howlett (1914-2003)
Osborne, Jackie
Osborne, Judy Barnhill
Osborne, Katie
Osborne, Luther
Osborne, Nellie
Osborne, Ott
Parigin, Janie Ragsdale (1946-)
Parrish, Terrie
Polk, Audrey (Andrews)
Polk, Callie E. (1880-1930)
Polk, Delilah Johnson (1839-1911)
Polk, Felton (1917-1963)
Polk, Frances (1889-1976)
Polk, George Lee
Polk, Howlett
Polk, Ila (1901-)

Polk, John (1900-1960)
Polk, James Knox (1844-1931)
Polk, John Wesley (1840-1911)
Polk, John Wiley (1900-1950)
Polk, Julia Robinson (1854-1929)
Polk, Lillie Alice
Polk, Millard
Polk, Nelson (1898-1951)
Polk, Tom (1920-1982)
Polk, Walter
Pope, Cora Blackburn
Pope, Ed C. (1840-1912)
Pope, Matthew (1873-1951)
Pope, Mittie Akin (1873-1960)
Pope, Raleigh
Pope, Sarah Elizabeth Sparkman (1848-1870)
Pope, William C. (1833-1910)
Pope, William E. (1868-1968)
Primm, Opal Johnson (1927-2018)
Prowell, Andrew
Prowell, Sara Mays
Rader, Cathryn Johnson
Rader, William
Ragsdale, Carroll (1863-1923)
Ragsdale, Joe Clellon (1905-1967)
Ragsdale, Columbus
Ragsdale, Daniel (1787-1841)
Ragsdale, Danny (1938-2014)
Ragsdale, Deliah Johnson (1862-1927)
Ragsdale, Doc (1899-1984)
Ragsdale, Elcain
Ragsdale, Ephraim (1872-1956)
Ragsdale, Ethel (1901-1969)
Ragsdale, Harvey H. (1835-1880)
Ragsdale, Hattie Johnson (1878-1946)
Ragsdale, Henry (1866-1942)
Ragsdale, Joe (1905-1967)
Ragsdale, John H. (1863-1940)
Ragsdale, Lemuel (1903-1997)
Ragsdale, Lillie (1901-1969)
Ragsdale, Mannie (1899-1984)
Ragsdale, Margaret Hewton (1795-1870)
Ragsdale, Myrtle (1856-1968)
Ragsdale, Rebecca (1916-1988)
Ragsdale, Reedy (1898-1969)
Ragsdale, William (1866-1942)
Ragsdale, Zula (1912-2005)
Rainey, Greenie (1901-1983)
Rainey, Myrtle Martin (1898-1976)
Redford, Kenneth (1898-1969)
Redford, Kenneth G. (1895-1973)
Redford, Ollie Pope (1900-1985)
Robinson, Carroll (1864-1940)
Robinson, Sarah (1826-1875)
Robinson Shadrach (1825-1879)
Robinson, W.A. "Bill" (1859-1932)

Shaw, Barkley
Shaw, Elizabeth (1849-1930)
Shaw, Mary Gee Thweatt (1876-1943)
Shaw, Oscar J. (1845-1934)
Shaw, William Greer (1907-1934)
Sparkman, Alice Evelyn Jones
Sparkman, Mrs. C.S.
Sparkman, Claude (1912-1996)
Sparkman, Cliff (1922-2001)
Sparkman, Gertrude Dodd (1888-1976)
Sparkman, Gus (1853-1944)
Sparkman, Joe
Sparkman, Mary Ann Robinson (1815-1892)
Sparkman, Nell (1888-1963)
Sparkman, Ollie (1884-1959)
Sparkman, Ollie Joe, III
Sparkman, Ollie "Toodlum," Jr.
Sparkman, Tishie Beasley (1872-1962)
Stovall, Dudley (1930-2018)
Stovall, Earl (1891-1970)

Stovall, Earl, Jr. (-1979)
Stovall, Gertrude Andrews (1925-2013)
Stovall, James Martin (1870-1926)
Stovall, Ray (1941-1971)
Stovall, Tennessee Virginia Nix (1853-1909)
Stovall, Wallace "Stovepipe" (1922-2011)
Stovall, William Franklin (1883-1911)
Sudberry, Hershel (1890-1960)
Sudberry, Lena Hassell (1896–1988)
Sudberry, M.E. (1924-1925)
Sullivan, Bobby
Sullivan, Hattie Barnhill (1889-1964)
Sweeney, Viola Osborne (1923-2013)
Thomas, Judy Gray
Tidwell, Annie Lou
Walls, Elmer (1950-2024)
Walls, Neil
Walls, Velmer (1950-)
Waller, Maggie Lee Baker
Woody, Jean (1922-2002)

FAMILIAR FACES

Johnson Hollow Folks – On the ground: Taylor Jones, Leslie Jones, Ophelia Jones, Eugene Johnson, Mallie Lena Johnson, and Eva Johnson Polk (seated in white); Standing: Wiley B. Johnson, Tom Polk, Wiley Jones, James Cliffton Jones, Emery James Johnson, Lela Jones-Johnson, Estella Johnson Baker, and Gus Sparkman on the horse.

William A. Kelly with Oscar and Susie Kelly; sitting, Ollie; standing, Vallie, Beulah, Nora, and Beal Kelly.

Bessie Leola Chandler Johnson, Aline Caldwell, Irene Caldwell

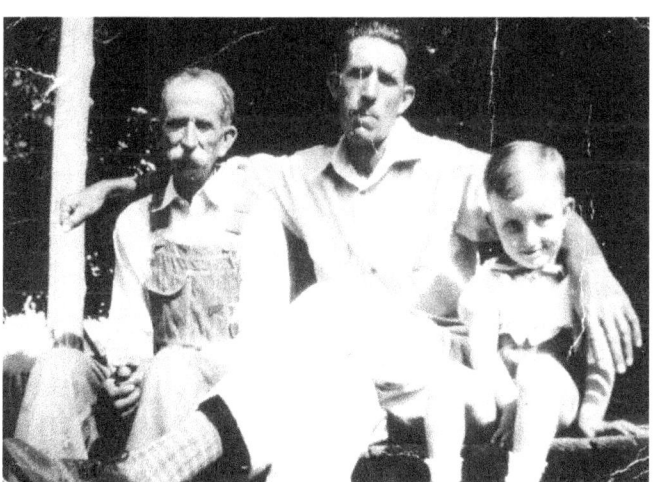

Ephraim, Clellon, and Danny Ragsdale. Three generations.

Joe Carl, Rollie, and John Ben Johnson, sons of Lemuel and Jennie Johnson

John Ben Johnson, Carl Johnson, Rollie Johnson, Floyd Johnson; standing, Lera Mai Fentress, Gertie Johnson, Elsie Jones, Bessie Andrews, Louella Jennette, children of Lemuel and Jennie Ragsdale Johnson

John Bolin Andrews, Joe Carl Johnson; standing, Melvin Fentress, Clellon Ragsdale, and Doc Ragsdale

Seth Johnson, son of Lemuel B. and Jennie Ragsdale Johnson

D.P. and Florence Polk Hargrove

Ollie Hassell Johnson, wife of Columbus Johnson

Nannie Marian Inman Johnson

Emmalee and Eva Johnson

William Samuel Marlin and sister Matilda Elizabeth Marlin Johnson

Bessie Leola Chandler and Emery James Johnson

Emery James Johnson with a team of mules

Jennie Ragsdale Johnson, wife of Lemuel Byrd Johnson

Mike Johnson, son of Harold and Martha Johnson

Tommy and Leta Hughes Byrd, parents of Clay Byrd

Rollie Gordon Johnson and Reedy Ragsdale

Lemuel Ragsdale, Lillie Ragsdale, Clellon Ragsdale, Ethel Ragsdale, Mannie Ragsdale

Ophelia Sophronia Johnson, wife of Robert Johnson

Robert Johnson and daughters – Lettie Capshaw, Bertha Hargrove, Ida Polk, Avie Inman

Byrd Johnson and Nannie Inman Johnson

Carolyn (Capshaw) and Milton "Buster" Johnson

John Oakley and Susan Byrd Johnson

Charles Green Johnson and Sally Holt Johnson

Wesley Samuel Inman

Fannie Hughes Barker

George Johnson and Kate Holt Johnson

James W. Gray, father of John B. Gray

Alexander W. Gray

Joseph A. and Loulie Russell Gray family of Gray Lane

Loulie Russell Gray and Joseph A. Gray

John Black Gray

John and Mahala Ragsdale Johnson. He is the son of Elcain Johnson, Sr. She is the daughter of Margaret Hewton Ragsdale.

Wiley Johnson, son of Hiram Johnson

John and Lera Atkins Polk Capshaw

The Robert and Ophelia Johnson family with Old Bessie

John Oakley (holding Lorene) Johnny, Milton, Kathryn, Mildred, and Susan Byrd Johnson

Bernice Johnson, son of Malachi, Sr., and Millie Polk Johnson

Ephraim Ragsdale and Hattie Johnson Ragsdale

Riley Lavender with grandchildren

Lera (1897-1985) and Timothy Terrell Akin, Jr. (1894-1944)

Esther Dodd

John L. and Nell Barker

Malachi Johnson family – Cub, Kathleen Garland, Millie Polk, Malachi, Sr., Lucille, Oakley, Barnett, Barkley, Bernice, Malachi, Jr., and Hayward Johnson

Elder Malachi Johnson and Millie Ann Polk Johnson

Garland family – Dewey, Daniel, Bobby, Cornelia Ann standing James Garland, Kathleen, Reda Mai, Zenith, Lois Garland

Sarah Elizabeth Sparkman Pope, daughter of Matthew and Mary Ann Robinson Sparkman, wife of Ed C. Pope

John P. and May Morrow

Delilah Johnson Polk and John Wesley Polk, Baxter's Artillery, CSA

Matthew Pope, Mittie Akin Pope, and Raleigh Pope

James Bruce Akin, Co G, 11th TN Cav., CSA

Myrtle Ragsdale

Mittie Akin Pope

Mansfield "Man" Akin

William E. Pope

Prentiss Crowson and Mansfield Akin

Ollie Pope, wife of Kenneth Redford, daughter of Mittie Akin and Matthew Pope

Mrs. C.S. Sparkman

Prentiss Crowson, Bob Clark, and Cam Akin

Bobby Dodd, son of Billy and Esther Dodd

Sam M. Clark, Ora Clark, and Ida May Akin Clark

Ollie Pope (Redford) and Raleigh Pope

Callie E. Polk

Claude and Lela Jones Johnson

Bill Jones and Grace Andrews Jones with Tim, Mildred, and Wilma are on the front row. In the back, Patsy, Richard, Larry, and Herbert Jones.

Claudie Jennette and sister, Dot Jennette Burke

Clifton Jones and sister, Annie Lela Jones

Dallas Johnson (Haley) and Gertrude Andrews (Stovall)

Danny Ragsdale, son of Clellon Ragsdale and grandson of Ephraim Ragsdale

Dorris and Dallas Johnson Haley with children, Claudine, Ronnie, and June Haley

Dallas Johnson (Haley), Abram Johnson, and Opal Johnson (Primm)

James Edward Johnson and Lela Snow Jones Johnson

Ken Huff and Dorothy Jones Elliott

Wallace "Stovepipe" Stovall and Joe Carl Andrews

Margaret Andrews (Stovall) on the Square

Clyde Andrews and Snow Hassell Andrews family – seated: Lena Geasley, Robert, and J.T.; standing: Anna, Clyde, Walter Howard, Grace Jones, Hazel Pentecost, Glover C. Andrews, and Millie Gibbs.

Abram Johnson, Clifton Jones, standing: Leslie Jones and Jim Jones

Wiley and Annie Williams Jones family: Bill, Mary Alice, Dot, Lela, J.B. and Cliff Jones

Fred Geasley and Lena Andrews Geasley with Louise Geasley, Wilma, and Mildred Jones

John Wesley Inman

Glover C., Robert, and J.T. Andrews

Grace Andrews Jones and brother Glover C. Andrews

Georgie Rainey, Autry Hassell holding Jimmy, Glover Clyde Andrews holding Ronnie, and Audra Harris Andrews

Vuna Johnson and Turner Jennette on their wedding day December 25, 1912

John T. Hassell and Annie Polk Hassell with Autry Hassell

Autry Hassell with M.E. Sudberry

Grace Andrews Jones, Clyde Andrews, with Wilma Jones, Albert Andrews, and Herbert Jones

Julie Robinson Polk and James K. Polk

John T. Hassell and Anna A. Polk Hassell

Catherine Coats Hassell, wife of W.J. Hassell

Hershel Sudberry and Lena Hassell Sudberry

Larry, Herbert, Richard, and Patsy Jones

Jessie Coates Andrews and Walter Howard Andrews, Lena Andrews Geasley and Fred Geasley

Bill Jones with Tim, Herbert, Patsy, Larry, and Richard Jones

John T. Hassell

Wiley F. Jones and Annie Williams Jones family. Standing: Louise Langford, Bill, Ruby, J.B., Mary Alice Potts, Cliff, Lela Johnson, and Dorothy Elliot

Aught Huff, son of Sam and Martha Harris Huff

Wiley F. Jones, Annie Lela Jones Johnson, and Joe Jones

Wiley Franklin Jones and Annie Williams Jones

James Knox Polk

Jim Taylor Jones and Ophelia Merritt Jones

Luther and Virginia Andrews McKee

Earl Stovall, father of Earl Jr., Dudley, Wallace, and Ray Stovall

Robert Park Huff

Miss Jean Woody

Elmer Walls, Robert Walls, and Neil Johnson, Burwood School

Rebecca Southall Harris and Fred Harris holding Anita Harris

Johnnie Ben Johnson, Cola Jennette Johnson, and Tommy Carroll Johnson

Richard H. Jennette

Ever Lena Marlin with child; standing are Terrie Parrish, Grace Martin, and Benton Martin

Grace Andrews Jones, Lena Andrews Geasley, and Kathleen Geasley

Henry Ragsdale

Joseph Bonapart Marlin, Co D 20th Inf CSA

Lillie Alice and Howlett Polk

Rennie Huff

Nell and Claude Sparkman

Myrtle Martin Rainey and Greenie Rainey

Clyde and Gertrude Fitzgerald

Bryant and Myrtle Harris with wagon

John Wesley Fry and Margaret Fry

Wiley Blount Merritt and Nelson Polk

Rhoda Merritt Johnson, the wife of Lemuel Byrd Johnson, denied Federal soldiers from taking her horse according to family lore.

Dixie Shaw Lockridge and Mary Lou Barker

Martha Robinson Johnson, wife of Hiram Johnson and mother of 14 children.

Lewis Johnson, Co E 55th TN Inf CSA

Wiley Blount Johnson holding Maggie Lee Baker (Waller); Mallie Lena Johnson holding Betsy Main Johnson (Cash)

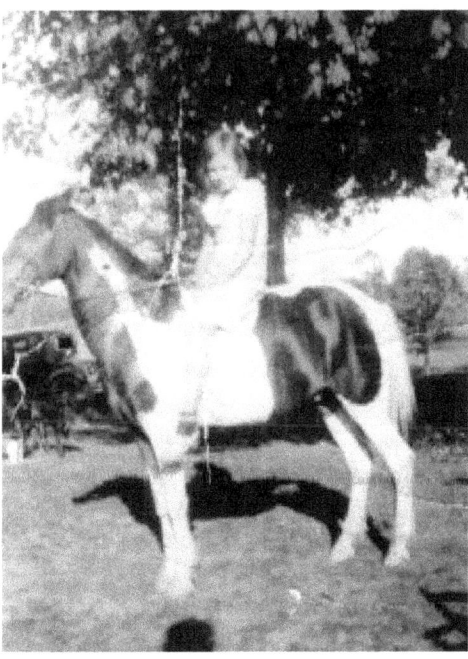

Hazel Johnson (Mrs. Carl Johnson and mother of Louise Byrd)

Louise Crane and Clay Byrd

Louise Crane Byrd and Janie Ragsdale Parigin

Rebecca, Zula, and Ethel Ragsdale

Annie Lou Barker Grigsby, beloved Burwood teacher

Jessie Grigsby Huff Cameron, beloved Burwood teacher

Jim and Judy Grigsby Hayes

Polly Barker Duncan, beloved Burwood teacher

Judy Grigsby Hayes

Jack Grigsby

Bud Osborne, Judy Barnhill Osborne, Jackie, Dawn, and Angie Osborne

Oneda Rainey and James Bruce Jones

Bud Osborne

Rollie and Rosie Lee Johnson

Johnson cousins – Ida Mai, Opal, Lucille, and Margaret

Rollie and Rosie Johnson family – 1st row: Arthur Byrd, Neil, Linda, Rollie; 2nd row: Judy and Jean; 3rd row: Rosie, Opal, Wilma, Herbert, William, Elton, Lucille, and James Johnson

Ragsdale brothers: Columbus, Elcain, Carroll, William, and John H. Ragsdale

Possibly Hiram Johnson and daughter, Callie Cathryn Johnson (Mrs. William Rader)

George Lee and Nelson Polk, Burwood cowboy wannabes

Brenda, John, Ken, Mae, and William Johnson, Christmas 1958

Neil, Jean, and Linda Johnson

Rhonda, Peewee, Byrd, and Barbara Johnson

Allie Lavender and Raymond Logan

Willie Gray and Jewell (Burnett) Gray family – Judy Thomas, Bill, Vivian Johnson, Pat Logan, Barbara Hughes, and Zula

Four generations – Raymond, Tandy with Amanda, and Ray Logan

Tandy, Raymond, Allie holding Patrick, and Sandy Logan

Brown Cannon

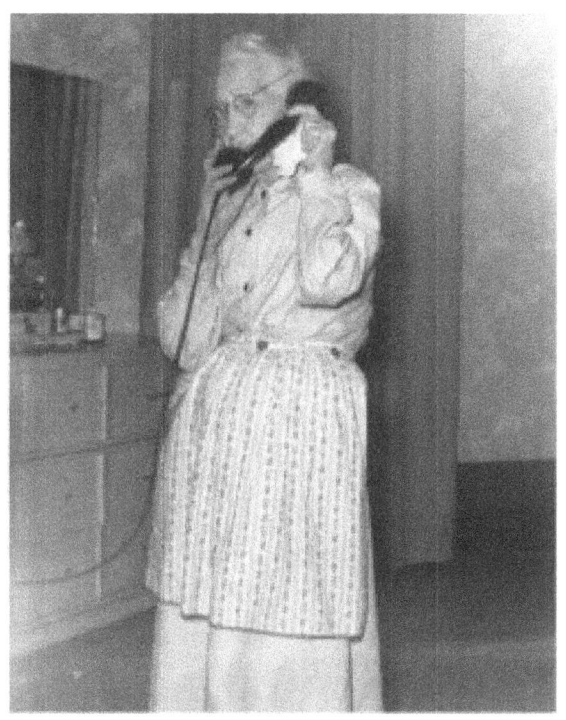

Millie Polk Johnson using the telephone for the first time.

Thomas J. Byrd

Glen Lavender

Tennessee Virginia Nix (Stovall); William Franklin Stovall, son; Rebecca Brown Nix, mother.

Hattie Stovall (Huff) and brother, James Martin Stovall

Frank Barker and Eula Barker standing in front of their humble home.

Abram Johnson and Doris Jennette

Sons of Jesse Jennette: Jesse and Porter, seated; Turner, Percy and Ben Jennette

Bobby Sullivan and Hobert Barnhill showing off a rattlesnake

Lou McClain and Ken Huff

J.B. Jones, Lou Huff, and Ken Huff

Nannie Myrt Jennette Huff and Robert Huff

Ken Huff and Robert Huff, Jr.

Bob and Lou Anna Gordon Harris family: Charlie, Lou Dora Tidwell, Effie Lee, Viola, Lillie Vaughn, and Henry Harris

Bob Harris with banjo

Hillsboro Hounds Dinner at Boston, 1933. J.T. Capley, guitar. Ike Capley, fiddle; Bob Harris, banjo.

Fulton, Bill, and Howlett Osborne

Charlie Harris on his horse

Henry Harris with his guitar

Mary Gee Thweatt Shaw

William Greer Shaw

William C. and Cora Blackburn Pope

Lula Shaw Akin

Sara Mays Prowell and Andrew Prowell Co C 44th TN CSA

Bettie Campbell. Ezekial Campbell, Charles Campbell, and Lula E. Campbell

Nelson Polk and Walter Polk

Familiar Faces

Barkley Shaw, teacher

Oscar J. Shaw and Elizabeth S. Shaw

James W. Hassell

James N. Akin

Kenneth and Ollie Pope Redford

James and Jessie Huff

Dean Johnson and Bessie Leola Johnson

Pearl, Blythe, Glen, and Riley Lavender

Ollie and Joe Sparkman on the lawnmower

Sara Andrews Beasley, wife of Andrew Craig Beasley, and g-granddaughter Mary Louise Lillie

Cain Polk with Felton, Audrey Andrews Polk, and Millard Polk

Willie Mai Beasley and Ridley Jones

Familiar Faces

Richard Jones

Larry Jones

J.B. Jones

Alice Eveline Beasley Sparkman, Ollie Joe Sparkman, III, and Ollie "Toodlum" Sparkman, Jr.

The world changes year to year
And friends from day to day,
But never will the ones we loved
From memory fade away.

Ellen Dodson Barker

Lewis Johnson

Albert and Frances Polk Andrews and family

Mannie, Delilah Johnson Ragsdale, and Joe Ragsdale

L.D. Barnhill

Bessie Mae Sparkman Barnhill

Carroll Robinson, Julia Robinson Polk, and W.A. Bill Robinson, children of Shadrach and Sarah Robinson

Deliah Johnson Polk, wife of John Wiley Polk

James Huff, Ollie Grigsby, Leonard Grigsby and Glen Grigsby

Carl Johnson, Hazel Johnson, Lodus Neil Johnson, Joe Johnson, Louise Byrd, Gary Fewell, and Dianne Johnson

Cliff Sparkman

Frances Polk Andrews

Sarah Polk Jennette and Joseph Jennette

Albert Jackson Andrews

Betsy, Harvey, Nellie, Faye, Ott, and Katie Osborne

Ott Osborne, Ray Martin, Copperhead Osborne, Luther Osborne, and Harvey Osborne

Allen Wayne Johnson

Russell Sparkman

Tom Osborne

Bill Osborne

Billy Dodd and Hilda Barker, Neil Barker and Esther Dodd

Familiar Faces

Scrapbook Sketches

BY RUBY RIGGIN DODD

The End.

Index

11th TN Cav., CSA, 327
20th TN Inf. CSA, 344
44th TN CSA, 364
55th TN Inf. CSA, 347
126th Infantry, 32nd division, 185

A

Abram, George, 217
Abram, Johnson, 308
Adair, Kenneth, 288
Adkisson, Joe Thomas, 93
A.H. Stephens family, 281
Akin, Adeline Craig, 274
Akin, Arthur Stewart, 7, 274
Akin, Betsey, 274
Akin, Bob, 271
Akin, Callie, 35
Akin, Cam, 30, 150, 271, 329
Akin, Cammie, 29, 59, 81–83, 271, 307
Akin, Carolyn Riggin, 150
Akin, Cornelia, 152
Akin, Dora, 271
Akin, Dorcas Starr, 7, 273–74
Akin, E.B., 271
Akin, Ed, 145
Akin, Edith, 274
Akin, Elizabeth, 92
Akin, Ethel, 271
Akin, Greg, 267
Akin, Ida, 145, 271
Akin, James, 274
Akin, James Bruce, 133, 145, 270–71, 307, 327
Akin, James Hull, 150
Akin, James N., 307, 366
Akin, J.B., 81, 90, 92, 96, 146–48, 150, 270
Akin, J.B., Jr., 59
Akin, J.B., Sr., 59
Akin, J.B. and Carolyn Riggin, 150
Akin, Jim, 35, 145, 150, 271
Akin, Jimmy, 304
Akin, Joella, 59, 83, 92, 148, 270–71
Akin, John, 7, 10–14, 22–23, 59, 82, 160–61, 134, 163, 165, 176, 178–79, 188, 202, 204–6, 259–60, 274, 307–10, 322
Akin, John Will, 82
Akin, Katherine Beckett, 147
Akin, Kattie Hattie, 271
Akin, Leana, 145
Akin, Lena, 271
Akin, Lera, 83, 268, 295, 324
Akin, Lera Mai Thweatt, 307
Akin, Lila Mae, 59, 90
Akin, Lilia Mai, 82
Akin, Lucille, 92
Akin, Lula Shaw, 307, 363
Akin, Lula Boyd, 147, 270-271
Akin, Madison, 271
Akin, Maggie, 271
Akin, Maggie Mae, 81, 90
Akin, Mamie, 271
Akin, Mann, 271
Akin, Mansfield "Man," 307, 328
Akin, Marion, 288, 305
Akin, Marion, Lera and Ted, 268
Akin, Mary, 59
Akin, Mary Terrell, 219
Akin, Mat, 271
Akin, Matilda Starr, 274
Akin, Mattie Mai, 92
Akin, Millard, 7, 23–24, 35, 38, 145–47, 152, 271
Akin, Millard F., 270
Akin, Mittie, 271, 328
Akin, Mr. and Mrs. R.V., 59
Akin, Nancy Carolyn, 145, 148
Akin, Nellie, 274
Akin, Ollie Mai, 271
Akin, Ora, 271
Akin, Polly Vance, 274
Akin, Rebecca, 274
Akin, Robbie, 271
Akin, Robert, 59, 90, 148, 270
Akin, Robert Vance, 149–50, 152
Akin, Ruth, 59, 81, 83, 90, 92, 148, 270
Akin, R.V., 15, 17, 146, 289
Akin, R.V., Jr., 90, 152, 153
Akin, Samuel, 6–7, 14, 57, 242, 271, 273–74
Akin, Samuel W., 274
Akin, Ted, 296
Akin, Tic, 96
Akin, Timothy Terrell, 17, 59, 90, 92, 267–68, 268, 274, 307, 324
Akin, Vance, 7, 35, 38, 40, 145–47, 149–50, 271
Akin, Vance, III, 153
Akin, Will, 23, 43, 293
Akin, William, 219
Akin, William M., 10, 274
Akin, William P., 133
Akin, William T., 272
Akin, W.J. (Uncle Will), 7, 296
Akin-Boyd-Dodd Home, 219–20
Akin Brothers' Store, 18
Akin family, 35
Akin-Hutcherson-Norman Home, 270
Akin-Ragsdale Home, 272
Akin Store, 38
Akin-Tomlinson Home, 273–74
Alexander, Eliza C., 274
Alexander, James M., 274
Alexander, Miss Ruth, 17
Alexander, Ruth, 95
Alexander, W.G., 128
Alexander W. Gray, 321
Alice, Lillie, 344
Alice, Mary, 335
Allen, 17, 235, 308
Allen, Mac, 48
Allison, James, 9–10, 43, 215
Allison, James P., 133
Allison, Leigh Perkins, 215
Allison, William, 215
Alma Sparkman, 85
Ambrose, Barbara, 100

American Legion, John E. Stephens Post, 185
Amos, Curtis, 50, 52
Amos, Elizabeth, 127
Amos, Jonas, 287
Amos, Sam, 60
Anderson, Chapman, 171
Anderson, Daniel, 240
Anderson, Eula Mai, 91
Anderson, John B., 285
Anderson, Thomas, 21, 247
Anderson Buckner, 96, 99, 289
Anderson's Big Spring, 58
Andrews, 136, 138, 307, 310, 334, 336
Andrews, Albert, 337, 370
Andrews, Albert and Clyde, 262
Andrews, Albert Jackson, 307, 373
Andrews, Anna, 334
Andrews, Audra Harris, 307, 336
Andrews, Bessie, 307, 314
Andrews, Bo, 115
Andrews, Clyde, 52, 262, 334, 337
Andrews, Era, 262
Andrews, Frances Polk, 307, 370
Andrews, Frances Polk , 370, 373
Andrews, Gertrude, 87, 331
Andrews, Glover Clyde, 136, 307, 336
Andrews, Howard, Walter, 334
Andrews, Jennie, 52
Andrews, Jessie Coates, 307, 339
Andrews, Joe Carl, 74, 87, 90, 307, 333
Andrews, John Bolin, 307, 315
Andrews, J.T., 307, 336
Andrews, Kenneth, 104
Andrews, Mannie, 370
Andrews, Margaret, 333
Andrews, Margaret Johnson, 307
Andrews, Nancy, 69
Andrews, Pam, 101
Andrews, Robert, 138, 307, 334, 336
Andrews, Ronnie, 307, 336
Andrews, Sandra, 101
Andrews, Snow Hassell, 307, 334
Andrews, Tiny, 59
Andrews, Walter Howard, 307, 339
Andrews, William, 69
Anglin, Delton, 78
Anglin, Grace, 77–78
Anglin, Marie, 78
Anglin, Sharon, 144
Anglin, William, 77
Antebellum Churches, 56
Armstrong, Martin, 240
Arnold, Clayton, 146, 185
Ashland City High School, 147
Ashworth, A.L., 158
Ashworth, Bolton, 158, 225
Ashworth, Charles, 225
Ashworth, Charlie, 158
Ashworth, Emily, 34
Ashworth, Fate, 224–25, 293, 296
Ashworth, Grandpa, 26
Ashworth, James, 158, 225
Ashworth, Jessie, 91
Ashworth, Jettie, 94
Ashworth, Jim, 34
Ashworth, Joe, 79
Ashworth, Joseph, 157
Ashworth, Josephus, 33, 158, 224
Ashworth, Locke, 158
Ashworth, Lottie Carter, 25, 107-8, 154-6
Ashworth, Nannie, 34
Ashworth, Perlina Locke, 157–58, 225
Ashworth, Susan Mahala, 34
Ashworth, Virginia, 157
Ashworth, Walter, 34, 158, 225
Ashworth, Willie, 34
Ashworth, Wilson, 30, 34, 158, 225
Ashworth Home, 34, 224
Association for the Preservation of Virginia Antiquities, 227
Atwood, John, 168

B
Bailey, Louise, 75
Bailey, Robert A., 168
Baker, Estella Johnson, 59, 231, 312
Baker, Jessie Ruth, 88
Baker, Maggie Lee, 347
Baker, Nelda, 101
Baker's Company of Holman's Cavalry, 248
Ball, Jimmy, 33
Ball, Laura, 33
Banks, L.H., 10
Banks, Thomas, 10
Baptist Church, 23, 62
Baptist Pallets, 23
Barker, Annie Lou, 175, 239, 244, 349
Barker, Blanche Lavender, 160, 163, 174-5, 307
Barker, Christine, 175
Barker, Cornelia Shaw, 34, 175
Barker, Ellen Dodson, 307, 370
Barker, Eula, 358
Barker, Eula Sparkman, 307
Barker, Eva, 239, 307
Barker, Fannie Hughes, 83, 307, 320
Barker, Frank, 307, 358
Barker, Franklin, Jr., 296
Barker, George H., 133
Barker, George Hightower, 236–37
Barker, George Roy, 160, 162
Barker, George W., 79
Barker, Georgia, 17
Barker, Georgie, 94
Barker, G.W, 160
Barker, Hilda, 239, 253, 307, 376
Barker, Hilda Stokes, 296
Barker, Houston, 175
Barker, Jerry, 3
Barker, John, 160, 163, 175
Barker, John L., 83, 175, 307
Barker, John L. and Nell, 324
Barker, John W. , 94, 162, 236–37
Barker, John William, 162
Barker, Larry, 3
Barker, Lottie, 174
Barker, Lottie Lee, 175, 307
Barker, Lottie Lee Lavender, 239
Barker, Margaret, 175
Barker, Mary Lou, 307, 346
Barker, Miss Annie Lou, 76
Barker, Nancy, Sandy, Hilda, and Neil, 253
Barker, Neil, 99, 138, 239, 253, 307, 376
Barker, Neil and Hilda, 253
Barker, Nell, 307
Barker, Pauline, 87
Barker, Pearl Troope, 160
Barker, Polly, 175
Barker, R.H., 138, 200, 307
Barker, R.H., Jr, 239
Barker, R. H., Sr., 134, 239
Barker, R.H., Sr., 53, 134–35, 238
Barker, Robbie Lee, 91, 175
Barker, Robert H., 239

Barker, Roy, 81, 83, 92, 96, 99, 160, 175
Barker, Roy, George, 160
Barker, Roy Edwin, 162
Barker, Ruth, 17, 175, 239
Barker. Blanch Lavender, 162, 237
Barker families, 173
Barker family, 307
Barker Home, 252
Barker-Lavender family, 175
Barker-Plemons Home, 236
Barker Road, 163
Barnett, Dr., 285
Barnhill, Bessie Mai Sparkman, 275, 307, 371
Barnhill, Billy, 275
Barnhill, Carl, 223
Barnhill, Cully, 223
Barnhill, Curtis, 48, 223
Barnhill, Dora E. Rainey, 223
Barnhill, Esther, 99, 223
Barnhill, Flossie, 48
Barnhill, Hobert, 223, 307, 359
Barnhill, Jeanne, 94, 223
Barnhill, Laura Bradford, 222–23
Barnhill, L.D., 39, 223, 275, 307, 371
Barnhill, Marie, 93, 223
Barnhill, Neil, 36, 275
Barnhill, Neil "Big Dog," 51
Barnhill, Rainy, 223
Barnhill, Reese, 223
Barnhill, Vachel I., 222
Barnhill, V.I., 223
Barnhill's poolroom, 40
Baseball Team of Burwood, 304
Battle, Thelma, 3, 130
Battle Ground Academy, 147, 184
Baugh, Phillip, 10
Baugh family, 248
Baxter, Martha Ann, 303
Baxter's Artillery, CSA, 326
Beal Kelley, 85
Bear Creek Road, 71, 302
Beard, Boyd Beard, 77
Beard, Doyle, 77
Beard, Elvis, 105
Beard, Glen, 104
Beard, James, 103
Beard, J.B., 93
Beard, Leslie, 96, 99
Beard, Margaret, 95
Beard, Mildred, 77–78

Beard, Odell, 96, 99
Beard, Prudie, 77
Beard, Vernon, 186
Beasley, Albert, 183, 190
Beasley, Alfreda, 123
Beasley, Andrew Craig, 367
Beasley, Andrews Craig, 307
Beasley, Barney, 190
Beasley, Dixie, 82
Beasley, Dwight, 123
Beasley, Earlie, 190
Beasley, Emily McKee, 234–35
Beasley, Emma Cowan, 188, 190
Beasley, Ernest, 190
Beasley, Eveline Hunt, 277
Beasley, Evie Hunt, 278
Beasley, John, 190
Beasley, John J., 234
Beasley, Lou Anna, 82
Beasley, Mrs. N.C., 277
Beasley, N.C., 17, 65
Beasley, Newton Cannon, 278
Beasley, Percy "Perk," 60, 127, 137
Beasley, Riley, 123
Beasley, Rosie Lee, 60
Beasley, SamElla, 277
Beasley, Sara Andrews, 307, 367
Beasley, William, 190
Beasley, William D., 109
Beasley, Willie Mai, 83, 277–78, 368
Beasley, W.M., 217
Beasley, Zachariah W., 277
Beasley Families, 119–20, 122
Beasley-Hunt-Sparkman Home, 276, 278
Beaver Spring, 132, 189
Beers Map, 37, 43, 232
Berry, Amanda, 214
Berry, C.D., 165
Berry, C. Dewees, 210, 212, 214
Berry, C. Dewees, III, 213
Berry, Douglas, 214
Berry, Mary Susan, 214
Berry, Mary Tillman, 213
Berry, Mary Washington Tillman, 212
Berry, Sue, 210
Berry, Will, 214
Berry, William Tyler, 212–13
Bethel Methodist Church, 167, 212–13
Biggers, James, 60
Bill Shor's Store, 42
Bingham, 31

Bizwell, Lucy, 190
Blackburn, Elwin, 214
Blackburn, Kenneth, 91, 214
Blackburn, Montie, 214
Blackburn, Mr. and Mrs. Kenneth, 214
Blackburn, Opal, 90
Black Students, 72
Blair, Betty Jo, 77
Blue Ribbon Day, 97-8
Bond, Thomas B., 9–10
Bond, Thomas H., 9–10
Booker, Elizabeth, 60
Booker-Davis, Janet, 3
Boston community, 27, 28, 33, 289, 298
Boulware, Mrs., 160
Bowden, Nancy Fitzgerald, 259
Bowman, Jane, 75
Bowman, Virginia McDaniel, 201, 203, 210, 214, 240, 243, 249, 258, 260
Boxley, Thomas, 9
Boxley, Thomas S. and D.W., 10
Boyce, Brownie, 92
Boyd, Abner, 148
Boyd, Azile, 90, 92
Boyd, Azille, 83
Boyd, Cora Akin, 219
Boyd, Dr. Willis B., 289
Boyd, Lillian, 90, 92
Boyd, Lou Willie, 83
Boyd, Noble, 59
Boyd, Sophronia, 148
Boyd Ridley Critz home, 164, 166
Boys Basketball Team: 103
Bradley, Robert, 62
Branham and Hughes, 184
Breezy Hill, 270–71
Brenda Harrison, 105, 116
Brice, Maurice, 60
Brick Church, 56
Brickell, Matthias, 180
Brickell, Rachel Noailles, 180
Brickell, Sarah, 180
Briggs, George I., 147
Brittain, William, 289
Brooks, Bessie, 74
Brooks, Bobby, 235
Brooks, Buck, 74
Brooks, James, 74
Brown, Curtis, 139
Brown, Delores, 115
Brown, Leroy, 60
Brown, Myles, 41

Brown, T.C., 101
Brown, Velma, 106
Brown Cannon Farm, 217
Bruce, James, 271
Bruer, Frank, 288, 295–96
Bruer, Vicki, 295
Buchanan, Frances, 147
Buckner, Anderson, 96, 99, 289
Burcham, Aura, 92
Burke, Dot Jennette, 307, 331
Burnett, Ann, 10
Burnett, Col. Joseph, 232
Burnett, Frances, 90, 92
Burnett, J.J., 10
Burnett, John, 61
Burnett, Joseph, Col., 232
Burnett, Major, 8
Burnett, Mary Campbell, 90, 232
Burnett, William W., 133
Burnett, W.W., 10, 232
Burnett Cemetery, 232
Burnett Home, 232
Burns, Alberta, 108
Burns, Christine, 36
Burns, David, 115
Burns, Deborah, 115
Burns, Early, 108
Burns, Elizabeth, 108
Burns, L.E., 108
Burns, Mike, 106
Burns, Ollie, 129–30
Burns, Walter and Sadie, 287
Burwood, name of, 24, 58, 242
Burwood and Thompson Station, 18
Burwood and Thompson Station Company of Men, 18, 295
Burwood Boys Baseball team, 305
Burwood Boys Basketball, 103–4
Burwood Community, 1, 2, 8, 15–16, 18, 37, 119, 226, 290
Burwood Community Center, 2
Burwood Demonstration Club, 148
Burwood Girls Basketball, 101–2
Burwood High School, 17, 89
Burwood Methodist Church, 7, 15, 148, 152
Burwood Presbyterian Church, 24, 91
Burwood Ride-A-Thon, 289–90, 294
Burwood's Baseball Team, 304

Burwood School, 28, 46, 72, 89–100, 102, 104–6, 148, 153, 176, 289, 342
Burwood School Blue Ribbon Day Event, 97–98
Burwood United Methodist Church, 2, 57–58, 274
Businesses, 37–38, 40, 42, 44, 46
Butler, Joe, 81
Byers, W.W., 79
Byrd, Arthur, 352
Byrd, Clay, 77, 307, 317, 348
Byrd, Ethel, 90
Byrd, Eva, 86, 90
Byrd, Kate, 262
Byrd, Leta Hughes, 307
Byrd, Lois, 94
Byrd, Louise, 3, 347, 372
Byrd, Louise Crane, 307, 348
Byrd, Lucille, 90
Byrd, Robert, 40, 91
Byrd, Thomas, 99, 307
Byrd, Thomas Henry, 133
Byrd, Thomas J., 357
Byrd, Thomas J., Jr., 307
Byrd, Tom, 27, 263
Byrd, Tommy and Leta Hughes, 317
Byrd-Venable-Huff home, 263-4

C
Cain, Eva Myers, 114
Cain Polk Home, 261–62
Caldwell, Agnes, 257
Caldwell, Aline, 307, 313
Caldwell, Irene, 313
Caldwell, Robert, 94
Calhoun, Rev. Frank A., 178
Cameron, Jessie Grigsby Huff, 307, 349
Cameron, Jim, 75
Campbell, Alberta, 122
Campbell, Bettie, 307, 364
Campbell, Charles, 307, 364
Campbell, Duncan, 274
Campbell, Ezekial, 364
Campbell, Ezekiel, 307
Campbell, James, 11
Campbell, Johnnie G., 109
Campbell, John R., 202
Campbell, Judge David, 212
Campbell, Katie, 109
Campbell, Lula E., 307, 364
Campbell, Mary Louise, 95
Campbell, Rebecca, 202
Campbell, Robert A., 109

Campbell, Will, 121, 128
Campbell Station, 248
Camp Hood, 140
Camp Peary, Virginia, 194
Candler, Jerry, 105
Cannon, Brown, 47, 51, 96, 216–17, 307, 357
Cannon, Ed, 3
Cannon, Edgar Brown, 216
Cannon, James H., 216
Cannon, Janie Mai, 114
Cannon, Jim, 9, 129, 170, 181, 184, 216
Cannon, Leila, 92
Cannon, Mary, 216
Cannon, Mary Lou, 99
Cannon, Newton, 181
Cannon, Newton, Gov., 216
Cannon, Sam, 74
Cannon, Samuel Perkins, 133, 216
Cannon, Sara, 216
Cannon, Susan Agatha Perkins, 215
Cannon, William Perkins, 215–16
Cannon, Wilmoth Pointer, 216
Cannon, W.P., 9, 73
Cannon Brothers meat packers, 168
Cannon Farm, 19, 215
Cannon Home, 215–16
Cannonsburg, 181
Capley, Ike, 361
Capley, Ike and J.T., 307, 361
Capley, J.T., 361
Capshaw, Carolyn (Johnson), 307
Capshaw, Edward Leon, 143
Capshaw, Hasting, 95
Capshaw, John, 322
Capshaw family, 95, 307, 319
Capshaw, R.B., 95
Carl, Clara, 74
Carl, O.B., 74, 90
Carlton, Gail, 106
Carothers, Annie Lee, 108
Carothers, Annie Pearl, 108
Carothers, Cam Alexine, 108
Carothers, Docia, 108
Carothers, Dorothy, 108
Carothers, Henry, 61
Carothers, Howard, 108
Carothers, John H., 63
Carothers, Linda, 102
Carothers, Sadie, 108

Carothers, William, 108
Carter, Benjamin, 6, 132, 240, 274
Carter, Daniel, 132
Carter, Dianne, 3
Carter, Eules, 108
Carter, Fred, 63
Carter's Creek, 28, 132
Carter's Creek Pike, 2, 8–9, 37, 41, 72–73, 79, 183, 189, 215, 219, 229–30, 267, 270
Carter's Creek Post Office, 232
Cash, Betsy Mai Johnson, 307
Cayce, Dr. Newman, 286
Cayce, John M., 133, 287
Cayce, John Wm., 287
Cayce, Matthew, 287
Cayce, Shadrack, 248
Cayce, Virginia, 287
Cayce, William, 10, 284, 287
Cayce, William and Shadrack, 248
Cayce, Wm., 285
Cayce Resort Hotel, 287
Cayce Springs, 8, 24, 129, 151, 243, 248, 284–87
Cayce Springs blacksmith, 118
Cayce Springs Resort, 286
Chadwell, Wayne, 71
Chairs, J.W., 10
Chandler, Bessie Leola, 316
Chaney, David S., 10, 133
Chaney, Ezekiel, 281
Chaney, William T., 133
Chapell, Pate, 83
Chappell, Vernetta, 83
Chapman & Morris, 10
Cheerleaders, 102–3
Cherry, Bill, 215
Chi Sigma Phi, 147
Church, A.B., 59, 143, 218
Church, Abe, 59, 81, 218
Church, Abraham, 65
Church, Abram Baker, 217
Church, Abram George, 217
Church, Elizabeth, 91
Church, Elmer, 59, 90
Church, George Abram, 217
Church, Mary, 218
Church, Odell, 81, 217
Church, Reba, 218
Church, Sam, 162
Church, Savantha, 217
Church, Willie, 218
Church, Willie Mai, 250

Church of Christ, 15, 68, 119, 163, 185
Civil War, 18, 34, 248
Clark, Bob, 23, 43, 307, 329
Clark, Ethel, 30, 59, 81–83, 92
Clark, Ewell, 59, 82, 271
Clark, George Milton "Mutt," 139
Clark, Ida May Akin, 307, 329
Clark, Lena Aline, 150
Clark, Milton, 43, 140–41
Clark, Mutt, 140
Clark, Ora, 329
Clark, Robbie, 30, 59, 82–83, 92
Clark, Sam M., 307, 329
Claud, John W., 11
Claude Lavender, 174–75
Claude Southall, 96, 177, 305
Clellon Ragsdale, 315, 318
Cliff Sparkman, 289
Clyde, 334, 345
Clyde Caldwell, 94
Coleman, India, 170
Col. Hardy Murfree cemetery, 215
Col. Hardy Murfree Cemetery, 182
Collins, Elizabeth Thweatt, 204
Collins, Ernest, 205
Collins, George, 205, 308
Collins, Harry, 204-5
Collins, John, 204
Collins, John and Elizabeth, 205
Collins, Leroy, 205
Colored Methodist Episcopal Church, 63
Colquit, John R., 10
Community Club, 17
Confederate Army, 133
Confederate Memorial Literary Society, 227
Confederate Veteran, 226–27
Cooke, Bessie, 75
Cooke, Lemuel, 75
Cooper, Freeman, 114
Cooper's Cavalry CSA, 224
Core, J.G., 10
Cornelia Ann Shaw Lavender, 171, 175
Cottage Home, 232
Cotton, Howard Hatcher, 143
Cotton, William, 10
Cowsert, B.F., 10
Cox, Dr., 26
Cox, Terry, 105
Craft, Donnie Joe, 88

Crafton, Joe, 88
Crafton, Mary Gray, 248
Crafton, Patty, 102-3
Crafton, Ralph, 88
Crafton, Ricky, 105
Craig, Nancy Barker, 3
Crane, Louise, 348
Crawford, J.W., 11
Creath, Mable, 165
Critz, Boyd Ridley, 166, 212
Critz, Frances, 212
Critz, Irene, 212
Critz, Jacob, 10
Critz, John, 10, 165
Critz, John M., 255
Critz, Joseph, Jr., 254
Critz, Joseph, Sr., 254
Critz, Julia Ridley, 165, 167
Critz, Juliet, 212
Critz, Juliette, 165
Critz, Lillie Mai, 165
Critz, Ruth, 212
Critz, Sallie Ridley, 165
Critz, Thomas L., 167
Critz, Thomas L. and Juliet, family, 166
Critz, Tom, 165, 170, 250, 310
Critz, Zachariah, 10
Critz family, 212–13, 248
Critz home, 167
Critz House, 254
Critz, Julia Ridley, 165, 167
Critz-Lazenby home, 254
Critz-Lazenby Home, 254
Critz Place, the, 212
Cross, Christopher C., 114
Crowson, Prentiss, 307, 328–29
Crump, E.E., 11
Crump, Martha, 11
Crump, Robert "Deedie," 109
Crump, William J., 109
Crutcher, Debbie, 101
Crutcher, Linda, 102–3
Cub Johnson, 86
Cumberland Presbyterian Church, 39
Cunningham, Sumner Archibald, 227
Cunnington, Hugh, 179
Curry, Dorothy, 106, 115
Curry, John, 105, 115
Curry, Nannie, 115
Curtis, Jessie, 88
Curtis, Shirley, 88
Custer, Jack, 191
Cyclone, 15, 166, 172, 212, 213

Cyrus, Billy Ray, 111

D
Dalton, Bob, Deputy Sheriff, 299
Daniels, Mrs. E.W., 161
Darby, Elva Mayo, 180
Darden, Lish, 60
David Crutcher, 104
Davidson County, 6, 273
Davis, Dee Dee, 115
Davis, Ellis, 78
Davis, Ernest, 51
Davis, James, 144
Davis, Laura, 190
Davis, L.T., 115
Davis, Mattie Lou, 77
Davis, Mrs. Burton, 190
Davis, Mrs. Pete, 295
Davis, Randal, 51
Davis, Ricky, 103
Davis, Wanda, 115
Davis, Wayne, 51
Dedman, Louise Shannon, 19, 243
Dee, Edward, 231
DeGraffenreid, L.D., 11
Dennis Martin, 143–44
Deputy Sheriff Bob Dalton, 299
Dickinson, Fanny M., 182
Disciples of Christians, 55
Dodd, Adron, 221, 230
Dodd, Bill, 96, 220
Dodd, Billy, 30, 31, 33, 41, 99, 305, 307, 329, 376
Dodd, Billy Zan, 99, 304, 305
Dodd, Bobby, 33, 36, 307, 329
Dodd, Brown, 231
Dodd, C.A., Jr., 231
Dodd, Cal, 96, 99, 141–42, 161
Dodd, Calvin, 23, 35, 65, 140–41, 220
Dodd, Calvin Washington, 35, 220
Dodd, Carl, 30–31, 59, 65, 81, 83, 85, 221, 269
Dodd, Carl S., 30
Dodd, Carl Shannon, 35
Dodd, Clarence Adron, 231
Dodd, C.W., 221
Dodd, Edward D., 95, 305
Dodd, Emily, 220
Dodd, Esther, 33, 41, 88, 324, 329, 376
Dodd, Esther Barnhill, 307
Dodd, Evelyn, 93, 95
Dodd, George, 95
Dodd, Gertrude, 311
Dodd, Hugh, 99, 231, 235
Dodd, Ida Beasley, 35, 220–21
Dodd, Jane, 220
Dodd, J.C., 231, 289
Dodd, Jenny, 220
Dodd, Jessica, 36
Dodd, John Alexander "Zan," 135
Dodd, Junior, 94
Dodd, Louise, 219–20
Dodd, Louise Shaw, 220–21
Dodd, Luther, 95
Dodd, Otis, 95, 231
Dodd, Rebecca, 220
Dodd, Rose Xena, 231
Dodd, Ruby, 31, 269
Dodd, Ruby Ava Riggin, 26
Dodd, Ruby Riggin, 3, 7, 14, 21, 25, 29, 30, 31, 70, 221, 225, 249, 261, 311, 376
Dodd, Ruth, 231
Dodd, Ruth Sparkman, 221
Dodd, Ruth Zane, 93, 231
Dodd, Sam Allen, 3, 31, 33, 36, 51, 88
Dodd, Samuel, 132
Dodd, Sue, 36
Dodd, Vance, 35
Dodd, Zan, 83, 85, 140, 219–21
Dodd family, 17, 26, 35, 65, 85, 94, 134–35, 140, 289, 307
Dodd Family Tidbits, 35
Dodd Home, 269
Dodd-Tomlinson House, 275
Dodge pickup truck, 155
Dodson, Elizabeth Fitzgerald, 259
Dodson, Ellen, 307
Dodson, Jana, 60
Dodson, Joe, 128
Dodson, Joshua, 60
Dodson, Polly Fitzgerald, 259
Dodson, Rebecca Lucretia, 237
Dodson family, 11, 260
Dortch, O.L., 147
Dortch Stoveworks, 127, 147
Dotson, Alice, 110
Dotson, Bird, 133
Dotson, Mary Alice, 110
Dotson, Mattie Sallie, 108
Dotson, Presley, 133
Dotson, Sarah, 108
Dotson, Willie Kinnard, 114
Douglass Methodist Church, 213
Drake, G.M., 11
Drake, James, 286
Drake, Lynn, 101
Drake, Zachariah M., 133
Drake House, 248
Drake-Martin cemetery, 248
Drumright, Grace, 90
Drury Lamb-John W. Lawrence home, 206
Duck River Ridge, 2, 14, 19, 22, 219, 241
Duff, Janice Inman, 3, 206
Duncan, Herman, 238–39
Duncan, Jon, 295
Duncan, Mrs. Herman, 294
Duncan, Mrs. H.T., 295
Duncan, Polly Barker (Pauline), 65, 87, 200, 238–39, 292, 295, 307, 349
Dunn, Charles, 288
Dunn, Charles F., 295

E
Eastview, 20–21, 240, 242, 244
Edgmon, Ethel, 213
Edwards, Teresa, 105
Eggleston, J.C., 301
Eleventh Tennessee Cavalry, 248
Elizabeth Sparkman, 96, 303
Elliot, Dorothy, 340
Elliott, Dorothy Jones, 307, 333
Ellis, Davis, 77
Elmore, Bernard, 59
Elmore, Chappell, 82
Elmore, J.D., 91
Elmore, Jennie Lee, 59, 83
Elmore, Jessie, 83
Elmore, John Ella, 82
Elmore, Johnnie, 83
Elmore, Johnnie Lee, 82
Elmore, Johnny, 59
Elmore, Marie, 83
Elmore, Prentice, 59, 82
Elmore, Vallie, 82
Elmore, Willie Beth, 83
Emanuel Pentecostal Church, 68
England, Linda, 101
England, Martha, 104
Evans, Daniel, 259
Evans, Rhoda Griffith, 259
Evans, Susanna, 259
Evergreen, 1, 14, 21, 112–14, 125
Evergreen community, 8
Evergreen Primitive Baptist Church, 60, 119

Evergreen Road, 26, 60, 65, 72, 111, 119, 121–23, 226, 247, 249
Evergreen School, 34, 72, 111–12, 114, 116
Ewell Farm in Spring Hill, 248

F
Fairview (home), 201–3
Falk, Gerald, 106
Farmer, Mike, 106
Farnsworth (S.E.) and Company, 194
Faw & Crockett, 301
Federal soldiers, 248, 346
Fentress, Lera Mai, 307, 314
Fentress, Melvin, 307, 315
Ferguson, Fay, 288
Ferguson, Faye, 88, 292, 296
Ferguson, William, 274
Fewell, Gary, 69, 103, 308, 372
Fiesta's Winning Riders, 296
Fitzgerald, Bessie, 282
Fitzgerald, Bird, 9, 260
Fitzgerald, Clyde, 292, 308, 345
Fitzgerald, Denae, 60
Fitzgerald, Denise, 60
Fitzgerald, Dennis, 60
Fitzgerald, Fannie Mae, 44
Fitzgerald, Gertrude, 308, 345
Fitzgerald, James, 60, 147
Fitzgerald, Jasmine, 60
Fitzgerald, Joe, 37
Fitzgerald, John, 259–60
Fitzgerald, John and Bird, 259
Fitzgerald, John and Ellender, 259
Fitzgerald, Joseph, 44
Fitzgerald, Julia, 260
Fitzgerald, Mary E. Helms, 109
Fitzgerald, Trey, 60
Fitzgerald Family Cemetery, 260
Fleming, Betty, 115
Fleming, Elizabeth, 202
Fleming, Hattie, 109
Fleming, Jackie, 115
Fleming, John W., 109
Fleming, Ken, 112–13
Fleming, Robert, 116
Fleming, William and Mixey Thompson, 202
Flowers, Elmie, 92
Fly, Betty Sue, 104
Fly, Henry, 60
Fly, James, 60

Forest Hill, 1, 8, 10, 12, 14, 72–74, 76, 78, 184, 189, 204
Forest Hill community, 1, 8
Forest Hill Farm, 209, 215
Forest Hill Female Academy, 72–73
Forest Hill Plantation, 132
Forest Hill School, 72–78
Forest Hill Spring House, 191
Forrest, General Nathan Bedford, 18, 248
Fort Bragg, 140
Fort Lewis, 140
Fort Oglethorpe, 185
Forty-fourth Tennessee Infantry Regiment, CSA, 227
Fountain Creek (Maury Co.), 248
Fourth Civil District, 8, 14–15
Fox, Charley, 185
Fox, Judy, 100
Franklin Elementary School, 148, 153
Franklin High School, 33, 97, 125, 140, 144, 148, 162, 167, 184, 191, 193
Franklin Post Office, 171
Franklin Supply Company, 177
Fraser, Marcia, 3
Fry, Annie Lee, 86, 90
Fry, Deamie, 85
Fry, John Wesley, 308–10, 346
Fry, Margaret, 308, 346
Fry, Ola, 48
Fry, Thomas, 48, 91
Fuller, Bud, 65
Fulton Johnson, 136, 179

G
Gant, Ann, 11
Garland, Bobby, 308, 325
Garland, Cornelia Ann, 308, 325
Garland, Daniel, 308, 325
Garland, Dewey, 56, 281–82, 308, 325
Garland, Dewey and Melissa, 281
Garland, James, 308, 325
Garland, Kathleen Johnson, 308, 325
Garland, Lois, 308, 325
Garland, Melissa, 3, 281–82
Garland, Reda Mai, 308, 325
Garland, Zenith, 308, 325
Garner, Robert "Dit," 22
Gatlin, Missie Sparkman, 228

Gatlin, Mrs. Willis, 228
Geasley, Ed, 77
Geasley, Eva, 85
Geasley, Fred, 308, 335
Geasley, Heddy, 88
Geasley, John Mack, 137
Geasley, Kathleen, 308, 343
Geasley, Lena Andrews, 308, 334-5, 339, 343
Geasley, Louise, 308, 335
Geasley, Mildred, 308
Geasley, Milton, 77–78
Geasley, Miss Clydie, 88
Geasley, Odelene, 77
Geasley, Prince, 85
Geasley, Ross, 85
Geasley, Vicky, 106
Geasley, Wilma, 308
Gentry, Bobby, 304
Gentry, Jimmie, 114
Gibbs, Dr. A., 16
Gibbs, Millie, 334
Gibson, Steven, 116
Gibson, Stevie, 124
Gillespie, Kaye, 102–3
Gillespie, Kim, 103
Gillespie, Randy, 104
Gillespie, S.O., 127
Givens, Thomas, 62
Goad, William, Constable, 299
Goetze, Anne, 57
Gooch, Mary Jane, 303
Good, Christine, 90
Gray, Alexander, 73
Gray, Alexander N., 133
Gray, Alexander W., 308, 321
Gray, Bill, 308, 355
Gray, Cora, 308
Gray, Ethel, 75
Gray, James W., 308, 321
Gray, Jewell (Burnett), 355
Gray, Jewell Burnett, 308
Gray, John B., 82, 321
Gray, John Black, 308, 321
Gray, Joseph A., 308, 321
Gray, Joseph A. and Loulie Russell, 321
Gray, Judy, 311
Gray, Lena, 86, 308
Gray, Loulie Russell, 308, 321
Gray, Mabel, 75, 90
Gray, Pat, 310
Gray, Vivian, 77–78, 309
Gray, Will, 308
Gray, Willie, 308, 355
Gray, Zula, 355

Gray Drug Company, 161
Gray Lane, 321
Gray's Store, 31
Green, Oscar, 223
Green, Robert, 205
Greer, William, 311
Greer Shaw, O, 90
Griggs, Richard, 100, 105
Grigsby, Annie Lou Barker, 308, 349
Grigsby, Glen, 308, 372
Grigsby, Jack, 308, 350
Grigsby, Jack and Judy, 244
Grigsby, Judy, 47, 244, 308
Grigsby, L.B., 239
Grigsby, Leonard, 45, 243, 295–96, 308, 372
Grigsby, Leonard B., 21, 240, 244
Grigsby, Mr. and Mrs. Leonard, 243
Grigsby, Mrs. L.B., 295
Grigsby, Ollie, 308, 372
Grigsby family members, 65, 239, 292, 295, 308
Grissom, Anita Harris, 3, 308
Grundy, Felix, 182
Guffee, Harry, Dr., 234
Guinn, Otis, 109
Gunnells, Eunice, 178

H
Hackett, George, 148
Haley, Clarence, 95
Haley, Claudine, 308, 332
Haley, Corinne, 93
Haley, Dallas Johnson, 308, 332
Haley, Dorris, 308, 332
Haley, June, 308, 332
Haley, Ronnie, 308, 332
Haley, Sadie, 96
Hamby, Bennie, 77–78
Hamilton, James H., 142
Hardison, Leona, 83
Hardison, Rose, 75
Hardison, Wayne, 291–92
Hargrove, Benny, 139
Hargrove, Bertha, 86, 308, 319
Hargrove, Bob, 103
Hargrove, Cora Gray, 308
Hargrove, D.P., 308, 315
Hargrove, Erby D., 86
Hargrove, Florence Polk, 308, 315
Hargrove, Grover, 71
Hargrove, Mark, 103

Hargrove, Nellie, 104
Hargrove, O.B., 86
Hargrove, Odie, 136
Harmon, Birdie, 82
Harmon, Doug and Herschel, 283
Harold Johnson Home, 256
Harper, Polly, 106
Harpeth Valley Baseball League, 178
Harris, Anita, 101, 308, 342
Harris, Bob, 308, 361
Harris, Bob and Lou Anna Gordon, 361
Harris, Bryant, 308, 345
Harris, Charlie, 308, 362
Harris, Effie Lee, 361
Harris, Fred, 308, 342
Harris, Henry, 308, 361–62
Harris, Jon, 3
Harris, LouAnna Gordon, 308
Harris, Myrtle, 308, 345
Harris, Rebecca Southall, 251, 308, 342
Harris, Viola, 361
Harrison, Brenda, 105
Harrison, Charlene, 105, 116
Harrison, Charles, 116
Harrison, Eddie, 116
Harrison, Eddie Lee, 106
Harrison, Fay, 102
Harrison, John, 116
Harrison, Faye, 116
Hartley, Kaye, 106
Hasselbring, Jeri McLeland, 255
Hassell, Anna A. Polk, 338
Hassell, Annie A. Polk, 308
Hassell, Annie Polk, 337
Hassell, Autry, 308, 336–37
Hassell, Cal, 85
Hassell, Catherine Coats, 308, 338
Hassell, Elisha M., 133
Hassell, Georgie Rainey, 308, 336
Hassell, James A., 133
Hassell, James and Fannie, 200
Hassell, James W., 308, 365
Hassell, Jimmy, 336
Hassell, John T., 308, 337–39
Hassell, Lige, 157
Hassell, Mary Jones, 34
Hassell, Paul, 86
Hassell, Snow, 307
Hassell, W.J., 308, 338

Hassell family members, 308, 337–38
Hatcher, Howard, 143
Hatcher, Mrs., 292
Hawk, Charles/Charley, 39, 297–99, 301–2
Hawk, Fred, 134, 298, 300
Hawk, Fred and Charley, 39–40, 297–303, 308
Hawk, Jerry, 303
Hawk, Mary Jane Beasley, 303
Hawk, Sam, 300, 303
Hawk Brothers, 297–98, 300–303
Hawkins, Callie Mai, 29
Hawkins, John, 158
Hawkins, Nannie Ashworth, 158, 225
Hawley, Audrey Merl, 208
Hayes, Jim, 308
Hayes, Jim and Judy Grigsby, 349
Hayes, Judy, 3, 140
Hayes, Judy Grigsby, 80, 308, 350
Haynes, Christine, 136
Haynes, Lucille, 60
Headden, Bitsy and Henry, 269
Helm, Col., 243
Helm, Council, 63
Helm, Fielding, 11, 267
Helm, John Wesley, 110
Henderson, 11, 79, 240
Helms, Annie F., 109
Helms, Hattie, 109
Helms, Robert A., 109
Helms, Tommie Jean, 110
Henderson & Henderson, 301
Henderson Helm, 79, 240
Henry, Billy, 162
Henry P. Sparkman, 95
Henry Sparkman, 83
Herbert, 309, 339, 352
Hicks, Rev. Lawrence, 263–64
Hicks, Mattie Lee, 92
Hightower, R.R., 11
Hill, Rachel, 293
Hill, Steve, 293
Hilliard, Mary M., 182
Hillsboro, 27, 115, 190, 304
Hillsboro Hounds Dinner, 361
Hilltop Manor, 258, 260
Hobbs, Alice L. Rainey, 109
Holman's Tennessee Cavalry Battalion CSA, 256
Holt, Billy, 65

Holt, Bud, 85
Holt, Charles, 103
Holt, Clint, 71
Holt, Earnest, 85
Holt, Henry, 106
Holt, Linton, 99
Holt, Virginia, 101
Homestead Manor, 213
Hood, Gerald, 304
Hood's Army, 248
Hop Plemons House, 236
Howard, Ed, 147
Howard, Walter, 138, 307
Howard McLemore, 105, 117
Howell, Dillard, 71
Huckabee, Pauline, 91
Hudson, Julia Otey, 114
Huff, Arthur, 83
Huff, Aught, 308, 340
Huff, Betty, 100, 295, 308
Huff, Billy T., 39, 41
Huff, Birdie (Fry), 85
Huff, Bobby, 95
Huff, Buddy, 27, 76
Huff, Callie, 33–34, 295–96
Huff, Charlie, 35, 46, 226, back cover
Huff, Darnell, 96
Huff, Dorothy, 292
Huff, Dorothy Jean, 93
Huff, Dorris, 27
Huff, Dorris and Buddy, 27
Huff, Earl, 86
Huff, Era, 81
Huff, Eugene, 35
Huff, Eva, 83
Huff, Farris, 81, 90, 92, 261, 264, 288, 292, 295–96
Huff, Glen, 46, 99, 304
Huff, Glen, Robert, Jr., Milton "Mutt," and Ken, 257
Huff, Gordon, 86
Huff, Grace, 86
Huff, Hattie Stovall, 257
Huff, Ida, 86
Huff, Inez, 91
Huff, James, 41, 43, 81, 90, 296, 308, 366, 372
Huff, Jessie, 100, 308, 366
Huff, Jessie Grigsby, 43, 93
Huff, Jimmy, 288
Huff, John Ella, 59, 82
Huff, Ken, 24, 45–46, 304, 308, 333, 360, back cover
Huff, Kenneth, 95, 143, 305
Huff, Kennette, 102

Huff, Lou, 36, 45–46, 360
Huff, Lou McClain, 308
Huff, Marie, 3, 100
Huff, Martha Harris, 308, 340
Huff, Mrs. James, 17, 295
Huff, Mrs. Tom, 192
Huff, Nannie, 23, 72, 231
Huff, Nannie Jennette, 137
Huff, Nannie Myrt Jennette, 360
Huff, Park, 81–83
Huff, Polly, 280
Huff, Rennie, 308, 344
Huff, R.G., 39
Huff, R.G., Sr., 256, 304
Huff, Rob, 33
Huff, Robert, 23, 45, 360
Huff, Robert, Jr., 230, 304, 360
Huff, Robert and Hattie, 257
Huff, Robert G., 257
Huff, Robert G., Jr., 231, 308
Huff, Robert G., Sr., 308
Huff, Robert H., Sr., 304
Huff, Robert Park, 308, 342
Huff, Rose Marie, 100
Huff, Sam, 308, 340
Huff, Samuel H., 133
Huff, Tom, 34, 192
Huff, Verda, 81
Huff, William, 90
Huff, Alexine, 34
Huff, Louise, 35
Huff's Store, 2, 22, 37-8, 40
Hughes, A.C. family, 214
Hughes, Barbara, 355
Hugh Prince, 94
Hull, Cordell, 152
Hull, Frances Marion, 149
Hull, Margaret, 149
Hull, Mary Mangrum, 149
Hull, Roland, Rev., 152
Hunt, Ella, 276
Hunt, Eveline, 276
Hunt, J.B., 276
Hunter, Jane, 188
Hunter, Milton, 184, 187–88, 191
Hutcherson, Charlie, 82
Hutcherson, Cliff, 82
Hutcherson, Louise, 91

I
Ida Hay Johnson Home, 266
Indian Boundary Line, 19, 240
Indian Territory, 19
Ingram, Dianne, 102
Inman, Avie, 319
Inman, John Wesley, 308–9, 335

Inman, Josephine Lawrence, 206–7
Inman, Martha Sue, 99
Inman, Mary, 99
Inman, Robert, 207–8
Inman, Wesley, 85, 87
Inman, Wesley Samuel, 84, 308, 320

J
Jackson, Rebecca Dodd, 3
Jack Watson Place, 165
Jacobs, H., 234
Jacobs, Joseph R., 11, 234
Jacobs, Louise, 234
Jacobs-Beasley-Satterfield Cemetery, 234
Jacobs-Satterfield-Prince-Stanley-Brooks, 234
Jacob Thomas Martin, 248
James Bruce Akin, 133, 145, 327
James Bruce Jones, 351
James Drake Pope, 15, 21, 243
James Gang, 224
Jamison, Sarah, 108
J.C. Dodd, 94
Jefferson, Angela McCullough, 3
Jefferson, Mrs. Alva, 77
Jefferson McKennon, 137
Jenkins, John Thomas, 108
Jennette, Della, 68
Jennette, Ben, 308, 359
Jennette, Claudie, 308, 331
Jennette, Dan, 88
Jennette, Doris, 308, 359
Jennette, Ernie, 76
Jennette, Jesse, 135, 308, 359
Jennette, Joseph, 308, 373
Jennette, Lee, 103
Jennette, Louella, 85, 308, 314
Jennette, Nannie Myrt (Huff), 308
Jennette, Park, 85
Jennette, Percy, 134, 162, 308, 359
Jennette, Porter, 85, 308, 359
Jennette, Richard, 308
Jennette, Richard H., 343
Jennette, Sarah Polk, 308, 373
Jennette, Tina, 106
Jennette, Tommy, 138
Jennette, Turner, 134, 308, 337, 359
Jennette family, 68
Jessie Grigsby Huff, 93
Jessie Sparkman, 92
Jim Ball Home, 35

Joe Pope Road, 44
John Morrow Place, 23
John Pope, John, 58
John Shaw Store, 39
Johnson, Abram, 138–39, 332, 335, 359
Johnson, Ada, 74, 92, 266
Johnson, Alfred, 116
Johnson, Alice, 266
Johnson, Allen Wayne, 308, 375
Johnson, Anna, 262
Johnson, Annie Lela Jones, 309, 331, 340
Johnson, Arthur Byrd, 308, 352
Johnson, Barbara, 308, 354
Johnson, Barbara (Barker), 308
Johnson, Barkley, 91, 308, 325
Johnson, Barnett, 86, 308, 325
Johnson, Bernice, 91, 308, 323, 325
Johnson, Bessie Leola, 367
Johnson, Bessie Leola Chandler, 308, 313, 316
Johnson, Betsy Main, 347
Johnson, Betty Ann, 77–78
Johnson, Bob, 262
Johnson, Brenda, 308, 354
Johnson, Byrd, 308, 319, 354
Johnson, Callie Cathryn, 353
Johnson, Callie Rader, 231
Johnson, Calvin, 63
Johnson, Carl, 308, 314, 372
Johnson, Carolyn (Capshaw), 319
Johnson, Carolyn Capshaw, 319
Johnson, Cathryn, 310
Johnson, Charles Green, 308, 320
Johnson, Charlotte, 91
Johnson, Christine, 77
Johnson, Cindy, 229
Johnson, Claude, 30, 134–35, 173, 308, 311, 330
Johnson, Claude and Lela Jones, 330
Johnson, Clifton, 56
Johnson, Coach Howard, 101–4
Johnson, Cola Jennette, 308, 343
Johnson, Columbus, 308, 315
Johnson, Connie, 101
Johnson, Cub, 86, 308, 325
Johnson, Dallas, 87, 308, 331–32
Johnson, Dean, 309, 367
Johnson, Debra, 102
Johnson, Dianne, 308, 372
Johnson, Doss, 161

Johnson, Doug, 29
Johnson, Douglas, 228–29
Johnson, Elcain, 25, 322
Johnson, Elisha, 84, 297, 299
Johnson, Elizabeth Marlin, 231
Johnson, Elsie, 262
Johnson, Elton, 308, 352
Johnson, Emery Eugene, 143
Johnson, Emery James, 308, 312, 316–17
Johnson, Emily, 110
Johnson, Emma, 74, 92, 266
Johnson, Emmalee, 86, 308, 316
Johnson, Chris, 229
Johnson, Estella, 261
Johnson, Estelle F., 25
Johnson, Eugene, 231, 312
Johnson, Eva, 86, 266, 308, 316
Johnson, Faye, 104
Johnson, Floyd, 308, 314
Johnson, Frank, 266
Johnson, Fulton, 136, 179
Johnson, Gene, 86, 261, 304
Johnson, George, 308, 320
Johnson, Gerald "Mama," 304
Johnson, Gertie, 86, 309, 314
Johnson, Harold, 88, 256–57, 309, 317
Johnson, Hattie, 310
Johnson, Hayward, 309, 325
Johnson, Haywood, 295
Johnson, Hazel, 309, 347, 372
Johnson, Herbert, 309, 352
Johnson, Hiram, 230–31, 309, 322, 347, 353
Johnson, Howard, 106
Johnson, Ida Hay, 265–66
Johnson, Ida Mai, 309
Johnson, Ila, 86
Johnson, James, 139, 352
Johnson, James Edward, 137, 309, 333
Johnson, Jay Howard, 103
Johnson, J.C., 79
Johnson, Jean, 309, 352
Johnson, Jefferson, 133
Johnson, Jennie Ragsdale, 309, 313, 314–15, 317
Johnson, J. Howard, 106
Johnson, Jimmy, 288, 296
Johnson, Joe, 112, 309, 372
Johnson, Joe, Jr., 112
Johnson, Joe Carl, 309, 313, 315
Johnson, John, 309, 354
Johnson, John and Mahalia Ragsdale, 322

Johnson, John Ben, 309, 313–14
Johnson, John M., 309
Johnson, Johnnie Ben, 343
Johnson, Johnny, 323
Johnson, Johnny Fulton, 309
Johnson, John Oakley, 262, 309, 320
Johnson, John W., 287
Johnson, Judy, 295, 352
Johnson, Judy Sweeney, 309, 311
Johnson, Kate Holt, 309, 320
Johnson, Kathleen, 91, 308, 325
Johnson, Kathryn, 309, 323
Johnson, Kathy, 106
Johnson, Ken, 309, 354
Johnson, Lela Snow Jones, 30, 59, 309, 330, 333, 335, 340
Johnson, Lemuel, 309, 313–14, 315, 317, 333, 346
Johnson, Lemuel and Jennie Ragsdale, 314
Johnson, Lewis, 309, 347, 370
Johnson, Lewis L., 133
Johnson, Linda, 352, 354
Johnson, Linda (Allums), 309
Johnson, Lionel, 39–40, 297–302
Johnson, Lodus Neil, 309, 372
Johnson, Lorene, 323
Johnson, Lorne, 309
Johnson, Lucille, 51, 309, 325, 352
Johnson, Lula, 85
Johnson, Mae (Frost), 309, 354
Johnson, Mahalia Ragsdale, 309
Johnson, Malachi, 56, 309, 325
Johnson, Malachi, Jr., 309, 325
Johnson, Malachi, Sr., 323, 325
Johnson, Mallie Lena, 309, 312, 347
Johnson, Margaret, 307, 309
Johnson, Martha, 256, 309, 317
Johnson, Martha Robinson, 309, 347
Johnson, Martha Woodward, 309
Johnson, Matilda Elizabeth Marlin, 309, 316
Johnson, Mike, 106, 309, 317
Johnson, Mike, Monica, Raymond, and Jonathan, 256
Johnson, Mildred, 309, 323
Johnson, Millie Ann Polk, 325
Johnson, Millie Polk, 262, 323, 357
Johnson, Milton, 323

Johnson, Milton "Buster," 309, 319
Johnson, Monica, 105
Johnson, Mrs. Carl, 347
Johnson, Mrs. Tom, 295
Johnson, Nancy, 100
Johnson, Nannie Marian Inman, 309, 316, 319
Johnson, Neil, 309, 342, 352
Johnson, Oakley, 86, 309, 325
Johnson, Ollie Hassell, 309, 315
Johnson, Opal, 310, 332, 352
Johnson, Opal (Primm), 309
Johnson, Ophelia, 231, 322
Johnson, Ophelia Sophronia, 309, 319
Johnson, Pat, 228
Johnson, Pat Jones, 229
Johnson, Patsy, 29
Johnson, Paul, 74
Johnson, Peewee, 309, 354
Johnson, Rhoda Merritt, 309, 346
Johnson, Rhonda, 354
Johnson, Ricky, 103
Johnson, Robert, 309, 319, 322
Johnson, Robert and Ophelia, family, 322
Johnson, Rollie, 313–14, 352
Johnson, Rollie and Rosie, 352
Johnson, Rollie and Rosie Lee, 352
Johnson, Rollie Gordon, 309, 318
Johnson, Ronald, 104
Johnson, Ronnie, 69
Johnson, Rosie, 352
Johnson, Rosie Lee, 309
Johnson, R.S., 110
Johnson, Ruth, 266
Johnson, Sallie Holt, 309
Johnson, Sally Holt, 320
Johnson, Sam, 265–66
Johnson, Seth, 309, 315
Johnson, Susan, 84
Johnson, Susan Byrd, 309, 320, 323
Johnson, Theresa, 229
Johnson, Tommie, 173
Johnson, Tommy Carroll, 309, 343
Johnson, Vernon, 266
Johnson, Vickie, 102
Johnson, Vivian, 355
Johnson, Vivian Gray, 309
Johnson, Vuna, 85, 309, 337

Johnson, Vuna Jennette, 309
Johnson, Wayne, 88, 375
Johnson, Wiley, 261, 322
Johnson, Wiley B., 312
Johnson, Wiley Blount, 309, 347
Johnson, William, 139, 309, 352, 354
Johnson, William "Judge," 231
Johnson, Willis R., 133
Johnson, Wilma, 309, 352
Johnson Hollow, 2, 25, 72, 84, 230, 261, 312
Johnson, Lela, 30
Johnson-Morrow-Dodd-Huff home, 230
Johnson-Morrow-Dodd-Huff Home, 230
Jones, Alice, 309
Jones, Alice Evelyn, 278
Jones, Annie, 262
Jones, Annie Lela, 309, 331, 340
Jones, Annie Williams, 309, 335, 340
Jones, Bill, 309, 330, 335, 339–40
Jones, Bill Cherry, Farm, 215
Jones, By George, 168
Jones, Charlene, 102–3
Jones, Cliff, 59, 335, 340
Jones, Clifton, 134, 309, 331, 335
Jones, Connie Johnson, 3
Jones, Cynthia Cannon, 170
Jones, David, 59
Jones, D.B., 255
Jones, D.F., 192
Jones, Dock, 192
Jones, Dorothy, 87, 307
Jones, Dorothy (Elliott), 309
Jones, Dot, 309, 335
Jones, Earl E., 136
Jones, Elsie, 309, 314
Jones, Elsie Johnson, 85
Jones, Emery, 103
Jones, Eugene, 309
Jones, Grace, 48, 334
Jones, Grace Andrews, 309, 330, 336–37, 343
Jones, Gwen Booker, 120
Jones, Herbert, 309, 330, 337, 339
Jones, Inez Tywater, 68
Jones, James Bruce, 309
Jones, James Cliffton, 312
Jones, James Taylor, 309
Jones, J.B., 335, 340, 360, 369
Jones, Jim, 335
Jones, Jim Taylor, 341

Jones, Joe, 340
Jones, Larry, 309, 330, 339, 369
Jones, Sam H., 192
Jones, Lela, 309, 335
Jones, Leslie, 312, 335
Jones, Leslie Burton, 309
Jones, Lela, 87
Jones, Maggie, 59
Jones, Mary, 309
Jones, Mary Alice, 335
Jones, Mary Alice (Potts), 309
Jones, Mildred, 88, 330, 335
Jones, Mildred (Candler), 309
Jones, Mrs. Ridley, 277
Jones, Oliver, 158
Jones, Oneda Rainey, 309
Jones, Ophelia, 312
Jones, Ophelia Merritt, 309
Jones, Patsy, 331, 340
Jones, Patsy (Johnson), 309
Jones, Paul A., 135
Jones, Pvt. Clifton, 309
Jones, Richard, 309, 330, 339, 369
Jones, Ridley, 49, 278, 368
Jones, Ruby, 309, 340
Jones, Sam H., 192
Jones, Sarah, 33
Jones, Taylor, 309, 312
Jones, Teresa, 229
Jones, Tim, 309, 330, 339
Jones, W.C., 129, 168–69, 215
Jones, Wiley, 312, 335
Jones, Wiley, Mr. and Mrs., 69
Jones, Wiley F., 340
Jones, Wiley Franklin, 309, 340
Jones, Will, 49
Jones, William Coleman, 168, 170
Jones, Willie Mai Beasley, 83, 277–78, 368
Jones, Wilma, 88, 309, 330, 335, 337
Jones Chapel Nazarene Church, 69, 70
Jordan, Henry, Elder, 60
Jordan, John A., 171
Joseph Critz House, 254–55

K

Kate Norman Lawrence Kyle Home, 246
Kelly, Beal, 309, 313
Kelly, Beulah, 309, 313
Kelly, Nora, 309, 313
Kelly, Ollie, 85, 313
Kelly, Oscar, 313

Kelly, Susie, 309, 313
Kelly, Vallie, 309, 313
Kelly, William A. "Bill," 309, 313
Kerr, Katie Ross, 248
Kerr, William, 248
Kerr House, 248
Kerr's Springs, 284
King, Doc, 53
King, Henry H., 286
King, James, Sr., 11
King, Mrs. J.W., 144
King, Silva Harris Osborne, 309
Kinnard, Belafonte, 116
Kinnard, Brown, 75, 134, 201–3
Kinnard, Brown, Jr., 203
Kinnard, Brown and Cynthia, 203
Kinnard, Carolyn, 203
Kinnard, C.H., 73
Kinnard, Claiborne Holmes, Jr, 202
Kinnard, Claiborne Holmes, III, 203
Kinnard, Claiborne Holmes, Sr., 203
Kinnard, Cynthia, 75
Kinnard, Elizabeth Fleming, 201
Kinnard, Fred, 288
Kinnard, Ida, 203
Kinnard, Mrs. Claiborne H., Jr., 203
Kinnard, Rebekah, 202
Kinnard, Samuel, 73
Kinnard Springs, 132
Kittrell, Bob, 165
Kittrell, Chad, 60
Kittrell, Cheryl, 60
Kittrell, Janie, 60
Knob Spring, 211
Kukendall, Elam, 17
Kyle, Kate Norman Lawrence, 245–46

L

Ladd, Will, 166
Lamb, Dr., 24
Lamb, Drewrey, 12
Lamb, Elizabeth, 206
Lamb-Johnson home, 206
Lamb-Lawrence Home, 206, 208
Lampley, Wallace, 179
Landowners in Burwood, 9
Lane, Gray, 321
Langford, Dean Johnson, 309
Langford, Leigh, 309
Langford, Leonard, 309
Langford, Louise, 340

Langford, Louise (Jones), 309
Langford, Steve, 309
Langford, Wayne, 309
Langford, Wiley, 309
Largen, Rev., 17
Largen, Rev. W.O., 16
Larry, 330, 339
Latta, Blanche, 96
Latta, Clarence, 81, 83, 90, 92
Latta, Cliff, 81, 92
Latta, Dewey, 95, 305
Latta, Howard, 90
Latta, Kenneth, 99
Latta, William, 133
Laura Bradford Barnhill, 223
Lavender, Aline, 175
Lavender, Allie, 310, 356
Lavender, Alvin, 174–75, 309–10
Lavender, Ann, 295
Lavender, Bessie Mai, 175
Lavender, Bill, 94, 173, 175
Lavender, Blythe, 175, 309–10, 367
Lavender, Claude, 173–5
Lavender, Coley, 226–27, 296
Lavender, Colley, 175, 288, 296
Lavender, Cornelia Ann Shaw, 171, 172, 174, 175
Lavender, Glenn, 81, 83, 175, 310, 357, 367
Lavender, Gus, 171, 174
Lavender, Hattie, 175
Lavender, Jack, 173
Lavender, James A., 175
Lavender, Lottie Lee, 239
Lavender, Margaret, 175
Lavender, Mary, 226-7, 290
Lavender, Minnie, 175
Lavender, Mr. and Mrs. J.R., 292
Lavender, Mrs. Percy, 17
Lavender, Pearl, 175, 310, 367
Lavender, Percy, 17, 171, 173–75, 289
Lavender, Rachel Fitzgerald Parman, 173
Lavender, Riley, 29, 48, 65, 172, 174–75, 288, 292–93, 295–96, 310, 324, 367
Lavender, Russell, 175
Lavender, Thelma, 175
Lavender, Tish Dodd, 221
Lavender, Virginia, 175
Lavender's Store, 40, 297, 299–300
Lawrence, Blanche, 83

Lawrence, Charles W., 138
Lawrence, Charles Wilson, 208
Lawrence, Charles Woodard, 206, 208
Lawrence, Dora, 83, 206–8
Lawrence, Eddie E., 208
Lawrence, Elizabeth, 208
Lawrence, Eunice Gunnells, 178, 184, 187–88, 208
Lawrence, Henry Thomas, 208, 246
Lawrence, Herschel, 206, 208
Lawrence, Jack, 207
Lawrence, John Thomas "Red," 137, 176, 179, 206, 208
Lawrence, John Wilson, 206, 208
Lawrence, Josephine, 91, 177, 206–8
Lawrence, Lizzie, 82
Lawrence, Minnie Tomlinson, 206-8
Lawrence, Mrs. R.D., 59
Lawrence, Nathan, 138, 206–8
Lawrence, Ollie, 63, 66, 208
Lawrence, Pat, 207
Lawrence, Paul, 94, 246
Lawrence Percy, 137
Lawrence, Ray, 246
Lawrence, R.D., 59
Lawrence, Uncle Herschel, 206
Lawrence, Virginia, 207–8
Lawrence, Walter E., 208
Lawrence, Willie, 82, 108, 208
Lawrence, Woodie, 94, 206–8
Lawrence Grove Baptist Church, 16, 66–67, 206
Layne, Edward, 204
Layne, Elizabeth, 204
Layne, Harry, 205
Layne, Jim, 76, 204–5
Layne, Lula P. Collins, 184, 204, 295
Layne Home, 204
Lazenby, Daphne, 105
Lazenby, Daphne and Alex, 255
Lazenby, Mrs. Alex, 254
Leach, Fannie, 60
Leach, Janie, 60
Lee, Effie, 361
Lee, Emmer, 85
Lee, Evelyn, 116
Lee, Evelynn, 106
Lee, George, 353
Lee, Martha, 106, 116
Lee, Robert, 116
Leeper, Hugh, 132

Leggs, John Willie, 108
Leslie, Dr., 24
Lewis, Elizabeth, 194
Lewis, Mrs. W.T., 194
Lile, C.T., 12
Lillard, Milton, 144
Lillian Boyd, 90, 92
Lillie, Herman, 74–75
Lillie, Jack, 90
Lillie, Joe, 74
Lillie, Leonard, 74
Lillie, Mary Louise, 310, 367
Lillie, Sibyl, 74-5
Lionberger, Rebekah, 203
Little Jewell Class, 17
Little Store, 41
Litton, James, 188
Locke, Perlina Branch, 34
Locke, Sue Dodd, 33
Lockridge, Dixie Shaw, 310, 346
Logan, Allie, 288, 356
Logan, Allie Lavender, 310
Logan, Amanda, 310
Logan, Patricia Gray, 3, 287, 310, 355
Logan, Patrick, 312
Logan, Ray, 310, 287, 356
Logan, Raymond, 287, 310, 355
Logan, Sandy, 356
Logan, Sherry Still, 3, 310
Logan, Tandy, 3, 106, 310, 356
Logan, William, 287
Logan, William Raymond, 287
Logue, Mr., 28
Lucas, Ann, 19, 241
Lucille Sparkman Tomlinson, 275
Lukas, Ann, 16
Lunn & Garner Shoe, 22
Lyle's Station, 183, 188
Lynch, Billy, 304
Lynch, Charles, 259
Lynch, Clyde, 111, 113
Lynch, Louise, 287
Lynn, John, 86
Lynn Creek Primitive Baptist Association, 60
Lytle, Captain William, 181

M

Macon, Uncle Dave, 28
Magic Chef, 127–28
Major, Lula Fain, 55–58
Maney, Martha M., 182
Maney, Sallie M., 182
Maney, William, 182

Maple syrup, 25
Margart, Capt., 37
Marlin, Allen, 76
Marlin, Ever Lena, 310, 343
Marlin, George W., 133
Marlin, Glen, 76
Marlin, Herbert, 71
Marlin, Jacob Thomas, 133
Marlin, Jeffrey, 105
Marlin, Joseph, 12
Marlin, Joseph B., 133
Marlin, Joseph Bonaparte, 310, 344
Marlin, Lester, 76
Marlin, Melvin, 76
Marlin, William Samuel, 310, 316
Martin, Alton, 77–78
Martin, Benton, 77, 143–44, 310, 343
Martin, Bernice, 77–78
Martin, Buddy, 77
Martin, Carolyn, 144
Martin, Claudine, 77
Martin, Clifton, 87
Martin, Danny Gail, 144
Martin, David, 144
Martin, Debbie, 144
Martin, Delbert, 144
Martin, Delmer, 144
Martin, Dennis, 77–78, 143–44
Martin, Donald, 77, 144
Martin, Dorothy, 77
Martin, Doug, 130
Martin, Douglas, 77, 249, 287, 290–91
Martin, Eugene, 87
Martin, Faye Osborne, 3
Martin, Gillman, 144
Martin, Grace, 310, 343
Martin, Hattie, 287
Martin, Jacob, 248
Martin, Jacob, Capt., 249
Martin, Jacob and Susan, 249
Martin, Jacob Thomas, 248
Martin, Jake, 18, 248, 290
Martin, Janice, 144
Martin, Jean, 77
Martin, Jesse, Mr. and Mrs., 144
Martin, JoAnne, 101
Martin, Kenneth, 177, 208
Martin, Lela, 77
Martin, Lonnie, 87
Martin, Lonnie T., 136
Martin, Lorene, 77

Martin, Martha Jean, 78
Martin, Mary Rainey, 3
Martin, Mrs. Ever, 144
Martin, Olive, 249, 290–91
Martin, Ray, 310, 374
Martin, Susan Drake, 248
Martin, Teresa, 106
Martin, Ula, 89
Martin, Willie Mai, 77
Maury, Sam, 74
Mayberry, A.C., 12
Mayberry, Alexander Gray, 73
Mayberry, H.G.W., 73
Mayes, Anna M. Johnson, 109
Mayes, Nancy J., 274
McCampbell, Arthur "Si," 137, 280
McCampbell, Clayton, 76
McCampbell, Johnny, 76
McCampbell, Polly Huff, 186, 280
McCampbell, Si, 76, 137, 304
McCampbell, Si and Polly Huff, 279
McCampbell, Suzanne, 3, 103
McCampbell, Suzanne and Deborah, 280
McCandless, Adie, 86
McCandless, Bob, 86
McCandless, Ed, 86
McCandless, Jackie Osborne, 3
McCarty, James Love and Caroline, 248
McClain, Lou, 360
McCollum, Thrasher, 6, 273
McCollum, William Merrill, 12
McCorkle & White, 301
McCoy, Willie Bell (Geasley), 85
McCullough, Angela, 116
McCullough, Arlena, 116
McCullough, Sadie Louise Pope, 124
McCullough, T.C., 76
McCullough, Vanessa, 116
McDaniel, Virginia, 203, 214, 240, 243, 249, 260
McKee, Allen, 104
McKee, Dudley, 341
McKee, George, 65
McKee, James K.P., 133
McKee, Luther, 310, 341
McKee, Virginia Andrews, 310, 341
McKee, Wallace, 341
McKennon, Marvin F., 137
McKinnon, Mary Lou, 91

McKissack, Danny, 117
McKissack, James, 117
McKissack, Jamie, 117
McKissack, Josephine, 110
McKissack, Larry, 117
McKissack, Louise, 110
McKissack, Nathan, 105, 117
McKissack, Patricia, 117
McKissick, James, 105
McLemore, Dorothy, 257
McLemore, Howard, 105, 117
McLemore, Kenny, 105
McLemore, Patricia, 106
McMcullough, Sadie Louise "Ease" Pope, 128
McMeen, John A., 293
McMinn, Belle, 59
McMinn, Frank, 59
McMinn, Mary Lou, 59
McRae-Shaw-Lavender-Barker Home, 252
Meacham, Nathan, 274
Meaders, Homer, 30
Mealer, A.C., 304
Medicinal Springs, 284
Merrill, James, 12
Merritt, James H., 133
Merritt, Wiley, 133
Merritt, Wiley Blount, 310, 346
Methodist Church, 15, 22, 30
Methodist Woman's Missionary Society, 17
Meyers, Shelia Johnson, 3
Militia districts, 8
Millard Akin Place, 269
Miller, Delores, 105
Miller, Dr., 24
Mizelle, India Jones, 170
Mizelle, Lucy Merrell, 170
Mizelle, Robert, 170
Moore, John, 57, 242
Moran, John, 161
Moran's Drug Store, 161
Morrow, Ethel, 81, 92
Morrow, James R., 133
Morrow, John, 65
Morrow, John P., 310, 326
Morrow, May, 310, 326
Morrow, Ola Clark, 310
Morrow, Robert, 84, 230
Morton, Christine Barker, 160
Morton, Earl, 160
Morton, Joseph, 12
Morton, Samuel S., 73
Moss, Emily, 184
Moss, W.H., 9, 12

Mount Taber Lodge, 63
Mr. Douglas Martin, 290
Mrs. Duncan, 295
Mrs. Garner, 22
Mrs. W.H. Bizwell, 190
Mt. Lavergne Methodist Church, 63
Mt. Lavergne School, 72
Mueller, Nancy, 111
Murdic, William, 60
Murfree, Col. Hardy, 132, 180-2,241
Murfree, Elizabeth, 182
Murfree, Hardy, 180–82, 215
Murfree, Mary, 180
Murfree, Mathias B., 182
Murfree, Matthias B., 132
Murfree, Salley B., 182
Murfree, William, 180
Murfree, William Law, 215
Murfree's Fork, 1, 8, 22, 55, 248, 274
Murfree's Fork Creek, 215, 238, 248
Murfree's Fork on Perkins Road, 72
Murfree's Fork Primitive Baptist Church, 62, 119
Myles Manor, 193

N
Nashville Banner, 290, 298–99, 301
National Register of Historic Places, 255
Neely, Charles Lynch, 259
Neely, James and William Lynch, 259
Neely, Jane, 259
Neely, Jane Grymes, 258
Neely, John, 258–59
Neely, John L., 301
Neely, Rhoda, 259
Neely, Sarah Wells, 259
Neely, Sophia, 259
Neely family, 248, 259
Neely land, 259
Negroes, 15
Nellie, 374
Nellums, Dolly Pea, 34
Nelson Polk, 261, 353
Nesbett, W.B., 274
Nevils, Harold, 110
New Hope Baptist Church, 71
New Hope Church of Christ, 71
Newton, Otis Lee, 56

Newton Cannon Beasley, 278
Nicholas, Sunshine, 90
Nichols, Joe Greer, 81
Nichols, Malcolm, 93
Nichols, Patterson, 90
Nichols, Tommy, 82
Nichols, Virginia, 257
Nix, Rebecca Brown, 310, 358
Nix, Tennessee Virginia, 358
Noland, Will, 295
Nolen, Mary, 12
Nolen, Will, 296
Norman, Cornelia Barker, 160
Norman, Kate, 26
Norman, Knox, 160, 239
Norman, Robbie Barker, 239
Norman, Sally, 26
North, Amanda, 105, 114
North Carolina, 16, 20, 181, 242

O
Odell Beard, 96, 99
Oden, Carolyn, 106
Oden, Dorothy, 105
Oden, Dr. H., 73
Oden, Henry, 60
Oden, Sharon, 124
Oden, Sue Barton, 112
Old Bandy, 243
Old Burnett's Tavern, 232
Old Burwood School, 2, 89
Old City Cemetery, 1
Old Goshen Methodist Church, 157
One-room log schoolhouse, 72
O'Riley, Grace, 162
Ormes, Ada, 29, 33
Ormes, Ada Lee Riggin, 36
Ormes, Charles, 36
Ormes, Charlie, 33
Ormes, Eliza, 33
Ormes, Mrs. C.H., 192
Ormes, Ned, 33
Orr, Gilbert M., 289
Orr, Nonnie, 89
Osborne, Angie, 310
Osborne, Betsy, 310, 374
Osborne, Bill, 310, 362, 375
Osborne, Bud, 288, 310, 350–51
Osborne, Copperhead, 310, 374
Osborne, Dawn, 310, 350
Osborne, Effie Lee, 310
Osborne, Faye, 310, 374
Osborne, Fulton, 310, 362
Osborne, Harvey, 310, 374
Osborne, Howlett, 310, 362
Osborne, Jackie, 310, 350

Osborne, Judy Barnhill, 310, 350
Osborne, Katie, 310, 374
Osborne, Latha, 77–78
Osborne, Luther, 310, 374
Osborne, Nellie, 310, 374
Osborne, Ott, 310, 374
Osborne, Sue, 101
Osborne, Tom, 375
Overbey, Albert Glen, 134, 183, 190, 193–94, 370
Overbey, Aldea, 187
Overbey, Aleda, 191
Overbey, Annie, 184
Overbey, Beasley, 187–89, 191
Overbey, Beasley, Jr., 184
Overbey, Beverly, 184
Overbey, Beverly and Beasely, Jr., 187
Overbey, Daniel, 183
Overbey, Dorothy, 184, 187
Overbey, Emily Tyler, 184
Overbey, Emma, 74, 92, 184, 187
Overbey, Etta, 187, 190
Overbey, Etta Beasley, 184
Overbey, Eunice, 74, 90, 92, 184, 187–88
Overbey, Frank, 215
Overbey, Glen, 73, 184, 186–87, 189–91
Overbey, John, 188
Overbey, Jr., Daniel, 183
Overbey, Mary, 74, 90, 184, 187
Overbey, T.F., 157, 184, 187, 190
Overbey, Turman, 184
Overbey, Turman and Emily Moss, 188
Overbey, William, 184, 187, 190–91
Overbey, W.W., 188
Overbey Farm, 74
Overbey's Store, 73, 204
Owen, Jane, 146, 160, 168, 171, 183, 192

P

Pam Andrews, 101–2
Parham, E.J., 13
Parham, E.L., 12
Parham, Peter, 12
Parham, R.A., 12
Parigin, Janie Ragsdale, 310, 348
Park Huff, 81
Parks, Dr. Joe, 24
Parrish, Terrie, 310, 343
Parson John Pope, 16
Parson Pope, 16, 22, 80, 243
Parson Pope property, 80

Patton, Andrea, 60
Patton, Emma Bradford, 127
Patton, Fannie, 110
Patton, Geraldine, 110
Patton, James, 57, 242
Patton, J.B., 12
Patton, John, 127
Patton, Mable, 127
Patton, Ollie Mai, 124, 127
Patton, Susannah, 12
Patton, William B., 12
Pauline Stofel, 99
Paul Lawrence, 94, 246
Peach, Terry, 71
Pearce, Mary Shearer, 255
Pearly Hill, 61
Pearly Hill Baptist Church, 64
Pearly Hill Church of Christ, 61
Pearly Hill Lodge and School, 64
Pearly Hill School, 72, 108–10
Peartree, Wood, 28
Peckerwood Hollow, 132
Peddlers, 23–24, 27
Peg Raciti, 3
Pentecost, Hazel, 262, 334
Peoples, "Daddy," 147
Perkins, John Willie, 110
Perkins, Robert, 62
Perkins, Samuel, 215
Perkins, Samuel F., 133
Perkins, T.F., 215
Perkins, T.F., Sr., 73
Perkins, Thomas F., 9, 12, 55, 62, 132–33, 187, 209, 215
Perkins, Thomas F., Jr., 133
Perkins, W.O.N., 1
Perkins Road, 56
Pete Harris, 104
Petway, Mrs. O.B., 295
Pewitt, James, 96
Pewitt, Jean, 96
Pewitt, Marie, 93
Pewitt, Mary, 93
Pewitt, Mrs. L.B., 295
Pewitt, Sue, 249
Pewitt, Tony and Sue, 249
Phillips, Zandine, 63
Pleasant Dale, 56
Pleasant Dale Presbyterian Church, 56
Plemmons, Nancy, 100
Plemons, Betty, 41
Plemons, David, 41
Plemons, Hop, 237
Plemons, James Lee, 236
Plemons, Molly Ann, 236

Plemons, Myrtle Osborne, 237
Polk, Audrey (Andrews), 310
Polk, Audrey Andrews, 368
Polk, Cain, 261–62, 368
Polk, Callie E., 310, 330
Polk, Deliah Johnson, 371
Polk, Delilah Johnson, 310, 326
Polk, Eugene, 138
Polk, Eva Johnson, 312
Polk, Felton, 310, 368
Polk, Florence, 262
Polk, Frances, 307, 310
Polk, George Lee, 310
Polk, Howlett, 95, 310, 344
Polk, Ida, 319
Polk, Ila, 310
Polk, James K., 338
Polk, James Knox, 310, 341
Polk, John, 84, 135, 310
Polk, John and Lera Atkins, 322
Polk, John O., 109
Polk, John Wesley, 133, 310, 326
Polk, John Wiley, 310
Polk, J.T., 61
Polk, Julia Robinson, 310, 371
Polk, Julie Robinson, 338
Polk, Lennie, 74
Polk, Lera Atkins, 307`
Polk, Lillie Alice, 310, 344
Polk, Mabel, 74
Polk, Millard, 310, 368
Polk, Millie, 325
Polk, Nelson, 85, 261, 310, 346, 364
Polk, Robert, 61
Polk, Tom, 261, 310, 312
Polk, Walter, 137, 310, 364
Polk, William Augustus, 133
Pollard, "Miss Beulah," 213
Pope, Alowena, 127
Pope, Annie, 110
Pope, Ann Lucas, 241
Pope, Ann Whitaker, 241
Pope, Carrie, 16, 226, 243
Pope, Carrie Campbell, 227
Pope, Charles, 110
Pope, Cora Blackburn, 310
Pope, Damali, 243
Pope, Ed C., 310, 326
Pope, Edith, 16, 243
Pope, Edith D., 227
Pope, Edith Drake, 226
Pope, Elizabeth, 241
Pope, Elizabeth Jeffries, 241
Pope, Ethel, 44
Pope, Georgia, 23

Pope, Hardy, 134
Pope, Howard, 127
Pope, James Drake, 15, 21, 243
Pope, J.C., 44
Pope, Joe, 43–44, 60, 119, 127–28, 243
Pope, Joe and Leslie, 243
Pope, John, 6, 20, 57, 110, 127, 241–43, 274, 285–86
Pope, John, Rev., 240
Pope, John O., 16
Pope, John Osborne, 20
Pope, John W., 286
Pope, John Whitaker, 21, 243
Pope, Joseph, Jr., 44
Pope, Joseph Lucius, Sr., 44
Pope, Larissa, 25
Pope, Larissa Campbell, 109
Pope, Leslie, 108, 121, 124–25, 127–28, 243
Pope, Louis, 44, 60
Pope, Lucious, 110, 127
Pope, Mary, 16, 44, 243
Pope, Mary Caroline Drake, 227
Pope, Mary Elizabeth, 227
Pope, Mary Frances, 128
Pope, Mary Gray, 127
Pope, Matthew, 310, 326, 328
Pope, Miss Carrie, 20
Pope, Mittie Akin, 150, 310, 326–27
Pope, Old Bandy, 243
Pope, Ollie, 310, 328–29
Pope, Ollie Mae, 59, 128
Pope, Ormari, 243
Pope, Osborne, 44, 243
Pope, Parson John, 16
Pope, Patience, 44
Pope, Raleigh, 134–35, 271, 310, 326, 329
Pope, Rebecca Jane Campbell, 247
Pope, Reverend John, 19, 20, 240, 247
Pope, Robert, 44
Pope, Rollie, 82
Pope, Sarah Elizabeth Sparkman, 310, 326
Pope, Solomon, 61
Pope, Sorchum, 127
Pope, Squire Billy, 15
Pope, Thomas Anderson, 243
Pope, Thomas Anderson place, 249
Pope, Thomas and Rebecca, 247
Pope, Vallie, 127
Pope, Walter, 110
Pope, W.C., 79, 200, 238
Pope, William, 61
Pope, William Augustus, 247
Pope, William C., 310
Pope, William Campbell, 227
Pope, William C. and Cora Blackburn, 363
Pope, William E., 310, 328
Pope, William Henry, 127
Pope, Wm. & J.W., 285
Pope-Barker-Duncan House, 238
Pope-Beasley-Sparkman family, 276
Pope Family Cemetery, 241
Pope Home, 20, 226, 250
Pope-Lavender-Huff Home, 226
Pope-Martin-Pewitt Home, 247–48
Pope's Campground, 242
Pope's Chapel Church, 15, 16, 19, 22, 58, 242, 274
Pope's Chapel Road, 2, 21, 23, 37, 72, 80, 242–43, 245
Pope Sisters, 226–27
Pope-Southall Home, 250–51
Pope-Southall house, 250
Porter, Jim Elick, 26
Postmaster, 37, 232, 256
Potts, Evelyn, 193
Potts, Mary Alice, 340
Potts, Mr. and Mrs. H.J., 193
Poynor, Claudine Haley, 3
Price, Clarence, 135
Price, Effie, 86
Price, Leslie, 86
Price, Oakley, 86
Priest, Eloise, 292
Primitive Baptist Church, Leiper's Fork, 39, 54–55, 228
Primm, Opal Johnson, 310
Prince, Allen, 17, 234–35
Prince, C.W., 134
Prince, Hugh, 235
Prince, James, 99, 235
Prince, Joe, 235, 292
Prince, Maude, 235
Prince, Maude Thompson, 235
Prince, Mrs. Allen, 17, 289
Prince, Stella, 94, 234–35
Prince, Tom, 235
Prowell, Andrew, 310, 364
Prowell, "Possum," 185
Prowell, Sara Mays, 310, 364
P.T.A., 294
Puryear, Jordan, heirs, 13
Puryear, Mordecai, 210
Puryear, Sarah Reese, 210

R

Radcliffe, Thelma, 114
Rader, Cathryn Johnson, 310
Rader, Florena, 86
Rader, Hallie, 86
Rader, Herbert, 86
Rader, Jasper, 86
Rader, William, 310, 353
Ragsdale, Albert, 193–95
Ragsdale, Carroll, 310, 353
Ragsdale, Clellon, 86, 313, 318, 332
Ragsdale, Columbus, 310, 353
Ragsdale, Daniel, 310
Ragsdale, Danny, 310, 313, 332
Ragsdale, Deliah Johnson, 310
Ragsdale, Delilah Johnson, 370
Ragsdale, Doc, 310, 315
Ragsdale, Elcain, 310, 353
Ragsdale, Elizabeth Lewis, 195
Ragsdale, Eph, 59
Ragsdale, Ephraim, 310, 313, 323, 332
Ragsdale, Ephraim F., 133
Ragsdale, Ethel, 86, 310, 318
Ragsdale, Etta, 85
Ragsdale, Harvey H., 310
Ragsdale, Hattie Johnson, 310, 323
Ragsdale, Henry, 310, 344
Ragsdale, James, 45, 87
Ragsdale, Jane, 102
Ragsdale, Jim, 33–34
Ragsdale, Joe, 310, 370
Ragsdale, Joe Clellon, 310
Ragsdale, John, 13, 261
Ragsdale, John H., 310, 353
Ragsdale, Lem, 86
Ragsdale, Lemuel, 310, 313–15, 318
Ragsdale, Lilia Mai Akin, 6, 272
Ragsdale, Lillie, 310, 318
Ragsdale, Mack, 193
Ragsdale, Mannie, 310, 318
Ragsdale, Margaret Hewton, 310, 322
Ragsdale, Michael A., 133
Ragsdale, Mrs. J.C., 295
Ragsdale, Mrs. J.S., 192
Ragsdale, Myrt, 34, 296
Ragsdale, Myrtle, 194, 310, 327
Ragsdale, Myrtle Riggin, 192, 194–95, 295

Ragsdale, Myrt Riggin, 33
Ragsdale, Rebecca, 310, 348
Ragsdale, Reedy, 310, 318
Ragsdale, Vance, 85
Ragsdale, William, 310, 353
Ragsdale, Zula, 310, 348
Rainey, Mrs. C.A., 295
Rainey, Georgia, 336
Rainey, Greenie, 310, 345
Rainey, Myrtle Martin, 310, 345
Rainey, Oneda, 351
Rainey, O.V. "Jody," 138
Ray, Ann, 295
Read, Mr. and Mrs. J.L., 249
Reed, G.W., 90
Reams, Joshua, 13
Redd, Samella Terrell, 109
Redford, James, 3
Redford, Kenneth, 310, 328
Redford, Kenneth G., 310, 366
Redford, Ollie Pope, 310, 366
Red River, 34
Reed, Garret, 147
Reed, G.W., 90, 148
Reese, Patrick, 9, 13
Reese, Rufus, 63
Reese, Thomas J., 13
Revolutionary War, 180, 274
Revolutionary War service, 19, 132, 182-3
Reynolds, Sherry Booker, 120
Ride-a-thon, 24, 288, 293, 296
Ridley, Boyd, 164, 166–67
Ridley, J.B., 13
Ridley, John Boyd, 167
Ridley, Mack Fitzgerald, 167
Ridley, Marion Archer, 167
Ridley, Mary Jackson Fitzgerald, 260
Ridley, Mrs. John B., 165
Ridley, R. F., 217
Ridley, Sallie, 165
Ridley, Trainer Archer, 167
Ridley-Beasley-Church Home, 217–18
Ridley Jones, 49, 277–78
Riggin, Bob, 33
Riggin, Callie, 33
Riggin, Emily, 34
Riggin, Jim, 34
Riggin, Joel, 132
Riggin, Mahala, 27, 34, 296, 225
Riggin, Mahala and Will, 261
Riggin, Mrs. W.J., 157
Riggin, Myrt, 33
Riggin, Robert, 192

Riggin, Robert "Bob," 33-4
Riggin, Ruby, 34, 86, 90, 92
Riggin, Sarah Jones, 192, 194
Riggin, Sena, 34
Riggin, Walter, 34
Riggin, Will, 27, 30, 192, 293, 296
Riggin, William J., 26
Riggin, William Jonathan, 34
Riggin, Willie, 34
Riggin, Wilson, 34
Riggin, W.J., 34
Robert Elsmere (book title), 15, 243
Robertson, General James, 19
Robertson, James, 22, 201, 240, 259
Robinson, Bill, 371
Robinson, Boyd, 179
Robinson, Buford, 90
Robinson, Carroll, 310, 371
Robinson, Jim, 90
Robinson, Julia, 310
Robinson, Marsha, 59
Robinson, Martha, 81, 92, 231, 309
Robinson, Michael, 274
Robinson, Robert, 81, 83
Robinson, Ruth, 83
Robinson, S.A., 66
Robinson, Shadrach, 310, 371
Robinson, W.A. "Bill," 310, 371
Russell Cunningham, 109
Ryan, Arnie, 69
Samuel Akin place, 7, 274
Samuel Akin-Thomas Tomlinson house, 273
Samuel Perkins Cannon home, 215
Satterfield, Emily Jane, 234
Satterfield, Joseph, 234
Sawmill-cotton gin, 37
Scales, W.P., 74
Scott, Ella, 94
Scott, Evie, 94
Scott, Josephine, 94
Scott, S.T., 56
Scott, Theresa, 96
Scruggs, Dorothy, 110
Scruggs, Earl, 110
Scruggs, Hester, 110
Scruggs, William, 110
Sedberry, Ann Adair, 260
Sedberry, Barbara, 198
Sedberry, Barbara Faye, 198
Sedberry, Billy, Jr., 198

Sedberry, Billy, Sr., 131, 198
Sedberry, Carline, 198
Sedberry, Dolly, 198
Sedberry, Frances (Dolly) Green, 199, 260
Sedberry, Frances Carline, 260
Sedberry, James Franklin, 198, 260
Sedberry, James Hamilton, 199
Sedberry, Jessie Zulieme, 198, 260
Sedberry, J. Hamilton, 197
Sedberry, Jimmy, 198
Sedberry, William, 196–98
Sedberry, William, Jr. (Billy), 260
Sedberry, William H., 260
Sedberry, William H., Sr., 196, 199
Sedberry, William Hamilton, 196, 198, 260
Sedberry, Zulieme, 198-9, 260
Sewell, Bob, 95, 179
Sewell, Daisy, 190
Sewell, J.M., 179
Sewell, Mrs. R.E., 190
Sewell, Robert, 177, 179
Sewell, Robert E., 176, 179
Sewell Electric Company, 179
Shane Cemetery, 248
Shannon, Dr. J.O., 20, 23
Shaw, Barkley, 310, 365
Shaw, Bernard, 59, 82
Shaw, Burnice, 13
Shaw, Delilah Lavender, 256
Shaw, Dixie, 59, 81–83, 92, 310
Shaw, Edgar, 21, 59, 81, 83, 92
Shaw, Edgar, Mrs., 17
Shaw, Elizabeth, 310, 365
Shaw, George, 81, 83, 90, 92
Shaw, Greer, 81
Shaw, Gus, 15
Shaw, Henrietta, 33–34
Shaw, James, 65
Shaw, John, 23, 39
Shaw, John A., 171
Shaw, John Osborn, 133
Shaw, Louise, 59, 82–83
Shaw, Mary Gee Thweatt, 310, 363
Shaw, Mr. and Mrs. George, 289
Shaw, Mrs. W.A., 58
Shaw, Oscar, 33, 311, 365
Shaw, Thomas E., 133
Shaw, W.A., 37, 59, 65
Shaw, William, 23, 34
Shaw, William A., 146, 256

Shaw, William B., 134
Shaw, William Greer, 311, 363
Shaw, William H., 133
Shaw-Huff-Johnson home, 256
Shaw's Store, 39-40, 252, 256
Shawtown, 23
Shea, Johnnie, 162
Shedd, Randy, 106
Shelton, Ricky, 103
Sheriff Nevils, 297–98
Sherry Still Logan, 356
Short, Annie Lee, 39, 42
Short, Bill, 39, 42, 59, 83
Short, Ethel, 81, 83
Short, Frankie, 96, 99
Short, Margie, 96
Short, Ruth, 81, 83
Short, Walter Faw, 83
Short, W.H., 39
Short's Store, 39, 252
Simpson, Oscar, 177
Singing Classes, 24
Singleton, R.W., 13
Skelley, Emma, 303
Skelley, Mr. and Mrs. Henry, 188
Skelley, Mrs. C.C., 188
Skinner, James, 138
Skirmish at Spring Hill, 158
Skirmish at Thompson Station, 247
Slaves, 9, 20, 25, 210, 243, 259–60
Smith, Allie Mai, 74
Smith, Bessie, 86
Smith, W.J., 301
Smithson, Ora, 89
Snow Creek, 26
Southall, 29
Southall, Bates, 96, 99, 140–42
Southall, Claude, 96, 177, 305
Southall, Dayton, 91, 250
Southall, Dennis, 106
Southall, Gustavus, 250
Southall, Gustavus and Rebecca, 250–51
Southall, James, 99
Southall, J.R., 234
Southall, Mary E. Satterfield, 234
Southall, Maude, 136, 251
Southall, Oliver, 250
Southall, Phillip, 133
Southall, Rebecca Anderson, 250
South Margin Street, 173
Sowell, Felix, 17
Sparkman, Alice, 3

Sparkman, Alice Eveline Beasley, 369
Sparkman, Alice Evelyn Jones, 277, 311
Sparkman, Butler, 59
Sparkman, Calvin, 269
Sparkman, Carroll, 133
Sparkman, Claude, 59, 66, 311, 345
Sparkman, Cliff, 94, 289, 311, 373
Sparkman, Elizabeth, 96, 303
Sparkman, Finis, 117
Sparkman, Gertrude Dodd, 50, 221, 311
Sparkman, Glen, 29, 92, 250–51
Sparkman, Gus, 29, 228, 311–12
Sparkman, Henry, 81, 83
Sparkman, Henry Porter, 275
Sparkman, Jacob G., 133
Sparkman, James, 84
Sparkman, James Matt, 300, 303
Sparkman, Jessie, 83, 92
Sparkman, Joe, 147, 277–78, 311, 367
Sparkman, Lucy, 59
Sparkman, Mary Ann Robinson, 311, 326
Sparkman, Matthew, 326
Sparkman, Maude Southall, 250
Sparkman, Mintie McKee, 228
Sparkman, Missie, 82
Sparkman, Mrs. C.S., 311, 328
Sparkman, Mrs. Glenn, 17
Sparkman, Nell, 311, 345
Sparkman, Nona, 83
Sparkman, Ollie, 3, 275, 288, 311, 367
Sparkman, Ollie, Jr., 277–78
Sparkman, Ollie, Sr., 49–50
Sparkman, Ollie and Gertrude Dodd, 50
Sparkman, Ollie Joe, 369
Sparkman, Ollie Joe, III, 311
Sparkman, Ollie Porter, 59, 81, 83
Sparkman, Ollie "Toodlum" Jr., 311, 369
Sparkman, Iulas, 59
Sparkman, Percy, 91
Sparkman, Rena, 117
Sparkman, Ruby, 83
Sparkman, Russell, 375
Sparkman, Tishie Beasley, 59, 311
Sparkman, Toodlum, 369

Sparkman Farm, 228
Sparkman House, 31
Sparkman Place, 31
Sparkman Road, 50
Sparkman, Sallie Hawk, 298, 300, 303
Spiritualaires, The, 69
Spring Hill Cemetery, 274
Stafford, Tony, 71
Stanley, Howard, 92, 234
Stanley, Myrtle Marie, 235
Stanley, Stella Prince, 235
Steele, Dig, 63
Steele, John, 105
Steele, May Susie, 108
Steele, Pat, 105
Steele, Richard, 13
Steele, Vallie, 108
Steele, Wanda, 106, 117
Stephens, A.H., 282
Stephens, A.H. and Nannie Fitzgerald, 281
Stephens, John E., 185
Stephens, Louise, 282
Stephens, Nannie Fitzgerald, 282
Stephens, Nannie Page, 282
Stephens, Ollie, 282
Stephens, Rev. J.R., 162
Stephens, Sally, 282
Stephens, William, 286
Stephens-Garland Home, 281–82
Stewart, Jean, 167
Stewart, Robert, 167
Stewart, Ruth Critz, 167
Still, Alene, 93
Still, Claude, 96
Still, Sherry, 310
Stofel, Eugene, 99
Stofel, Louise, 94
Stofel, Lucille, 94
Stofel, Pauline, 87, 99
Stofel, Pud, 99
Stofel, Vivian, 87, 99
Stone's River, 180
Stovall, Dudley, 311
Stovall, Earl, 311, 341
Stovall, Earl, Jr., 311
Stovall, Earl Jr., 341
Stovall, Gertrude Andrews, 311
Stovall, Hattie, 358
Stovall, James Martin, 311, 358
Stovall, Joseph, 132
Stovall, Karen, 102–3

Stovall, Kathy, 101–3
Stovall, Ray, 311, 341
Stovall, Tennessee Virginia Nix, 311
Stovall, Wallace "Stovepipe," 311, 333
Stovall, William Franklin, 311, 358
Stovall George M., 133
Stutts, Tony, 106
Sudberry, Hershel, 311, 338
Sudberry, Lena Hassell, 311, 338
Sudberry, M.E., 311, 337
Sugar Ridge, 1, 8, 10, 12, 14, 22, 24–25, 29, 107–8, 154–55, 245
Sullivan, Bobby, 96, 99, 304–5, 311, 359
Sullivan, Brenda, 100
Sullivan, Calvin, 105
Sullivan, Carroll, 104
Sullivan, Celia, 95
Sullivan, Celie, 99
Sullivan, Geneve, 94
Sullivan, Guy, 99
Sullivan, Hattie Barnhill, 311
Sullivan, James, 106
Sullivan, Jerry, 104
Sullivan, Lon Bucky, 104
Sullivan, Louisa, 74
Sullivan, Margaret, 93
Sullivan, Molly, 99
Sullivan, Owen, 99
Sullivan, Peggy, 101
Sullivan, Sandra, 102
Sullivan, Sterling, 96
Sullivan, Tommy, 103
Sullivan, Vera, 94
Sullivan, Wilma, 95
Sulphur Springs, 8, 285
Swanson, Edward, 201–2
Swanson, Edward and James, 202
Swanson, James, 202
Sweeney, Kennette Huff, 3
Sweeney, Kerry, 106
Sweeney, Viola Osborne, 311
Sycamore community, 1, 8
Sycamore folks, 261
Sycamore Road, 71–72, 119
Sycamore School, 69, 72, 84–88

T
Tabernacle, old, 34
Tanner, Jim, 59
Tarbox School, 34
Tate, Elijah, 118
Tatum, Eph, 187
Tatum, Richard M., 13, 286
Taxidermist, 196, 260
Taylor, Doris, 100
Taylor, Floy, 160
Taylor, George, 91
Taylor, Georgia, 160
Taylor, James, 309
Taylor, Margaret Barker, 160
Tennessee & Alabama Railroad, 14
Tennessee Female College, 227
Tennessee Ride-at-thon, 289
Tennessee State Prison in Nashville, 302
Tennessee State University, 125, 155
Tennessee Walker, 48
Tennessee Walking Horses, 293
Tennessee Women's Press and Author's Club, 227
Tent Meeting, 59
Terrell, Elthomas, 109
Terrell, John W., 109
Terrell, Paul, 109
Terrill, Timothy, 307
Terrill heirs, 13
Theta, 26, 29
Thomas, Charles, 178
Thomas, John, 208
Thomas, Judy, 355
Thomas, Judy Gray, 311
Thomas Byrd, 96, 99
Thompson, Arvis, 304
Thompson, Daly, 177
Thompson, Grandmother, 235
Thompson, Jennette, 13
Thompson, Mickey, 151
Thompson, Peter, I, 13
Thompson's Station, 9, 23, 29, 72, 248, 258
Thompson's Station School, 72, 112, 213
Thompson Station Church, 167
Thompson Station Elementary School, 125
Thurman, Edwin, 90
Thweatt, Anola, 59, 83, 92
Thweatt, Ed, 59
Thweatt, James, 59, 81, 83
Thweatt, John Henry, 209
Thweatt, Lera, 81
Thweatt, Mary Allen, 209
Thweatt, Pleasant Samuel, 209
Thweatt, William Howard, 209
Thweatt, William Peter, 209
Tidwell, Annie Lou, 311
Tidwell, Lou Dora, 361
Tollgates, 14
Tomlinson, Bertha, 83
Tomlinson, Jerry, 275
Tomlinson, Lester, 275
Tomlinson, Louise Harper, 273
Tomlinson, Lucille Sparkman, 275
Tomlinson, Mrs. Thomas, 295
Tomlinson, Thomas, 273, 275, 295
Tomlinson, Thomas and Lucille Sparkman, 275
Tomlinson, Thomas J., 273
Tornado of 1910, 20, 58
Trimble, Clara, 92
Trimble, G.W., 13
Trimble, Velma, 92
Troope, Pearl, 162
Truett, J.M., 13
Tucker, Thomas, 13
Turman, Garrett, 183
Turnage, Cindy Johnson, 3
Turner, Gordon H., 294
Tyler, Emily, 183

U
Under the Flag of the Cross, 197
United Daughters of the Confederacy, 227
United Methodist Church, 2, 57–58
University of Tennessee, 153, 162
University of Tennessee Press, 227
Unknown, Demetria, 105
USS George Squires, 140

V
Vachel Barnhill Home, 222
Valley View Farm, 212, 214
Vance, Polly, 148
Vance, Thomas, Rev., 100
Vance Akin-Robert Byrd home, 153
Vaughn, Lillie, 361
Vaughn, Pete, 193
Veach, S.C., 89, 147
Velmer Walls, 100
Venable, Bob, 263
Venable, Bob and Lizzie Mae, 264
Venable, Jim, 263
Venable, Mattie, 263

Venable, Susan "Sook", 263
Village of Burwood, 37–38, 40, 42, 44, 46, 132, 238, 270

W

Waddey, Frank, 82
Waddey, Lilia Polk, 262
Wade, H.P., 14
Wade, James, 53
Wade, John F., 14
Wade, L.B., 14
Wade, Lucy, 14
Walker, Brenda, 105
Walker, Dr. J.O., son, 141
Walker, Dr. J.O.'s son, 141
Walker, Dwight, 117
Walker, George F., 136
Wall, Charles, 292
Wall, Harold and Dorris Wall, 296
Wall and Mooney School, 168
Waller, Maggie Lee Baker, 311, 347
Walls, Annie Lee, 77–78
Walls, Elmer, 3, 100, 342
Walls, Mary Inez, 100
Walls, Mary Nell, 77
Walls, Neil, 311
Walls, Robert, 342
Walls, Rosie, 100
Walls, Velmer, 100, 311
Walton, Jim, 82
Walton, Ollie Mai, 82
Ward, Humphrey, Mrs., 15, 243
Warf, Andy, 190
Warf, Mrs. Andy, 190
Warren, William, 14
Warwick, Richard/Rick, 3, 8, 255
Washington, Calvin, 35
Watson, James, 79, 206
Watson, Jane, 211
Watson, Jane Bradley, 211
Watson, Jane Reese, 210–11
Watson, John, 210–11
Watson, Katie, 108
Watson, Sally N., 206
Watson, Simon, 79
Watson, Stephen, 14
Watson, Susan Catherine Puryear, 210
Watson, Thomas, 14, 210–11
Watson, T.J., 9
Wayne, Harold, 296
Webb, William S., 15
Wesley, Thomas, 13
Wesley Inman, 85
West End Church, 17
West End School, 23, 65, 72, 82
West Harpeth, 8–9, 14, 164, 181, 210, 213, 240
West Harpeth River, 6
West Harpeth School, 213
Whitaker, Elizabeth Cary, 241
Whitaker, Richard and Elizabeth Cary, 241
White, Cynthia, 81
White, Ezekiel, 180–81
White, Lloyd, 88
Whitehead, Linda, 86
Whitehead, Rosie, 86
Whitfield, Nancy, 106
Whitley, Gladys, 74, 77–78
Whitley, Mrs., 74
Whitley's Class, 78, 302
Whittaker, Ann, 16
Whittaker, Melvin, 160
Wiley, John, 371
Wilkes, John, 14
Williams, Cornelia, 153
Williams, Eddie, 22
Williams, Fleming, Jr., 177
Williams, Gilliam, 88
Williams, Jeffery, 106
Williams, Louie G., 139
Williams, Melvin, 88
Williams, Travis, 56
Williams, William Washington, Dr., 20, 23, 79
Williams Academy, 72, 79–80, 82
Williamsburg, 15, 20–21, 23, 242
Williamson County Bank, 152
Williamson County Sportsmen's Club, 178
Williams Post Office, 79
Willie Lawrence, 108
Willows (home), 210–14
Wilson, Berry, 60
Wilson, Mary L., 109
Wise, Danny, 105
Wise, Lisa, 105
Witt, P.E., 14
Woman's Society of Christian Service, 152, 167
Women's Historical Association, 227
Women's Society of Christian Service, 152, 167
Woodard, Martha, 257
Woody, Jean, 311, 342
Woolsey, Bill, 196
World War II / WWII, 35, 136, 138–40, 142, 206, 253
World Wars, 131, 34, 176, 185, 190
Wren, William J., 13
Wright, Johnny, 28
Wright, Ruby, 90
WWI medic, 131

Y

Yates, Joseph, 8, 286–87
York, Ann, 257

www.ingramcontent.com/pod-product-compliance
Lightning Source LLC
Chambersburg PA
CBHW060537010526
44119CB00006B/183